# Shakespeare's Happy Comedies

*by the same author*

MILESTONES ON THE DOVER ROAD

JOHN DOVER WILSON, C.H.

# Shakespeare's
# Happy Comedies

FABER AND FABER
24 Russell Square
London

First published in 1962
by Faber and Faber Limited
24 Russell Square London W.C.1
First published in this edition 1969
Printed in Great Britain by
Latimer Trend & Co Ltd Whitstable

SBN 571 09023 0

TO
ALL WHO HAVE BEEN
MADE HAPPY BY THEM
FROM
ONE WHO HAS HIMSELF
FOUND HAPPINESS
IN THEM

# Contents

9

# *Preface*

On the 20th of January 1931, my friend Mr. Richard de la Mare of the firm of Faber and Faber, which had since 1927 been issuing facsimiles of First Folio texts under my editorship, suggested that I might be inclined to let them have a short life of Shakespeare. Such a book had long been in my mind, but realizing that the Syndics of the Cambridge University Press, for whom I was editing the 'New Shakespeare' with Sir Arthur Quiller-Couch, had a prior claim to anything I wrote on this subject, I felt I ought to consult them first, with the result that *The Essential Shakespeare* appeared in 1932 under their aegis. It happened however that 1931 saw the completion of the comedies for them with the publication of *The Winter's Tale*, at which point Sir Arthur Quiller-Couch resigned the co-editorship, leaving me to carry on alone. The delightful introductions he had contributed to the edition since its inception ten years earlier had deservedly won the admiration of a large public; but his partner, who bore responsibility for the text, commentary, and glossary, which involved the closest scrutiny of every line of the fourteen comedies, inevitably formed his own ideas about them which, while only once traversing, I think, those of Sir Arthur, suggested a rather different approach. And by the time *The Winter's Tale* was published in the series, these ideas had matured considerably. I was in fact ready, indeed anxious, to make a book out of them; and as such a book could obviously not be published at Cambridge, I was free to look elsewhere. Mr. de la Mare's letter of January 20th came to me therefore at an auspicious moment. I had not been able to let him have his short Life of Shakespeare but if he would be prepared to accept a book on Shakespearian comedy instead, I should be grateful if he would publish it. He welcomed the substitute and the agreement between us for the book that now follows was signed on the 27th of July 1931.

Other publishers have perhaps waited longer for author's copy—many for ever! But none can have shown Mr. de la Mare's patience, courtesy and good humour in the waiting. And when the author passed three score years and ten without honouring his promise, any other publisher would have given him up altogether. Yet I had not only been eager to get down to it in 1931, but seemed to see next year a very fair chance of being able to do so. For in 1932 an invitation came from the University of Liverpool to give one of their courses of Shute lectures on the Art of the Theatre. For various reasons, however, the lectures could not be given before the beginning of 1938, to be repeated in the winter of 1938–9 in Edinburgh as public lectures in aid of 'academic refugees' from Europe, on whose behalf they succeeded in raising £150. Yet when I came to deliver them I took care to speak from such full notes that the book on Shakespearian comedy seemed virtually already in draft. There were six lectures in all (An introduction dealing with the early Comedies; *The Merchant of Venice; The Merry Wives of Windsor; Much Ado about Nothing; As You Like It; Twelfth Night*). But war, that shatters all plans, broke out in 1939, and when it was over both the Cambridge University Press and I realized that unless I could press resolutely forward and concentrate all my energies upon their edition of the plays I should never live to finish it. The Press accordingly offered me generous terms which enabled me to retire from teaching six years before the usual period—a premature retirement eased by the kind offices of the University of Edinburgh and by the grant of a Leverhulme Fellowship. And I have been the willing employee of the Cambridge Syndics ever since.

The last play in the canon is however now in the press and I am at liberty, in my eightieth year, to realize how disgracefully I have treated Mr. de la Mare and to take another look at the lectures delivered twenty-one years ago. These I have of course now revised, expanding the introductory lecture into two chapters. All the same, I have often deliberately retained something of the atmosphere of the period in which they were originally delivered. The one, for example, on *The Merchant of Venice* in 1938 inevitably reflected the treatment of the Jews by the Nazis before the outbreak of war, though before the full horror of the concentration camps had been revealed; and it does not I think lose anything by so doing. There had been no lecture on *The Taming of the Shrew* and I have now contented myself with passing references to this, since it is only in part Shakespeare's. But *A Midsummer Night's Dream*, a happy comedy if ever there was one, had also been omitted, and this gap Mr. de la Mare has allowed me partially to fill by reprinting an essay on the subject I wrote, at his request, in contribution to the *Tribute to Walter de la Mare on his seventy-fifth Birthday*, which fell on 25th April 1948. It is 'but a trifle, and that triflingly handled', as was said of a much greater work by a much greater author. But I felt it a signal honour to be asked to write it and I am proud to be able to flaunt the honour before a larger public. Once started on the *Dream*, however, I found I had a good deal more to say about it. I have therefore now added two fresh sections which will, I fear, convince many of my critics that I shall never learn to mend my ways.

The only book on Shakespearian comedy which held the field in 1938 was Professor Charlton's, published in February just as I was beginning my course, though available earlier in the Bulletins of the John Rylands Library; and as it is still, I think, the standard treatment of the subject there

# Preface

is nothing out of date in my references to it—often, I am afraid, adverse. Apart, however, from George Gordon's charming little essay published in 1944[1] which, I was encouraged to find, picked out as I had done George Meredith and Bergson as examples of how *not* to regard Shakespeare's comedy, I must confess I have refrained from reading anything else on the subject that has appeared since Charlton's book.[2] The only excuse for my delinquency is that a man of eighty shrinks from the labour of recasting which a critical appraisal of recent writings might have involved. Perhaps fellow scholars will be inclined more readily to forgive me when I remind them that a book based upon popular lectures is intended to appeal not to scholars but to the general public.

The proofs have been read by four different friends whose combined learning and common sense have saved me from many errors and supplied not a few omissions. To all four, my most grateful thanks.

J. D. W.

[1] George Gordon, *Shakespearian Comedy and other Studies*, 1944.
[2] I was unhappily also luckless enough to miss Professor Alexander's *Shakespeare's Life and Art*, published in the same year as Charlton's, and full of pregnant observations upon the comedies.

# CHAPTER I

# The Neglect of Shakespearian Comedy; His Comic Genius

*(the general characteristics distinguishing it from that of other comic writers)*

Traditional Shakespearian criticism from Coleridge to Bradley has been almost entirely concerned with the tragedies. Nothing is more curious, for example, than the treatment meted out to the comedies in that representative and very influential Victorian critique, Dowden's *Shakespeare: his Mind and Art* (1875). In Chapter II, which gives a general survey of the plays as a whole, we have, as a matter of form, references to the comedies, while they are spoken of again in a later chapter on 'The Humour of Shakespeare'. But Dowden is only interested in them as supplying him with examples of humorous characters, or rather of Shakespeare's delight in the creation of such characters. For from beginning to end of the book he is preoccupied with Shakespeare's spiritual development, has nothing to tell us about the general qualities of his comedies, and deals so slightly with the greatest of them all, *Twelfth Night*, that its name is not even to be found in his index. And yet, as his title shows, he claimed to be enlightening the world on the principles of Shakespeare's art. Clearly it was the tragedies which chiefly interested him.

This concentration upon the tragedies to the neglect of

the comedies has had two unfortunate results. First of all, it has, despite Dowden, given us a false idea of Shakespeare's spiritual and artistic development. We look at him far too much through the tragic end of the telescope and so have belittled him. And in the second place, it has impaired our vision of the tragedies themselves. They were not written, like those of Greece, or those of France in the classical period, by one who only knew, or was only interested in, the tragic mood. His tragedies *grew out* of the comedies. The stuff of his 'mind and art' was first woven on the comic loom and it retained something of this comic texture right up to the end. Imagine *Hamlet* without Polonius or without the Prince's antic disposition; *Lear* without the Fool; *Macbeth* without the Porter (which Coleridge, insensitive to comedy, declared could not be Shakespeare's!), and the truth of this is obvious. On the other hand, he carried the tragic baton in his knapsack from the outset of his career. As we shall note, nearly all the comedies have something of a tragic strain about them. Shakespeare was all of a piece; and his development during the twenty years or so of his life as a dramatist, unparalleled for its range and rapidity, was an unbroken development. Can *Venus and Adonis*, we ask, have been written by the same man who gave us *Lear* and *The Tempest*? Yet no part of the canon is fully explicable without the rest; and the best commentary upon any one of his plays is furnished by all the others. As Whitehead has taught us: 'At the heart of the nature of things there are always the dream of youth and the harvest of tragedy. The Adventure of the Universe starts with the dream and reaps tragic Beauty. This is the secret of the union of Zest with Peace— that the suffering attains its end in a Harmony of Harmonies.'[1] Whitehead does not mention Shakespeare; perhaps did not even have him in mind. Yet this passage expresses in philosophical terms what the whole sweep of Shakespeare's dramatic production, culminating in the harmony of harmonies which is *The Tempest*, expresses sym-

[1] *Adventures of Ideas* (1932), p. 381.

bolically. When Keats wrote 'Shakespeare led a life of Allegory: his works are the comments on it',[1] he said the same thing in other words.

This comparative neglect of Shakespeare's comedies is partly due, however, to the neglect of comedy in general. Take the first two volumes of the probably exhaustive *Subject Index of the London Library* (which were all that had been issued when the present book was first drafted) and it will be found that while the titles of the books it then possessed on the theory of tragedy run to over a couple of columns, those on the theory of comedy occupy little more than a half-column; and the subject of most of these is 'the comic', that is to say they are mainly of the psychological or quasi-psychological type, explanations of laughter and the like, and appear to have nothing to do with comedy as a form of art. There is, in fact, as far as I know, even today no comprehensive study of the last beyond one or two half-forgotten Italian treatises written at the time of the Renaissance, and a brief discussion in Jonson's *Discoveries*.[2]

This only raises the further question: what has in this way held up all discussion of comedy as compared with that of tragedy? One answer, no doubt, would be that it is less interesting, less interesting especially to the philosophical type of mind to which we are indebted, perhaps unfortunately, for most of our literary theory. Both Plato and Aristotle, for example, regard comedy as a mere pastime, serviceable for recreation, but not, like tragedy, concerned with the supreme good or end of life.[3] This view was natural for the Greeks since Greek tragedy was profoundly religious, being in fact in itself a form of religious worship, while Aristophantic comedy, though quasi-religious, because connected with the worship of Dionysus, was an irreverent, satirical, hilarious public entertainment. This difference of attitude no longer obtains of course in the

---

[1] *Letters*, ed. Forman, p. 305.     [2] *Ben Jonson*, VIII, 643-4.
[3] S. H. Butcher, *Aristotle's Theory of Poetry and the Fine Arts* (4th ed.), 1920, p. 206.

modern world; but Greek philosophy left another mark on modern thought which has always weighted the scales against comedy, an influence which, in all likelihood originally purely accidental, has been reinforced by the sheep-like propensities of the human race. In a word, had the *Poetics* of Aristotle contained a section on comedy, there can be little doubt that we should today be in possession of a considerable body of critical discussion on the subject. As everyone knows, the *Poetics* is a fragmentary book of notes, probably lecture notes, on poetry, which, as it has come down to us, deals mainly with tragedy and epic. The history of comedy is briefly attended to in the fifth chapter by way of a statement that (unlike tragedy) it has had no historian because it has never been taken seriously. It seems tolerably certain, however, that the nature of comedy was considered, perhaps in passing, by Aristotle in the lost second book, which is known to have contained a more detailed account of Catharsis than is found elsewhere in the treatise. It seems therefore possible, perhaps likely, as has been argued,[1] that Aristotle claimed a catharsis for comedy as well as for tragedy; the difference probably being that whereas tragedy purged men's bosoms of pity and terror by representing an 'imitation' of them in the theatre, the purification effected by comedy was in respect of the tendency to excess of laughter and of scorn or contempt. This would mean that comedy was viewed by the Greeks, as they viewed everything else, from the political standpoint, that is to say as an aid to the production of that justice or temperance in the soul of man which would make him a good citizen in the city-state. A man overmuch given to spiteful laughter was a nuisance to his neighbours. The spectacle of comedy gave that tendency a harmless outlet; it regulated the indulgence of a natural, though (if excessive) an undesirable, propensity. In a word, it civilized.

There is also little doubt that to the Greeks laughter possessed a taint of unseemliness, if not of indecency, which it no longer of necessity has for us, since in that age its patron

[1] See Lane Cooper, *Aristotle's Theory of Comedy*, 1924.

# Faber & Faber

## have pleasure in sending for review

### a copy of

SHAKESPEARE'S HAPPY COMEDIES
by John Dover Wilson
(Faber Paper Covered Edition)

## which will be published on

2nd September 1969 at 15/-

*It is requested that the notice of the book shall not appear before the date of publication.*

*The publishers are glad, whenever possible, to lend photographs of authors and illustrative material.*

24 Russell Square, London W.C.1

was Dionysus, the wine-god. This is why Plato forbade his Guardians to laugh, and condemned Homer as blasphemous for ascribing laughter to the gods. The severance of laughter from obscenity, to which both historically and psychologically it was closely allied, is one of the many great debts which civilization owes to Puritanism, and under Puritanism I include, of course, the puritanism of the counter-Reformation and that of the Reformation alike. But how partial that severance still is may be seen by comparing the comic periodicals of our country with those so freely available on the Continent.

Let us now turn to the best-known, almost the only, discussion of comedy in English: I mean George Meredith's *Essay on Comedy*. Meredith does not mention Aristotle; nevertheless what he has to say is little more than an elaboration and a translation into modern terms of what Aristotle might have written. 'Laughter', Meredith tells us as he draws his conclusions:

> is open to perversion, like other good things; the scornful and the brutal sorts are not unknown to us; but the laughter directed by the Comic spirit is a harmless wine, conducing to sobriety in the degree that it enlivens. . . . Sensitiveness to the comic laugh is a step in civilization. To shrink from being an object of it is a step in cultivation. We know the degree of refinement in men by the matter they will laugh at, and the ring of the laugh; but we know likewise that the larger natures are distinguished by the great breadth of their power of laughter.'[1]

Aristotle would hardly have reckoned laughter among the 'good things' of life, or have agreed that the breadth of a man's power of laughter was one of the distinguishing features of magnanimity. But he might perhaps have subscribed to much else.

And yet all this, interesting and valuable from the point of view of sociology and psychology, is really of little relevance to literary criticism, which is mainly concerned with comedy as a species of artistic composition; with the differ-

[1] George Meredith, *Essay on Comedy*, 1903, pp. 92–4.

ent types of comedy; and with the means by which the
comic dramatist attains his success with his audience.
Comedy may be useful as a medicine for the soul; it may be,
as Meredith claims, the guardian spirit of common sense
hovering above our civilization with its 'slim feasting smile',
ready to 'cast an oblique light' upon our follies and absurdities, and to vent its 'volleys of silvery laughter'.[1] But if that
be taken as a description of what comedy actually effects, a
description which at once defines the character of those
effects and marks them off from those produced by other
forms of literary art, it is manifestly inadequate. And that
for a very obvious reason—it excludes Shakespeare!

Meredith has much to say about Aristophanes, Menander
and Terence, Molière and Congreve, even not a little concerning writers who were not dramatists at all or only so
incidentally, such as Fielding, Byron, Cervantes and Carlyle.
But to Shakespeare barely a page of the essay is devoted.[1]
And on that page he is politely but firmly turned out of the
commonwealth of comedy. It is true that Meredith begins
by calling him a 'well-spring of characters which are satur-
ated with the comic spirit'; but since he goes on to describe
these characters as 'creatures of the woods and wilds, not in
walled towns, not grouped and toned to pursue a comic
exhibition of the narrower world of society' (which 'narrower world' he spends the rest of the essay in trying to
show us as the essential feeding ground of the comic spirit),
it is clear that he has either left something unexplained, or is
manœuvring for ground and using 'comedy' in two senses
in order to get Shakespeare somehow into the picture. Even
so, the author of *Twelfth Night* is only brought in to be dismissed immediately after. For Meredith goes on at once to
speak of 'his comedy of incredible imbroglio', and slams the
door upon him in the following sentence, which Dryden
himself could have written: 'Had Shakespeare lived in a
later and less emotional, less heroical, period of our history,

[1] Ibid., pp. 89–90.　　　[2] Ibid., pp. 22–3.

he might have turned to the painting of manners as well as humanity.'[1]

This strange handling of one of the greatest of comic dramatists by one of the greatest of comic novelists reveals a serious, if not a fatal, flaw in the *Essay on Comedy* which would lead me to digress too far from my topic if I stopped to investigate it here. It reveals, however, something else which is more to the point. The brilliant generalizations of the *Essay*, relevant enough to most comic dramatists and anticipated in all probability, as we have seen, in the lost second book of the *Poetics*, do not fit Shakespeare. Equally inapplicable, as we shall see, are the generalizations of the perhaps even more famous essay by Bergson[2] which is based exclusively on the study of Molière and his successors in modern French comedy. The book does not contain a single reference to Falstaff—think of it!—and its title is *Laughter*! It is perhaps even more extraordinary that it excludes Rabelais also. Bergson's views on laughter, though interesting as far as they go, are reached from a very limited standpoint, as far as drama goes.

It would seem, then, that Shakespearian comedy differs, possibly fundamentally, from the comedy of most of the other comic dramatists in modern literature. In what does this difference consist? A cursory examination of the qualities which the comedies of these dramatists possess or display and those of Shakespeare do not, may help us to arrive at some useful preliminary conclusions about our theme before attempting to obtain positive results by the consideration of Shakespeare's comedies in detail.

Most modern comedy, from the 'comical satires' of Ben Jonson down to the plays of Ibsen and Bernard Shaw which ushered in the social and moral revolution that is the outstanding fact of our time, has been critical in purpose. The means and the object of attack have differed. Jonson lashes typical crimes and follies of the period: the Jacobean lust for

[1] Ibid., pp. 23.
[2] H. Bergson, *Laughter*, translated by Brereton and Rothwell (1911).

wealth in *Volpone*; social pestilences and their victims in *The Alchemist*. Molière, more subtly, exhibits to our view the springs of hypocrisy, of virtue driven by vanity into anti-social misanthropy, of hypochondria, of intellectual snobbery. Ibsen and Shaw expose, the one with mordant irony and the other with ridicule and brilliant wit, the conventions of a dying civilization and the hollow men of an outworn system of public life.

This type of comedy is often called classical; it is really *neo*-classical. No such seriousness of purpose infused the comedies of Greece and Rome after the death of the Old Comedy, which Aristophanes had graced. Modern neo-classical comedy was begotten by classical learning upon the traditions of the late medieval morality play. The doctrine of *instruction*—the typical doctrine of Renaissance dramatic theory—was imposed upon the classical dramatic form, and the result was an almost complete departure from the tone of classical comedy.

This is particularly evident in the *dénouement*. In the comedies of Plautus and Terence, who follow Menander, the intriguer (a slave), responsible for most of the complications of the plot, is generally pardoned at the end, and the end itself is usually a happy consummation. In modern (or neo-classical) comedy, in order that virtue, or common sense, or the revolutionary notions of the dramatist, may triumph, the intriguers and their dupes are generally brought to destruction, or the social inadequacy of their pretentions is ruthlessly exposed. Thus the 'happy ending' becomes the victory of virtue, or common sense, or social justice, in other words the victory of *society*, whether actual or desirable, over its enemies.

Shakespeare knows hardly anything of this. As a distinguished American critic puts it:

'Not only does he laugh as all England laughed, but he believes as all England believed, and no more of the critical spirit is there in him than must needs be in one so well-balanced and sane. That is reserved for individual cases; and not a single ideal, ethical judgment, or custom of his time does he question, thus losing a great source of comedy indispensable to the dramatist of our day. . . . By choice he accepted life; and his imagination comprehended more than it discriminated, though not indifferently. His imagination was an embrace.'[1]

I cannot go quite all the way with this, which seems an oversimplified representation of the spirit that gave us *Hamlet* and *Lear*, *Measure for Measure* and *Troilus and Cressida*. But it is undoubtedly true that Shakespearian comedy, up to 1601 at any rate, was not critical, or only so in a very limited sense. *Love's Labour's Lost*, itself a *jeu d'esprit* at the expense of neo-classical notions, comes nearest to the neo-classical ideal; and this is interesting, because it also comes nearest to neo-classical *form*. Yet Shakespeare was no innovator like Jonson, but rather the perfecter and sublimater of the old-fashioned type of comedy. His comedies belong to the same species (though refined to the point of genius, so that they became in the end something new), as the comedies of sixteenth-century Italy, which were themselves romanticized descendants of Plautus and Terence.[2] Thus, in a way, Shakespearian comedy has a better title to be called classical than has Jonsonian comedy.

Closely connected with the lack of social criticism in Shakespearian comedy is the fact that he laughs, or gets his audience to laugh, quite as often *with* his characters as *at* them. High spirits is one of the predominant notes of his happy plays. His principal characters often find themselves in absurd situations, and sometimes do ridiculous things, but though we laugh, *they* usually laugh too; and their escapades are performed to the accompaniment of such a running commentary of witty dialogue that we are kept perpetually admiring as well as smiling at them.[3] Most of the chief characters, in short, are delightful people. If they do not seem delightful to us, we have generally

[1] E. E. Stoll, *Shakespeare Studies* (1927), p. 186.
[2] See Charlton, *Shakespearian Comedy*, 1938, Chapter 2.
[3] Stoll (op. cit., pp. 156-7) has some excellent remarks on this.

23

misunderstood Shakespeare. In modern or neo-classical comedy, on the other hand, we are usually invited to laugh at or even to scorn the chief characters. Indeed, such plays are frequently without a single character that evokes our admiration or our sympathy. Except in Shaw they tend to be grim; Shakespeare's tend to be gay.

It is true that two leading figures, Shylock and Malvolio, cannot be so described and that among minor characters Shakespeare often gives us butts to be laughed at. Yet even they are seldom lacking in some trait or some final speech which reveals them and excites our sympathy, while it is remarkable that if they are laughed at, they are laughed at by other characters in the play as well as by the audience. Laughter on the stage is, in fact, one of the marks of Shakespearian comedy.

The importance of the Clown in relation to all this is obvious. The Clown or Fool had a long stage-history behind him when Shakespeare took him over.[1] But Shakespeare brought him to his perfection, and after Shakespeare he disappears and is seen no more in the theatre, or in literature —Wordsworth's *Idiot Boy* being a kind of abortive attempt to revive him. The Fool is fundamental to Shakespearian comedy—not only because Costard, and Launce, and Lancelot Gobbo, and Bottom, and Touchstone, and Feste furnish the very salt of the plays in which they appear, but also because they symbolize and embody what is one of the outstanding features of Shakespearian comedy in general. They are at once butts and critics, as the 'allowed Fool' had always been at court and in castle throughout the Middle Ages. 'He uses his folly', the Duke says of Touchstone, 'like a stalking-horse and under presentation of that he shoots his wit[2].' The Fool was an institution, we cannot doubt, which made a particular appeal to the mind of Shakespeare, as it did to that of Sir Thomas More, and he clung to it even after he had passed from comedy to tragedy. The subtlest

[1] Cf. Enid Welsford, *The Fool*, 1935.
[2] *As You Like It*, V, iv, 103–4

and tenderest of all fools is the Fool in *King Lear*, and the part he plays in the greatest of the world's tragedies will help us to understand his significance in the comedies.

You may say, if you will, that his function is that of the chorus in Greek drama; it is less than that and a great deal more. One who was himself a simpleton, who affected the shambling gait and vacant stare of the village idiot, who was the laughing-stock of all the other characters in the play, and yet whose comments upon them and upon matters in general proved him wiser than them all, was obviously an extraordinarily useful and effective type for a comic dramatist, and it is a great pity that he is lost to our stage.

Bergson points out that comedy is largely concerned with persons who make themselves ridiculous by becoming mechanical instead of human, typical instead of individual. The Fool was significant for exactly the opposite reason. Born witless, an automaton with almost automatic actions and a doll-like expression, he surprises and delights us by his sudden fits of sanity and penetration. *All Fools but the Fool*, the title of an unknown play by Chapman,[1] best perhaps describes his dramatic function. What there is of social satire in Shakespearian comedy is largely to be found in the sallies that fall from the Fool's lips.

In the Fool, I suspect, we come very close to Shakespeare's own standpoint as a comic dramatist. The idea that the deepest and greatest things in life may be hidden from the wise and prudent and be revealed unto children and fools; that however much the stupid and the simple may be overwhelmed by confusion and ignominy in the court of the world's laughter, they are allowed the right of appeal to a higher court; and that what counts, that is what wins our affection, is not rank or wealth or intellect, but humanity, native and unassuming; all this, as we shall find, forms the undertone, or one of the undertones, in Shakespeare's comedies. In other words, they appeal not to the intellect,

[1] See Henslowe's *Diary*, ed. Greg, II, 203 (1599). *All Fools* (1605) has no fool in it and therefore cannot be identical with the earlier drama.

but to what we call, for want of a better name, the heart. But if so, they are comedies of a totally different kind from the comedy of which Molière is the chief representative. Another quotation from Bergson shows this clearly: 'Laughter has no greater foe than emotion. . . . To produce the whole of its effect . . . the comic demands something like a momentary anaesthesia of the heart. Its appeal is to intelligence, pure and simple.'[1]

And there is yet another point to notice about the Clown or Fool which helps to make him central, as it were, to Shakespearian comedy. That two-sidedness, motley-mindedness, that ability, call it what you will, to flash suddenly upon us from behind his wooden mask a living beam which illuminates him and us and all the world, is not his alone, though especially his. All, or at any rate most, of Shakespeare's characters possess it in some measure. We must be on the look-out for it, if we are to understand these characters rightly—it helps us, for example, to solve the problem of Shylock. There are 'types' of various kinds to be found in Shakespeare's comedies; but they are always liable to 'come alive'. Do they thereby cease to be comic? If Bergson is to be believed, it would seem that they do. To quote him again:

> 'If we leave on one side, when dealing with human personality, that portion which interests our sensibility or appeals to our feelings, all the rest is capable of becoming comic. . . . Every comic character is a *type*. . . . Thus, to depict characters, that is to say, general types, is the object of high-class comedy. This has often been said. But it is as well to repeat it, since there could be no better definition of comedy.'[2]

Shakespearian comedy eludes the definition altogether.

It is natural to pass from this to a consideration of the relation of plot to character. When Meredith speaks half-contemptuously of Shakespeare's 'comedy of incredible imbroglio' he refers, of course, to the normal plot of Shakespeare's comedies, which, depending as it does largely upon

---

[1] H. Bergson, op. cit., pp. 4, 5, 139.     [2] Bergson, ibid., pp. 148-9.

mistakes and confusion brought about by disguise or family resemblance, has been almost universally deplored by critics as puerile and mechanical. They go on to compare it with the elaborate and well-motivated plots of Ben Jonson, which are usually wholly dependent upon the interaction of his characters—are often, indeed, made up of the intrigues or plots of different persons working secretly against each other. And what is true of Jonson is true also, *mutatis mutandis*, of Molière.

Now Shakespeare inherited his 'imbroglio' plots partly from the not infrequent use of family resemblance in Plautus—and he went so far as to double the twins of the *Menaechmi* in *The Comedy of Errors*; and partly from the Italian comedy or from the Italian and Spanish *novelle*, in which disguise was an exceedingly common device in the making of plots. The popularity of the disguise motive in Italian comedy, which was in the main the old Latin comedy brought up to date, was due to the fact that whereas female characters in Plautus and Terence were generally courtesans (because respectable women could not be encountered in the streets), the young men of sixteenth-century Italian plays generally set their hearts upon more reputable girls, who nevertheless were equally prevented by propriety from meeting their lovers in the open, unless they assumed male attire and passed as boys.[1] This does not explain, however, the frequent resort to the same device by Shakespeare and his contemporaries on the stage of England, where no such social purdah customs prevailed.

An American critic, Dr. Freeburg, in an interesting book entitled *Disguise Plots in Elizabethan Drama*[2] has pointed out that, artificial as the disguise motive may seem to modern spectators and critics nourished upon realistic drama, it was an accepted convention of the Elizabethan stage for which there was a good deal to be said. It was in fact dramatically highly effective, since it simultaneously

[1] Cf. R. Warwick Bond, *Early Plays from the Italian* (1911), p. xxxix.
[2] V. O. Freeburg, Columbia University Press, 1915.

set up complications in the plot, complications which might be most elaborate; gave full play to the expectations of the audience; and enabled the dramatist to accomplish that most difficult of his tasks, a neat termination of the play, with the greatest possible ease, inasmuch as he had only to expose the disguise to bring about the finale, and this he might do at any moment suitable to himself.

The same critic notes that disguise adds complication to character as well as to plot. A disguised character is practically two persons: (i) for the other characters in the play, who are deceived, and (ii) for the spectators who enjoy being in the know. And this two-sided situation, which reminds us of what we have just been saying about the Fool in Elizabethan drama, gives opportunity for all kinds of veiled allusion, double meaning, dramatic irony, and subtlety of dialogue generally.[1] From the purely theatrical point of view disguise had the further merit of affording occasion for frequent change of costume, and of enabling the boy-players to play women *as boys* for most of the time they were on the stage. Perhaps nothing gave the device more popularity than this last point, since not only must it have greatly eased the task of those who had to coach the boys in their parts, but also it added considerably to the piquancy of the situation for the audience.

Disguise, indeed, exercised in sixteenth- and seventeenth-century Europe a fascination upon circles far beyond the theatre walls. The courts of the Renaissance gave themselves up with zest to pageantry and display. The theatre itself, on the one hand, lived and flourished upon court patronage, and on the other play-acting, generally in the form of masques, was one of the chief amusements of courtiers and nobility, an amusement that became almost a passion at the court of the first two Stuarts, inspired mainly

---

[1] As in the case of the Fool, the extreme instance of this doubling by means of disguise is to be found in *King Lear* in the character of Edgar, which puts a little strain on our credulity since we are not accustomed to the device, as Shakespeare's audiences were.

by Queen Anne and ennobled by the art of Inigo Jones and Ben Jonson; both, it will be noted, primarily men of the theatre. And the fun of such masques for the princes and courtiers performing them lay of course chiefly in the 'dressing up' and especially in the disguises the participants delighted to assume, partly because they gave free play to flirtation and love-making, as had the traditional 'impromptu masking' which had roots both in Italy and in the medieval English 'mummery'.[1] All this is also naturally reflected in the arcadian and other romances. To make love, and to be made love to, masked, was one of the principal sports of the age, and one never likely to drop entirely out of favour as long as fashionable societies are to be found with time to waste on amusements. Such a society existed in London in the reign of Edward VII, and the account given in Sir Edward Marsh's correspondence (1903–10) of masked balls in London and of the flirtation involved is very Elizabethan.[2]

Among Dr. Freeburg's useful observations concerning plot and character, one consideration which affects the relation between the two had, it seems, escaped him. The disguise-plot, just because it is largely mechanical and *external* to the life and action of the characters, gives the dramatist far greater freedom with his characters than the more naturalistic plots of realistic comedy, which are, as we have seen, entirely dependent upon the interaction of those characters. In Jonson and Molière plot and character are all of a piece, different but inseparable portions of the same dramatic pattern; and because *to be comic* their characters must be types, be mechanical, it is all the more necessary that the plot should bear the unmistakable stamp of verisimilitude. With Shakespeare it is exactly the reverse. His characters are

---

[1] See Enid Welsford, *The Court Masque* (1927), p. 102. In the masking scense of *Romeo and Juliet* (I, iv), *Much Ado* (2, i), *Love's Labour's Lost* (V, ii) and *Henry VIII* (I, iv) we have vivid representations of 'impromptu maskings' on the stage.

[2] See Christopher Hassall, *Edward Marsh* (1959), Chapter VII.

no abstractions but creatures of seeming flesh and blood; his plots are either mechanical or non-existent. And it is just because he is not obliged to fit his characters into the pattern of a rigid plot that he has scope to give them life. As we shall find, *Love's Labour's Lost* is apparently, but only apparently, an exception to this.

A naturalistic plot was part of that decorum of which we hear so much in Renaissance dramatic theory, and which the neo-classical drama succeeded in imposing upon the playwrights of Europe. The 'three unities' erroneously supposed to have been laid down by Aristotle were the most notorious of the rules of this decorum, and likewise made for naturalism of effect.[1] It is probable that Shakespeare smiled when the 'Unities' were preached at him, as no doubt they were; for though *Errors* and *Love's Labour's Lost* observe them, perhaps owing to the circumstances of their original production, as also does *The Tempest*, which may have been first performed under circumstances of a similar nature, none of the plays that lie between these two distant points in his dramatic career pays the least attention to them.

But, besides the unities of place, time, and action, the Renaissance critics considered under 'action' a fourth, that of dramatic species. Sir Philip Sidney complains that English plays in his day

> be neither right Tragedies, nor right Comedies, mingling Kings and Clownes, not because the matter so carrieth it, but thrust in Clownes by head and shoulder, to play a part in majesticall matters, with neither decencie nor discretion: so as neither the admiration and commiseration, nor the right sportfulness is by their mongrell Tragicomedie obtained.

And he adds,

[1] Cf. Rapin, *Réflexions sur la poétique*, 1672, §xii: 'I make no pretence of justifying the necessity, justice and truth of these rules. . . . I take all that for granted. I only say that, if you consider them well, you will find that they are merely made to methodize Nature, to follow her step by step. . . . If there is not unity of place, time, and action in poems, there is no verisimilitude.' (Cited from Saintsbury, *Loci Critici* (1903), pp. 140-1.)

I knowe the Auncients haue one or two examples of Tragicomedies, as Plautus hath *Amphitrio*. But if we marke them well we shall find, that they neuer, or very daintily, match horne Pipes and Funeralls.[1]

This was written about 1581, long before any of Shakespeare's plays reached the stage; and the future lay with Sidney, for Ben Jonson was a rigid upholder of the rule which forbade the mixture of serious elements in comedy, however saturnine his own comedies may have been in practice. But 'Elizabethan drama' and Shakespeare came between. Here, once again, it was the neo-classicists who raised the standard of revolt, in the name of a Return to the Past as all wise revolutionaries claim; and Shakespeare who was the traditionalist and conservative, his 'mongrell tragicomedie' being doubly descended from the Middle Ages. For its 'comedie' was a heritage of the miracle plays, in which comic elements were freely mingled with the most solemn matters of religious history, in order to satisfy the popular craving for a little fun amidst so much seriousness, the dramatists being able to 'count with certainty upon finding in their audience a childlike capacity for making a quick transition from laughter to tears'.[2] On the other hand, the type itself was in part a relic of the meaning given to the words 'comedy' and 'tragedy' in the Middle Ages. These terms were not applied to the religious drama just spoken of. Indeed, not until the Renaissance was it realized that they had once possessed a theatrical significance. For, with the old classical theatre gone out of mind, medieval man

'had come to regard comedy and tragedy, not as names for specific dramatic types, but as names for emotional narratives coming respectively to happy and to sad endings. When at the Renascence, emotional drama grew up again on the basis of medieval narrative, it became the natural heir of the same distinction. The stress of emotion is common to Elizabethan tragedy and Elizabethan comedy,

[1] *The Defence of Poesie*, edited by Albert Feuillerat, 1923, pp. 39–40. See Johnson, *Rambler*, 156, for a half-hearted defence of tragi-comedy in Shakespeare.

[2] Creizenach, *The English Drama in the Age of Shakespeare*, 1916, p. 238. See his footnote for contemporary theoretic attempts to defend this mingling.

but while in tragedy it issues in pity and terror and the funeral procession, in comedy it gathers only to pass away and dissolve in triumph and laughter and the clash of marriage-bells. For such emotional or romantic comedy as distinct from comedy proper, "tragicomedy", which the Elizabethans sometimes used, is perhaps the happiest term.'

I quote from E. K. Chambers[1] who has here given us the best account of Shakespeare's 'tragicomedie' I know, and I shall not hesitate to adopt it as a leading idea in the investigation that follows. Yet while it is obviously apt to *The Merchant of Venice*, in the context of which it was written, and may even be applied to *Much Ado*, the term 'tragicomedie' must be stretched a good deal to cover *Love's Labour's Lost*, *As You Like It*, or *Twelfth Night*, which indeed contain serious elements that move towards an emotional crisis, to be, however, resolved in the end, but nothing in the least 'tragic'. Yet these comedies clearly belong to the same species as the others and are shaped by the same traditional formulas, with which tragedy has but slight connexion.

What then, to conclude, is the fundamental difference between the comic genius of the traditionalist Shakespeare and that of neo-classicists like Jonson and Molière? Shakespeare's comedy is emotional, fanciful, tender, human; Jonson's and Molière's is intellectual, realistic, critical. This is not to deny that the latter is poetic; *Volpone* and *Le Misanthrope* are both poems. Compare, for example, what is admittedly Shakespeare's greatest comic creation, Sir John Falstaff, with the Alchemist or Tartuffe. The leading characters of Jonson and Molière are comic types, magnificently realized and presented with ruthless force for our inspection. Had Falstaff been similarly conceived he might well have been exhibited for our scorn as a comic type exposing the seamy side of Elizabethan London, since he is actually revealed in the text as a filthy old ruffian, physically repulsive, as disorderly in morals as in dress, in short, a liar, a sot, a coward, and a whoremaster. Yet Shakespeare cloaks all this

---

[1] *Shakespeare: a Survey*, 1925, p. 111.

by enduing him right from the beginning with such gaiety and animation, such nimbleness of wit, such a varied flow of imagery, such perfect poise and self-assurance, and above all with such magnificent vitality, that so far from being repulsive in our eyes he has become, as I have written elsewhere, a kind of god in the mythology of modern man, a god who does for our imagination very much what Bacchus or Silenus did for that of the Ancients.[1] He teaches us nothing; and is so far from 'realism' and a comic type that no one has ever been like him or can ever be like him. Yet we may receive much medicine for the spirit from the contemplation of an imaginary being free of all the conventions, codes and moral obligations that control us as members of human society; a medicine which Meredith, when not theorizing, himself describes in a sonnet on 'The Spirit of Shakespeare' as:

> Thunders of laughter clearing air and heart.

Falstaff, in a word, is a supreme comic poem whom we enjoy imaginatively and who evokes in us the emotions of delight, wonder, admiration and exaltation.

The comedy of Jonson and the other realistic comic writers appeals then to the intellect. It is a comedy of ideas; Shakespeare's comedy is a comedy of the emotions—a fundamental distinction. And in this, too, Shakespeare was all of a piece. For what is true of his comedies is true also of his tragedies, is true indeed of Elizabethan tragedy in general, in which, as Edmund Chambers has written, 'the artist endeavours to transfer to the audience not his own judgments, but his own emotional states, through the medium of their sympathies with the woes and exultations of the characters whom he fashions for the purpose'.[2] It seems that in looking for the secret of Shakespeare's comic genius we have stumbled upon the secret of his dramatic art as a whole.

---

[1] *The Essential Shakespeare* (1932), p. 88; *The Fortunes of Falstaff* (1943), p. 128.
[2] E. K. Chambers, op. cit., p. 111.

# CHAPTER II

# Shakespeare's Happy Comedies; Their Origin and Special Quality

F alstaff is Shakespeare's greatest comic character. However, the main subject of this book is not comic character but comedy—comedy as a form of dramatic art; and *Henry IV*, which W. P. Ker[1] described as 'something like a large roomy novel', is not in any sense a comedy. Thus while it will be impossible to avoid all reference to Prince Hal's fat friend, just as it will be difficult not to mention the comic scenes in *Romeo and Juliet* or the Bastard in *King John*, we shall not be concerned directly with that Falstaff at all. On the other hand, his far less interesting cousin of Windsor who masquerades under the same name because it suited Shakespeare's book to palm him off upon the Queen as the genuine Sir John, falls well within our purview because he happens to hold the central place in a comedy, the delightful and in some ways unique comedy of *The Merry Wives of Windsor*.

And I am to narrow the issue still further, for I shall be asking my readers to consider not so much Shakespearian comedy in general as a special kind of Shakespearian comedy, namely the ten comedies he wrote first, which it is generally agreed constitute a class of their own. These are: *The Comedy of Errors, The Taming of the Shrew, The Two*

[1] W. P. Ker, *Form and Style in Poetry* (1928), p. 343.

## Their Origin and Special Quality

Gentlemen of Verona, Love's Labour's Lost, A Midsummer Night's Dream, The Merchant of Venice, Much Ado about Nothing, As You Like It, Twelfth Night, and The Merry Wives of Windsor, which possess a character and tone in common that clearly mark them off from the two later groups of comedy: that comprising Troilus and Cressida, All's Well, and Measure for Measure, which date from the opening years of the seventeenth century, and the four plays of the last phase, Pericles, Cymbeline, A Winter's Tale, and The Tempest. These second and third groups are generally described respectively as the Bitter Comedies or Problem Plays and the Romances. No such satisfactorily comprehensive label has, however, become attached so far to the plays of the first group. For the term 'romantic' often applied to them lacks precision, seeing that all Shakespeare's comedies are in a sense 'romantic', and is further liable to confusion with the more or less accepted title for the last group. The 'Elizabethan Comedies' will not do either, inasmuch as Troilus and Cressida at any rate, if not All's Well, was produced during the reign of the great Queen.[1]

Pondering this question of titles when preparing the lectures which formed the first draft of this book, I consulted a critic of a younger generation, not a critic known to other Shakespearian critics, a critic on the hearth in fact. How would you, I asked, describe Shakespearian comedy? The reply I got was this:

> What attracts me about the comedies of Shakespeare is just that you can't label them, that they are a glorious rich blend of all types of comedy—witty dialogue, fanciful poetry, true realistic comedy etc. etc.—mysteriously made into a harmony, in which each type is heightened and yet transformed by the influence of the other types and all combined to express a certain very real view of the world, which it's impossible to analyse. Ben Jonson's plays do not give me any sense of reality; I mean they fail to move me. But reading a Shakespearian comedy puts me into a mood in which I feel the world as a unity, as I also do in a tragedy, though in a different way of

[1] E. K. Chambers, William Shakespeare (1930), i, 270-1, dates Troilus and Cressida, 1601-2 and All's Well, 1602-3.

course. What it boils down to, I suppose, is this. I like Shakespeare's comedies because they make me feel fine and the world is a jolly place—and surprisingly beautiful at times; and I don't like Ben Jonson's because they make me feel petty or just unreal.

Despite his refusal, my critic had given me the label I sought for. The quality the first ten comedies have in common is happiness, a serene happiness, liable to develop into merriment in the conclusion, yet threatening to become serious at times, otherwise there would be no play. And, though my critic does not say so, this quality is only found in these first comedies. No one could call *Measure for Measure*, *Troilus and Cressida* or *All's Well* either serene or happy, while the mood we are left with at the end of one of the Romances may be serenity, but not happiness so much as beatitude. Compare the concluding passage of *The Merchant* with that of *A Winter's Tale* or *The Tempest*, and the point is obvious. The former calls Boccaccio to mind, the latter Heaven.

But, as my critic hints, most Shakespearian comedy is a blend of many dramatic types and devices, drawn from a variety of sources, so fused that they have become well-nigh indistinguishable. Yet if we think of the happy comedies from *Errors* to *Twelfth Night* for a moment as ten panels of the same tapestry, we may discern certain main patterns which, though not of course all found in every play, run through most. All but one of Shakespeare's comedies, indeed, including those of the two later groups, are woven on a foreign canvas which is generally Italian, though a forest in France or near Athens or again a royal park in Navarre served equally well: and it is mainly this foreign background or atmosphere that has earned the title of 'romantic' for Shakespeare's comedies in general. It is in fact one of the marks that serves to distinguish the 'romantic' from the 'realistic' category of drama; in which connexion it is significant that Ben Jonson's earliest humour play, *Everyman in his Humour*, was in the original draft of the 1601 Quarto located in Italy, and furnished with Italian character names, but transferred to London and the names anglicized in the revised version that appeared in the Folio text of 1616 —a change which may be taken to mark the birth of modern English realistic comedy.

Moreover it is important to observe that in this foreign setting Shakespeare was merely following tradition, since the scenes in both the old Latin and the later Italian comedies from which his sprang were naturally laid in some Mediterranean town. Equally traditional were the clowns and fools that he introduced into them all, and so formed a second strand in the general pattern. This element was medieval in origin, though not without features reminiscent of, if not akin to, the mischievous slaves in Plautus and Terence. Two other traditional elements, common to most of the plays in question, may be called structural, since they furnish the leading themes or subjects about which the plays were built, I mean the business and domestic affairs of the merchant class and the love affairs and friendships of the gentry in the class above. Aspects of both are commonly found in all ten, but there are two in which each is dealt with separately. These are *The Comedy of Errors* and *The Two Gentlemen of Verona*, which are generally regarded as the earliest comedies for which Shakespeare was wholly responsible. For though *The Taming of the Shrew* which Chambers places between them[1] must be reckoned a happy comedy, it was as he shows only Shakespeare's in part.

The first recorded performance of *Errors* was one given as an item in a Christmas-tide student jollification at Gray's Inn on 28th December 1594, but allusions in it to the civil war between Henry of Navarre and the Catholic League in France make it pretty clear that it was written two or three years before.[2] *The Two Gentlemen* offers no such clues and its date is really quite uncertain, as Chambers admits though being inclined to put it at 1594–5. For myself I find it

[1] E. K. Chambers, op. cit. (1930), i, Chapter VIII, 'The Problem of Chronology', pp. 270–1, 325.
[2] See note on III, ii, 123–4 in New Cambridge edition.

difficult to believe that these two very short plays were not composed at much the same period or at any rate for the same company and the same type of stage, whether in a private house or at court. However this may be, Shakespeare, it seems, began his career as a writer of comedy with two diploma pieces upon quite different themes, and having thus tried them out experimentally, so to speak, he resorted to them for any characters, motives or situations he might need when he came to the composition of their brilliant sequels. In a word, *The Comedy of Errors* and *The Two Gentlemen of Verona* are the basic plays of the happy comedies. And this being so, a brief account of them both in the light of their sources forms an appropriate introduction to what comes later, the more appropriate indeed because at times Shakespeare went back to the source behind the basic play for something he required.

*The Comedy of Errors* is a drama of merchant life at a seaport in the Mediterranean. The male characters apart from the Duke, the two Dromios, and Pinch the schoolmaster, comprise no fewer than seven merchants. And the whole play, the scenes of which take place in or near the marketplace, revolves round the doings of merchants, their womenfolk, and servants. We have only to add that one of the characters is a courtesan to complete its resemblance to the old Latin comedy; and in fact, as has always been known, it is a free adaptation of the *Menaechmi* by Plautus.[1] But it is a Plautine comedy enlarged, and became an Elizabethan play while retaining its foreign appearance. In Plautus twin brothers, accidentally separated soon after birth and losing all trace of each other for twenty-five years, are as accidentally brought together again, without knowing it, in the same town, where their resemblance gives rise to a series of absurd and comical situations. Shakespeare changes the name of the twins from Menaechmus to Antipholus and more than doubles the confusion, and hence the entertainment of

[1] In his Introduction to *Errors* in the New Shakespeare edition, Q furnishes a full and lively paraphrase of the Plautus play.

the audience, by giving the twin Antipholuses twin servants who had been separated at the same time and in the same way as their masters. The twin servants, whom he calls Dromio,[1] were probably suggested by Sosia, the slave in *Amphitruo*, another play by Plautus; there being a parasite but no slave in *Menaechmi*. Furthermore one of Shakespeare's most hilarious scenes is that in which Antipholus of Ephesus is shut out of his house while Antipholus of Syracuse is being entertained at dinner by the Ephesian wife who takes him for her husband, while Dromio of Syracuse who has gone in with his master jeers at Dromio of Ephesus through the hatch of the bolted door, and Luce, the kitchen maid, joins in the raillery from a gallery above. This too, as has long been realized, Shakespeare took from *Amphitruo*, another comedy based on mistaken identity. In *Amphitruo*, however, the resultant confusion is due, not to a natural resemblance between twins but to one deliberately assumed as a disguise by Jupiter, and by Mercury who acts as his servant, in order that the heavenly father, in love with Amphitryon's wife, and transforming himself into the similitude of her absent lord, may be entertained by her at board and bed. Whereupon the real Amphitryon, returning from the wars, finds himself shut out like Shakespeare's Antipholus in III, i of *Errors*, and jeered at from above the door by Mercury disguised as the slave Sosia—as one Dromio is jeered at by the other. As a matter of fact there are twins too in *Amphitruo*, since Alcmena, Amphitryon's wife, gives birth to them at the end of the play, one of them being Jupiter's son Hercules. But twins were a favourite device with Plautus; we get twin sisters for example in the *Bacchides*.

Anyhow it is obvious that Shakespeare knew *Amphitruo* well. But how did he know it? In the original Latin or in an English translation? One must ask the same question also about *Menaechmi*. For though a translation by William Warner was published in 1595, that is far too late for *Errors*,

---

[1] Is this a version, perhaps a misprint, of Dromo, the name of the slave in Terence's *Adelphi*?

yet the printer of the book tells his readers in a preface that *Menaechmi* was only one of 'divers of this Poettes Comedies Englished [by Warner] for the use and delight of his private friendes'. Was Shakespeare one of these friends? If so, he may possibly have read both the comedies he wanted for *Errors* in Warner's manuscript.

However this may be, when he came to write his play he not only improved upon the plot of *Menaechmi* in the fashion just mentioned, but while preserving its classical accidentals he gave it a flavour at once Christian, Elizabethan and romantic. In Plautus the father of the Menaechmi dies before the play opens; Shakespeare brings him to life as Aegeon and so begins his play with a highly unclassical picture of a pathetic old man condemned to death for seeking a long lost son in an enemy country, and rounds the play off with a tender and equally unclassical picture of family reunion and reconciliation. Thus the rollicking farce inherited from Plautus is, as it were, framed within a moving little domestic drama. Finally, the invention of a sister for the wife of Antipholus of Ephesus and of a mother (at first seen as an Abbess) for the twin Antipholuses enables Shakespeare to give expression to the duty of a husband on the one hand to a wife and of a wife on the other to her husband. And if he enlarges more eloquently upon the latter in *The Taming of the Shrew*, that was required by the exigences of the plot and need not in fairness to the author be set down to the account of Anne Hathaway.

*The Two Gentlemen of Verona* is a complete contrast to *The Comedy of Errors.* The background is still Mediterranean and the sea is again not far off, almost omnipresent indeed, seeing that one of the 'gentlemen' takes ship at Verona, an inland city, to travel to Milan, still further inland. And each 'gentleman' is attended by a clownish servant as is each Antipholus by his Dromio. But it does not contain a single merchant; the two gentlemen are both noble, their ladies noble ladies, and Sir Eglamour seems to walk straight out of Malory. As for the source, there is nothing classical about it, being a tale of disappointed love taken from a Spanish source of the early sixteenth century. At least, the *Diana* of Jorge de Montemayor, the most famous pastoral romance of the age, or rather the tale of Felix and Felismena as related therein, is in Chambers's opinion the only 'clear source'. A translation of *Diana* was published in 1598 by Bartholomew Young with a dedication to Lady Rich, Sidney's 'Stella', and sister to the Earl of Essex; but according to Young's preface it had then already been in existence for sixteen years. If therefore Shakespeare could not read Spanish it is possible that he had access to a manuscript copy of Young, or he may have used a play entitled *Felix and Philomena*, performed by the Queen's players at court in 1585 but now lost, which was obviously derived from the same story.[1] Professor Pruvost has recently argued that Shakespeare appears to have been familiar with the well-known Italian comedy commonly called *Gl'Ingannati* from which Montemayor borrowed the story, since it relates details not found in *Diana* though utilized by Shakespeare in *Twelfth Night*,[2] though this would be explained if the details in question were present in the English *Felix and Philomena*. Not that the ultimate source is a matter of great moment. That Shakespeare knew of Montemayor's volume, apart from the story of Don Felix, is proved by Rosalind's jesting boast that if Orlando wooed her seriously she would play all sorts of shrewish tricks upon him; for example 'weep for nothing like Diana in the fountain' and do it when he is 'disposed to be merry' (*As You Like It*, IV, i, 148-9), an allusion which escaped the commentators until Paul Reyher[3] pointed out that it referred to Montemayor's heroine, a heartless enchantress of divine loveliness, who would sit by a fountain shedding copious tears as she swore oaths of

[1] E. K. Chambers, i, 331.

[2] *Etudes Anglaises*, xiii, No. 1.

[3] Paul Reyher, '*The Two Gentlemen of Verona* et *Twelfth Night*, leurs sources communes', *Revue de l'Enseignement des Langues Vivantes*, XLI (1924), pp. 438-46, and his *Idées dans l'Oeuvre de Shakespeare* (1947), pp. 23-4.

constancy to one lover while preparing to marry another.[1]

In any case Shakespeare seems to follow Montemayor pretty closely. The incident, for example, in which Lucetta drops Proteus' letter under the eyes of her mistress, who thereupon hurriedly snatches it up,[2] is an almost exact reproduction of the account of a similar trick to excite the curiosity of Felismena by her maid Rosina. In the novel as in Shakespeare the faithless lover goes off to the imperial court where he makes love to another lady. In both the lady left behind follows him to court disguised as a youth; in both she lodges at a hostelry and from there overhears her lover serenading her rival; in both she takes service with him as a page and he employs her as a go-between to convey letters and tokens to the new mistress; and in both the new mistress having heard of the old one discusses her with the latter disguised as a page. But she does not in *The Two Gentlemen* fall passionately in love with the page as in Montemayor; Shakespeare reserves that for *Twelfth Night*, where however the *Felix and Felismena* story is but slightly drawn upon as a single thread in a more fine-spun texture.

Not of course that the story was the sole source of *The Two Gentlemen*, since it only accounts for Proteus and covers what is after all merely the sub-plot; the main plot being concerned with the love of Valentine for Silvia, her imprisonment by her father in a high tower, Valentine's design of rescuing her by means of a rope-ladder, its discovery by the father, her escape nevertheless in company with Sir Eglamour, her capture by outlaws in the forest, re-capture by Proteus, and finally the extraordinary scene in which Valentine comes upon them as Proteus is attempting to rape her, and hands her over to him, after he shows signs of repentance. Most of this except the last incident is the merest commonplace of romance, which, if not Shakespeare's invention, he might have picked up anywhere; the rope-ladder for example later used in *Romeo and Juliet* is to be

[1] See p. 2 of Young's translation.
[2] I, ii, 67 ff.

42

found in Brooke's *Romeus and Juliet* with which he was probably already familiar at this date. Silvia, however, is faintly adumbrated in Montemayor's Celia, the lady at the imperial court to whom the fickle Felix makes love, while by introducing Valentine into the story and representing him as the bosom friend of Proteus, to whom he is prepared to surrender Silvia in the final scene, Shakespeare greatly enriched his plot which now turned upon a conflict between Love and Friendship.

This, however, is a theme not fully understood by critics because Elizabethan ideas about love and about friendship and about the relationship between the two, are all strange to our modern minds. 'Shakespeare', Chambers[1] notes, 'is obsessed by this theme in the *Sonnets*', and as will be noted in a moment, in one point the *Sonnets* and *The Two Gentlemen* are remarkably similar. Speaking generally, however, as Chambers admits, the theme is almost a literary commonplace at the time of the Renaissance, so much so that he suggests it is idle to look for its source in parallels like Lyly's *Euphues*. Reyher, on the other hand, has no hesitation in doing so,[2] and it seems likely enough that Shakespeare owed something here to a book that he must have known very well indeed. Nevertheless his two gentlemen and ladies belong to a distinctly higher class than Lyly's,[3] while the love Valentine offers Silvia and Proteus outrages, is high-flown compared with anything in Lyly or with the courtship of ordinary Elizabethans, though still holding its appeal for them especially in the romances they delighted to read. Furthermore, few critics seem to have observed that the equally high-flown friendship between Valentine and Proteus belongs likewise to a traditional ideal as expressed in Cicero's noble *De Amicitia* and exemplified earlier in the love of David for Jonathan 'passing the love of women', and during the Middle Ages in the tale of the

[1] Op. cit., i, 331.
[2] Reyher, loc. cit.
[3] Philautus is 'a town born child' (Bond's *Lyly*, i, 190).

devoted friendship between two knights like Palamon and
Arcite, immortalized first by Chaucer in *The Knight's Tale*;
and then by Shakespeare and Fletcher in *Two Noble Kinsmen*,
or again in classical stories like *Damon and Pithias* or the
quasi-classical *Titus and Gisippus*, both of which had been
dramatized before Shakespeare's *Two Gentlemen* was produced.[1] Indeed it seems pretty clear that he had the last
story in mind as he wrote, inasmuch as Valentine's surrender
of Silvia to Proteus in the last act is closely paralleled by a
similar action on the part of Gisippus. And it is very likely
that Shakespeare had read the story in Sir Thomas Elyot's
*Governour* (1531) a book with which he was certainly
familiar,[2] probably more so than with the eighth novel of
the Tenth Day in Boccaccio's *Decameron*, from which Elyot
presumably took it.

Elyot, who writes to expound and illustrate the various
qualities it is desirable a 'governor' or ruler should possess,
relates 'the wonderful history of Titus and Gisippus' in order
to exhibit 'the figure of perfect amity' or friendship;[3] and
in his 'history' both the paragons exhibit this 'perfect amity'
in turn. First Gisippus, discovering that Titus has fallen in
love with the woman he is just about to marry, arranges
that his friend shall take his place on the nuptial couch at the
first night and publicly hands her over to him as his wife the
following morning. And, later on in the tale, Titus, finding
Gisippus accused of murder—falsely, as we are told—and
just about to be executed, declares in the court of justice
that he is himself the murderer and desires the death penalty.
Like Gisippus, Valentine hands his beloved over to his
friend, saying

---

[1] *Damon and Pithias*, by Edwardes, was published in 1564 and probably played
at Court on Christmas Day, 1564. A play on the same theme is recorded as
Chettle's in Henslowe's *Diary* (ed. Greg, ii, 211) while the *Revels Accounts*
records a performance of *Titus and Gisippus* by the 'Children of St. Paules' on
19th February 1577. (See Chambers, *Elizabethan Stage*, IV, 93, 152.)

[2] See *Henry V* (New Cambridge edition), notes on I, ii, 180 ff.

[3] Book II, Chapter XII.

And that my love may appear plain and free
All that was mine in Silvia I give thee

which seems to echo the very words of Gisippus:

> Here I renounce to you clearly all my title and interest
> that I now have or might have in that faire maydon.[1]

Thus both proclaim the triumph of Friendship over Love. But there the parallel ends, for Proteus is a double traitor, false friend and false lover, which however renders the sacrifice to Friendship all the more admirable on Valentine's part.

And Valentine the perfect friend is also the perfect lover. Like the knights of old or the heroes of romance he always addresses Silvia as his 'mistress', speaks of himself as her 'servant', and, when he introduces his friend, begs her to 'entertain him' as his 'fellow-servant'—language significantly never found in Shakespeare's other love scenes. Charlton sees this as a reflection of the medieval *amour courtois* and even quotes from Chrétien de Troyes in support of his contention. Surely that is far-fetched in more senses than one. For romantic love had long since superseded 'courtly love', which was implicitly adulterous.[2] Indeed, as C. S. Lewis[3] notes, Spenser was celebrating the 'final defeat' of the latter in Book III of the *Faerie Queene*, published in 1590. Valentine's adoration of Silvia was a shade highfalutin; or perhaps 'literary' would be the better term, since it was probably due to the dramatist's inexperience at that date of the way gentlemen and ladies actually made love or even spoke to each other. When he wrote *Love's Labour's Lost* he had become more intimate with the 'divers of worship' who stood by him in 1592 and so learnt to exchange 'taffeta phrases, silken terms precise' for 'russet yeas and honest kersey noes'; and after Berowne there was no return to Valentine.

---

[1] *The Governour*, Everyman Library, p. 172.
[2] See C. S. Lewis, *The Allegory of Love* (1936), Chapter I.
[3] Op. cit., p. 298.

But if Valentine is the perfect lover, Proteus as I said is the traitor to love. The soliloquy he utters after his first meeting with Silvia is the very negation of the self-effacing love that Valentine stands for, and when he attempts to 'force' Silvia in the forest he shows that self-satisfaction is what 'love' means to him. Moreover by treating a lady as if she were a peasant girl, as indeed peasant girls were almost normally treated by young gentlemen until the nineteenth century, he sins against the code of a gentleman.[1] No doubt the incident of the attempted violation is managed with a crudity we do not expect from Shakespeare. No doubt too the repentance of Proteus that follows Valentine's forgiveness and the subsequent surrender of Silvia are huddled one upon the other with incredible speed. It is rough technique that seems to contrast strangely with the rest of the play which, if less subtle than *As You Like It* or *Twelfth Night*, is constructed with considerable skill, and gives an effect of great charm on the stage when well produced. The apparent crudity of the last scene may be partly due, I believe, to textual corruption, but the almost universal condemnation of it at the hands of modern critics is also due to their inability or refusal to view the scene through Elizabethan eyes as a young poet's rather high-flown representation of the triumph of Friendship over Love.

And yet might there not be something personal behind it after all? According to the reckoning of most critics, about the time the dramatist was composing his *Two Gentlemen*, the poet was beginning to address sonnet-letters to his friend who, when introduced to the poet's lady, plays the traitor as Proteus does and is freely forgiven as Valentine forgives Proteus. But 'we ask and ask'. . . .

With the help of this survey of the character and sources of the two basic plays we can now sum up the main ingredients or elements that went to the composition of the Happy Comedies.

[1] Cf. C. S. Lewis, op. cit., p. 35, citing the tale in Malory (Bk. III, Chapter III) of how King Pellinode begat Tor on the daughter of a cowherd.

I. A continental or Mediterranean background in all except *The Merry Wives of Windsor*; for though Falstaff might proclaim himself 'Sir John to all Europe', to have made an Italian or Spanish knight of him would have exceeded even Shakespeare's powers.

II. *Clownage and Foolery.* The importance of this has already been insisted upon in general terms. At least two, often more, clowns or fools are to be found in each play, viz. the Dromios in *Errors*, Launce and Speed in *The Two Gentlemen*, Costard and Dull in *Love's Labour's Lost*, the two Gobbos in *The Merchant of Venice*, the servants Rugby and Simple in *The Merry Wives*, Dogberry and Verges in *Much Ado*, Touchstone and William in *As You Like It*, Grumio and Curtis in *The Shrew*, Feste and Fabian in *Twelfth Night*, and finally Bottom, Quince, etc. in *A Midsummer Night's Dream*. And though Shakespeare makes no distinction between clown and fool in the texts, it is clear that in certain plays, notably in *As You Like It* and *Twelfth Night*, there was a marked distinction in costume between the Fool proper with cap, bells and bauble, and the clown or clowns dressed like yokels or mechanicals. Touchstone, as I have already quoted, uses his folly like a stalking-horse and under the presentation of that shoots his wit. William, on the other hand, in the same play is little more than a butt to be laughed at. Both kinds 'play upon the word', but the mere clown blunders ridiculously. Old Gobbo for example says 'infection' for 'affection' and 'defect' for 'effect'. Lancelot on the other hand is a 'wit-snapper', deliberately picking up by the wrong sense words or phrases his interlocutor has uttered. And the dialogue between him and Lorenzo in III, v of *The Merchant of Venice* not only provides an excellent illustration of wit-snapping in action but shows that while such quipping was the usual stock in trade of stage fools of that period, the man who played the fool in Shakespeare's company was a past master. For after a series of quibbling replies in which Lancelot keeps up the game of mis-taking everything that Lorenzo says to him, the latter admiringly exclaims:

O dear discretion! how his words are suited!
The fool hath planted in his memory
An army of good words, and I do know
A many fools that stand in better place
Garnished like him, that for a tricksy word
Defy the matter.

                                        III, v, 60–5.

That is to say: Lancelot's words are matched to their context with great discrimination whilst other fools higher in favour (? at court) sacrifice the sense to mere word-play. Incidentally the expression 'garnished like him' refers, I take it, to the Fool's costume, and if so places Lancelot in the same class as Touchstone and Feste.

In an interesting footnote to an essay on 'Feste, the jester', A. C. Bradley distinguishes between 'Fools proper' i.e. professional fools attached to a court or house[1] and humorists like Launce and Lancelot Gobbo, or 'low characters unintentionally humorous'. But it is not always easy to draw the line. I think Lancelot Gobbo is probably a borderline case.

III. *Quibbling by the gentry.* While to the delight of their audience the fools thus skilfully keep sense at bay and the clowns mishandle the language through ignorance, their betters endlessly toss the language to and fro. Dr. Johnson declared that a quibble was to Shakespeare 'the fatal Cleopatra for whom he lost the world and was content to lose it'. In fact, the relationship was more intimate and more respectable; for in time it became the very stuff of Shakespeare's thought. And it shows how little the Restoration understood Shakespeare when we find Dryden complaining that Shakespeare's style was 'pestered'[2] with imagery. Yet imagery was with him no native ornament or mannerism of style, for it grew upon him as play followed play. There is very little of it in the early plays; and it seems likely that he may have learned it from himself, i.e. from the quibbling dialogue of the wit-mongers in his early comedies. Modern

---

[1] Gollancz, *A Book of Homage to Shakespeare*, 1916.     [2] i.e. clogged.

readers are apt to pass over this witty dialogue quickly as so much dead wood, but it must have seemed full of sap to contemporary auditors;[1] and an editor whose business is to wrestle with the sense of his author word by word, cannot help being struck by the quantity of verbal sparring in the comedies. If we go by the clock, how much of the two or three hours' traffic of the stage was devoted to it! And in *Love's Labour's Lost* virtually a whole play, in which we shall see the dialogue consists mainly of 'sets of wit well played'[2] and 'fine volleys of words quickly shot off?[3]

There can be no doubt that Shakespeare gave his mind to such quibbling very seriously and very frequently. He derived something of it from Lyly, but in his own day it was probably regarded as his most original and essential contribution to comic drama; and it was apparently by its means that he first attracted the attention of the educated and 'judicious'. Witness Chettle's references in 1592 to the praises he had won for his 'facetious grace'[4] from 'divers of worship'. And it is probable too that his reputation in the same quarters rested largely upon this foundation right up to the accession of James I. And it is not difficult to see that the 'divers of worship' were young. Play after play contains its party of dashing young bucks, generally hunting in threes—Mercutio, Romeo, Benvolio; Berowne, Longaville, Dumain; Antonio, Bassanio, Gratiano. The other two themes, less general and more structural in character, are immediately derived as we have seen from the basic comedies and their sources.

IV. *Merchants and mercantile life* (after Plautus). Apart from *Errors*, already dealt with, *The Taming of the Shrew* and

---

[1] See below, pp. 61 and 87, and for these linguistic fashions in general, G. D. Willcock, *Shakespeare as Critic of Language*, Shakespeare Association, 1934; and a recent book on *Shakespeare's Wordplay* by M. M. Mahood.

[2] V, ii, 29.

[3] *Two Gentlemen*, II, iv, 32-3.

[4] For the full meaning of 'facetious' cf. Strype's *Cranmer* (1694), p. 512 (ed. Oxford, 1812): 'a very facetious man who delivered his reproofs and counsels under witty and pleasant (jocular) discourse'.

*The Merry Wives of Windsor* are the predominantly merchant plays. In the former Baptista, the father of Katharine and Bianca, is a wealthy merchant of Padua, and the scenes at his house give us an intimate picture of merchant family life. For though the characters call each other 'gentlemen', they are clearly intended to be merchant princes such as were found in most Italian cities at that period, and could be paralleled among the city fathers of Shakespeare's London. And when Gremio, an aged suitor for the hand of Bianca, describes the household goods he will endow her with (II, i, 339–55), we get a glimpse of the furniture, plate, etc. in a well-to-do merchant's house of the day. Furthermore, in speaking of merchant princes it is hardly necessary to mention *The Merchant of Venice*, the central figure in which is the very wealthy Antonio, which introduces the usurer, a stock character in Terentian comedy, and which opens magnificently on the quay-side with talk of 'argosies with portly sail' and of 'ventures' upon the ocean.

As for *The Merry Wives* one has only to read Stratford for Windsor to realize that Shakespeare had a personal interest in merchant life. For the Fords and the Pages might be the Quineys and Sadlers and Shakespeares of his native town.[1]

The only other Happy Comedy exhibiting the influence of Plautus is *Twelfth Night*, the imbroglio of which arises from twins becoming separated and then arriving in the same town without knowledge of each other's presence. And as in *Errors*, though not in *Menaechmi*, the cause of separation is a shipwreck, while since the twins are brother and sister, not brothers as in the Plautus play, the sister is disguised as a page. This however links the play with *The Two Gentlemen* which is its true forerunner.

V. *Love and Friendship among persons of high rank* (after Montemayor). Marlowe's 'saw',

Who ever loved that loved not at first sight,

---

[1] Cf. Smart, *Shakespeare—Truth and Tradition* (1928), p. 56.

which the shepherdess quotes in *As You Like It*, and its corollary:

> The course of true love never did run smooth,

by which Lysander foreshadows the troubles that come upon the young people in *A Midsummer Night's Dream*, constitute the leading themes of most of the Happy Comedies; while the grand conclusion towards which they all inevitably move is best expressed in Puck's jingle:

> Jack shall have Jill,
> Nought shall go ill,
> The man shall have his mare again and all shall be well.

The marriage bells crown the happy plays with happiness; it is the obstacles that hinder and protract that consummation for the best part of five acts which make the comedy. And these obstacles are not the natural obstructions that Hermia and Lysander enumerate in the opening scene of *A Midsummer Night's Dream*, viz. difference of race, inequality in rank, disparity of age, an enforced marriage by the choice of friends or guardians, the calamity of war, death or sickness, but just that 'incredible imbroglio' that Meredith scoffed at.

The basic theme of love and friendship, as first worked out in *The Two Gentlemen*, involves a quartet of characters, two men and two women, moving in a kind of stately minuet against a romantic background. The dramatic conflict is provided by the rival claims of love and friendship and the characters play the traditional roles in this conflict, being on the one hand the hero and heroine destined to fall in love with each other, and on the other hand the hero's false friend who makes love to the hero's lady and is followed about by his forlorn lady generally disguised as a boy; the disguise giving rise to the cross-purposes or imbroglio which, when exposed, brings the play to its conclusion. This theme or pattern, derived from one of the basic plays, may be called the basic pattern which as a whole or in part and in different forms or variations is found in seven out of the ten happy comedies. This pattern or formula may be set forth in quasi-diagrammatic fashion thus:

### The Two Gentlemen

Valentine and Silvia: Proteus, the false friend, and Julia, his forlorn lady.

Friendship and love pull in different directions.

### Love's Labour's Lost

This, which probably originally followed close upon *The Two Gentlemen* and therefore forms the subject of the next lecture, gives us the most obvious variation of the basic pattern, since no fewer than four gentlemen and four ladies are involved, and the doubling of the principals is accompanied by a doubling of the pace at which they move, while the characters keep changing partners, changing costumes, and assuming different disguises which give rise to a series of imbroglios, resolved in the end by the confessions of the partners brought to repentance by the messenger of death.

### A Midsummer Night's Dream

Lysander and Hermia: Demetrius and Helena.

Here the friendship motif is weak and belongs to the ladies, not to the men, while each lady becomes forlorn in turn. The imbroglio is accidentally created by Puck's mistake with Cupid's magic flower and is later resolved by Oberon with 'Dian's bud'.

### The Merchant of Venice

Bassanio and Portia: Antonio.

Only one lady, but the friendship between the men is so strong that it even threatens the hero's love for a moment or two.

A trivial but amusing double imbroglio is created by the assumed disguise of Portia and Nerissa, and resolved by the restoration of the rings.

# Their Origin and Special Quality

## Much Ado

Benedick and Beatrice: Claudio and Hero.

The men are friends but not rivals: Hero becomes Claudio's forlorn lady for a time. An imbroglio that threatens the happiness of all four lovers arises from Hero's maid disguising herself as her mistress, and is resolved by the constables.

## As You Like It

Orlando and Rosalind: (? Celia and Oliver).

The women are friends but not rivals; Rosalind and Celia disguise themselves as boys for most of the play, which could not have existed without Rosalind's disguise, exposed by her fainting at the sight of Orlando's blood. But when Shakespeare came to this play he had no need to draw on Montemayor, since he found in Lodge's *Rosalynde* a pastoral romance with a plot so well suited to his needs that though Lodge does not appear to have owed anything to Montemayor, the play falls quite naturally into its place as one of the disguise-and-imbroglio series. In particular, the half-pretence love-making between Orlando and Ganymede (Rosalind) makes a fine variation on the disguise motif of the earlier plays.

## Twelfth Night

Elements from Plautus and Montemayor are here blended, the latter's influence predominating and going back behind *The Two Gentlemen* to the Felix and Felismena story itself. Orsino, the hero, pays court to Olivia the heroine, and she falls in love with Viola who, disguised as a page, courts Olivia for Orsino, and so fills the role of the forlorn lady, being herself in love with Orsino and eventually marrying him. The friendship motif (Antonio's strong affection for Sebastian) is only introduced towards the end of the play in order to precipitate the *dénouement*, by exposing Viola's disguise. On the other hand, Viola and Sebastian, twin brother and sister, separated by shipwreck but both arriving in Illyria unknown to each other, lead us, as has been noted above, back to *The Comedy of Errors*. Such is the groundwork of this most delicate and subtle comedy.

# CHAPTER III

# *Love's Labour's Lost:*
# *The Story of a Conversion*

T he reputation of *Love's Labour's Lost* is one of the curiosities of dramatic history. In Elizabethan and Jacobean times it seems to have been among the more popular of Shakespeare's plays—at any rate in court circles. Sir Arthur Quiller-Couch and I suggested in our edition (1923) that it may have been first written for a private performance at Christmas 1593, possibly for Southampton and his friends. Certainly it was played before Queen Elizabeth at Christmas 1597, perhaps in revised form. But the opinion in which it was held emerges most clearly from the fact that during the Christmas season 1604–5, Burbadge picked it out for special recommendation as a play to be given at the Earl of Southampton's house before Queen Anne, declaring that 'for wytt & mirthe' it 'will please her exceedingly'.[1] It is true that Shakespeare's company appears at this time to have been deliberately reviving old Elizabethan plays which James and Anne had not seen. But Burbadge's confidence in the attraction of *Love's Labour's Lost* is none the less remarkable, inasmuch as it was then ten or twelve years old, and is now regarded as essentially a topical play. Yet if the title-page of the second edition of the Quarto (1631) is to be believed, it still held the

[1] Chambers, *Eliz. Stage*, iv, 139; *William Shakespeare*, ii, 332.

stage after Shakespeare's death, being acted both at the Blackfriars and at the Globe. After that it just drops out. Nothing is known of it in the theatre for two hundred years, and though revivals took place during the nineteenth century, only three are recorded in this country and two in the United States, none of which seem to have been very successful.

As for its reputation among the critics, Dryden set the fashion, which is still to a large extent that of modern commentary. His *Essay on the Dramatic Poetry of the Last Age* (1672), in which he seeks to demonstrate the superiority in wit, language and conversation of his own times to that of Shakespeare, a superiority which he attributed to improvements in 'gallantry and civility', includes *Love's Labour's Lost* among those plays which, he reminds his readers, 'were so *meanly* written that the comedy neither caused your mirth, nor the serious part your concernment'.[1]

This judgment was echoed a hundred years later by Dr. Johnson:

> In this play, which all the editors have concurred to censure, and some have rejected as unworthy of our Poet, it must be confessed that there are many passages *mean*, childish and vulgar; and some which ought not to have been exhibited, as we are told they were, to a maiden queen. But [he feels compelled to add] there are scattered through the whole many sparks of genius; nor is there any play that has more evident marks of the hands of Shakespeare.[2]

And there save for one exception the position stood in this country[3] until a few years ago. The exception, a remarkable one, is an essay by Walter Pater published in his *Appreciations* (1889), which comes very near to what I believe is the truth. He writes:

[1] *Essays of John Dryden*, ed. by W. P. Ker (1926), i, 165.
[2] *The Plays of William Shakespeare*, ed. by Samuel Johnson (1765), ii, p. 224.
[3] It is noteworthy that the young Goethe and his friends at Strassburg, rejoicing in Shakespeare, made a special study of *Love's Labour's Lost* both in translation and the original, delighting even in its 'quibbles'. See *Dichtung und Wahrheit*, Book XI (1770–71).

# Love's Labour's Lost: The Story of a Conversion

The unity of the play is not so much the unity of a drama as that of a series of pictorial groups, in which the same figures reappear, in different combinations but on the same background. It is as if Shakespeare had intended to bind together, by some inventive conceit, the devices of an ancient tapestry and give voice to its figures.[1]

But Pater's was a voice crying in a wilderness of neglect and depreciation. The accusation of 'meanness' which Dryden and Johnson both levelled at the play is based in the main upon the quantity of quibbling it contains. This is borne out by Dryden's condemnation of this fault in Ben Jonson, which occurs in the same essay. Jonson's wit, he declares, was excellent enough so long as he borrowed from the classics. But 'when he trusted himself alone, he often fell into meanness of expression. Nay, he was not free from the lowest and most grovelling kind of art, which we call clenches, of which *Every Man in his Humour* is infinitely full; and, which is worse, the wittiest persons in the drama speak them.'[2]

The puns he instances from Jonson, e.g. 'Aristarchus' and 'stark ass', 'limbs of satin or rather Satan', are certainly 'mean', if not 'grovelling'. But there is nothing of this sort in *Love's Labour's Lost*. Indeed, Shakespeare usually avoided what may be called the straight pun, Falstaff's notorious pun of 'gravy' on 'gravity'[3] being the exception that proves the rule. What he chiefly indulged in was, as we have seen above, rather the Quibble—a term that needs definition, and which I should define as a kind of word-play in which one character makes a remark or utters a word, and another immediately picks it up and uses it or replies to it in a different sense—even at times in two or three different senses. Such quibbling is one of the main roots of Shakespearian repartee, and there are pages of it in *Love's Labour's Lost*. This is how Boyet comments upon it:

> The tongues of mocking wenches are as keen
>   As is the razor's edge invisible,

[1] Ed. 1907, p. 163.      [2] Dryden, op. cit., i, 173.
[3] *2 Henry IV*, I, ii, 160.

Cutting a smaller hair than may be seen,
Above the sense of sense; so sensible
Seemeth their conference, their conceits have wings
Fleeter than arrows, bullets, wind, thought, swifter things.[1]

And the description must be allowed true.

Take one example only: Katharine, masked and pretending to be Maria, who is the lady of Lord Longaville's choice, mocks that young gentleman, himself vizarded and disguised as a Muscovite. And the following dialogue then takes place, the main point of which is that, while he thinks she is Maria, she knows very well that he is Longaville. To encourage the bashful lover, she opens with

KATHARINE. What, was your vizard made without a tongue?
   [This refers to the practice, still found in Christmas crackers, of
   making masks with long paper tongues which shot out at will.]
LONGAVILLE. I know the reason, lady, why you ask.
KATHARINE. O, for your reason! quickly, sir—I long.
LONGAVILLE. You have a double tongue within your mask,
               And would afford my speechless vizard half.
   [In other words Katharine has the double (= deceitful) tongue
   that all women possess and is therefore ready to lend a tongue to
   him. But in saying 'I long' Katharine had uttered the first syllable
   of Longaville's name and had thus 'afforded his speechless vizard
   half' in another sense. It is this sense she now picks up in her
   reply, which is a multiple quibble, since it speaks the other half
   of his name, appears to applaud his jest by saying 'Well!' after the
   comic pronunciation of contemporary Dutch or German merchants
   in London, and enables her to insult him at the same time.]
KATHARINE. 'Veal' quoth the Dutchman. Is not 'veal' a calf?
LONGAVILLE. A calf, fair lady?
KATHARINE.               No, a fair lord calf.
   [Longaville, finding himself getting the worst of it, now suggests
   a change of subject.]
LONGAVILLE. Let's part the word. [Part = give up. Thus he means
   'Let's have done with this "veal" business.' Whereupon Katharine, pretending he means 'let us divide or split the word "calf",'
   which would give the first two letters of her own name, retorts.]
KATHARINE. No. I'll not be your half [i.e. your better half].
   Take all and wean it—it may prove an ox [i.e., a fool].[2]

[1] V, ii, 56–62.                          [2] V, ii, 241–50.

With the mention of 'ox' the quibblers have arrived at the goal of most Elizabethan jesting, viz. horns, and the dialogue drifts off into a series of jokes on the subject of cuckoldry, which to the Elizabethans seems to have been as irresistibly laughable as the mother-in-law was to readers and spectators in Victorian England.

Such verbal ingenuity, fine-spun and carried forward from speech to speech, trivial as it may seem to us, undoubtedly cost Shakespeare much thought, and often embraced in *Love's Labour's Lost* a good deal of indelicate innuendo. Today we need elaborate commentary to understand it even in part. Could the Elizabethans follow it in the rapid give-and-take of the stage? We must suppose they did, otherwise Shakespeare would hardly have put himself to the pains of placing it in the mouths of his characters, which he does, not only in *Love's Labour's Lost*, but in play after play, until it reached its culmination in the sallies of Hamlet, anticly disposed.[1]

No doubt the sport had become stale by the time Dryden was writing. But he goes far astray in attributing Shakespeare's love of it to his lack of social opportunity. 'In the age wherein those poets lived', he remarks, with the accustomed air of superiority which the Restoration writers assumed in speaking of their predecessors, 'there was less of gallantry than in ours; neither did they keep the best company of theirs. . . . I cannot find that any of them had been conversant in courts, except Ben Johnson.'[2] We should not perhaps pay too much attention to these words, seeing that they lead up to a paragraph dedicated to the praises of Charles II who 'at his return . . . found a nation lost as much in barbarism as in rebellion: and, as the excellency of his nature forgave the one, so the excellency of his manners reformed the other'.[3] In any event, the truth as regards *Love's*

[1] Cf. G. D. Willcock, op. cit., and *Hamlet* (New Cambridge) Introduction, pp. xxxv–xliii.

[2] Dryden, op. cit., i, 175; 'Ben Johnson' is his spelling.

[3] Dryden, op. cit., p. 176.

*Labour's Lost* was the exact opposite of what Dryden states. It was essentially a court play, could have been written only by one thoroughly 'conversant' with the 'wit, language and conversation', the manners and badinage of court life, and for that very reason among others, it fell rapidly out of favour, when the fashions changed. Hazlitt, who was too much taken with the figures in the underplot of the play to 'set a mark of reprobation on it' as a whole, observed nevertheless that 'Shakespear has set himself to imitate the tone of polite society then prevailing among the fair, the witty, and the learned, and he has imitated it but too faithfully.'[1]

And there are two other features of the play, which must have contributed greatly to its popularity among the young noblemen and inns-of-court men for whom it was composed, but seriously detract from its reputation with posterity.

First, it was Shakespeare's most elaborate and sustained essay in satire and burlesque. It teems with topical allusions to persons known to the original audience—allusions bound to fade with the passing hour and with the fading memories of the persons concerned; never very explicit, even at the outset. Anything in the nature of direct lampooning of the great, however much out of favour at the moment, would be most inadvisable, so swift and sudden were the revolutions of Fortune's wheel at the court of those times. Hints were dropped—scattered broadcast indeed—and personal traits were perhaps aped upon the stage; but, if the spectators put two and two together and made five—that was their own look-out. As Jaques puts it in a later play,

> I must have liberty
> Withal, as large a charter as the wind,
> To blow on whom I please, for so fools have;
> And they that most are galléd with my folly,
> They most must laugh; and why, sir, must they so?

[1] William Hazlitt, *Characters of Shakespeare's Plays*, 1817.

> The 'why' is plain as way to parish church:
> He that a fool doth very wisely hit
> Doth very foolishly, although he smart,
> Not to seam senseless of the bob: if not,
> The wise man's folly is anatomized
> Even by the squand'ring glances of the fool.[1]

And in the second place, *Love's Labour's Lost* is 'a great feast of language'. The English tongue was not only changing with unparalleled rapidity in the early nineties, at which period it was written, but the English people were peculiarly conscious of it. A fresh stream of words was pouring into the language, drawing its tributaries from many sources; all sorts of new experiments were being tried out, some of them high-flown and most egregious; and the effect of all this was the bewilderment of the uneducated, who made up the bulk of the nation, and the recreation of the educated, who found in it a game which they played with unflagging zest.

And of all the games played with the English tongue in the theatre of that age, *Love's Labour's Lost* was the most zestful, and must have seemed to contemporaries the most fascinating. It exemplifies and holds up to ridicule at least three distinct types of linguistic extravagance or corruption:

(a) the stilted preciosity of court circles in Armado, whose pretentious eloquence is thus described by a rival rhetorician: 'His humour is lofty, his discourse peremptory, his tongue filed, his eye ambitious, his gait majestical, and his general behaviour vain, ridiculous and thrasonical. He is too picked, too spruce, too affected, too odd as it were, too peregrinate, as I may call it.'[2]

(b) then there is the pedantic affectation of Holofernes, the schoolmaster, who speaks the words just quoted, the affectation of the dictionary and the school-book of colloquies. His 'epithets are sweetly varied' and his shadow the curate, who follows him about reverently with his table-book ready to 'draw' at any moment for the noting down of the 'singular and choice epithets' that fall from his lips,

---

[1] *As You Like It*, II, vii, 47–57.  [2] V, i, 9–14.

sums him up (by contrast) in his description of the unlettered Dull:

> 'Sir, he hath never fed of the dainties that are bred in a book; he hath
> not eat paper, as it were, he hath not drunk ink; his intellect is not
> replenished, he is only an animal, only sensible in the duller parts:
>> And such barren plants are set before us that we thankful should
>> be,
>> Which we of taste and feeling are, for those parts that do fruc-
>> tify in us more than he.[1]

(c) lastly there is Dull himself, and Costard the King's
fool,[2] who represents the rustic misunderstanding and misuse,
or the deliberate distortion by the jester, of the new wealth
of words.

But if all this be so; if *Love's Labour's Lost* is replete with
satirical hints about dead persons, some of them hardly
known by name to scholars today, with parodies of fashions
in speech demoded three centuries ago, and with three- or
four-piled verbal ingenuities which can only be recon-
structed (though hardly brought back to life) by the most
laborious explanation—what possible significance or interest
can it have for us in the twentieth century? To Charlton,
who edited the play in 1917,

> It is deficient in plot and in characterisation. There is little story in it.
> Its situations do not present successive incidents in an ordered plot.
> . . . Four men take an oath to segregate themselves from the society
> of women for a term of years: circumstance at once compels them
> to a formal interview with four women; they break their oath. That
> is the whole story. . . . Clearly a story as simple as is this permits of little
> elaboration in the dramatic plotting of it. The oath is patently absurd.
> . . . Clearly it must be broken, and the only interest aroused is in the
> manner of the breach.
>> All four men might forswear themselves in chorus, and have done
> with it; but by letting each lover try to hide his lapse from his
> fellows, a way is made for progressive revelations in the one scene
> of the play which is really diverting as a dramatic situation. . . .
> There are other scenes in which the actions and the words contribute
> equally to the theatrical interest; for example, that in which the men

[1] IV, ii, 23–9.                              [2] See pp. 71–2.

are led to a wrong identification of the masqued [*sic*] ladies; but they are accidental to the working out of the story, not really different in kind from the pageants, the masques, and the dances which make the padding of the play.

But the worst consequences of the poverty of the story appear in the persons who perform it. The four courtiers could not but resemble each other in a wooden conformity; for they all have to do the same thing, and have all to be guilty of an act of almost incredible stupidity. . . . To the eye, at all events, the ladies of *Love's Labour's Lost* are a little more individualised than are the men; for being ladies, the colour of the hair and the texture of the skin are indispensable items in the inventory. . . . Yet under the skin, these ladies are as empty and as uniform as are their wooers. . . .

No profound apprehension of life will be expected from *Love's Labour's Lost*. . . . So much and so little was Shakespeare when he began.[1]

So much and so little, one is tempted to retort, can one understand about a play when one has only read it in a book. And in saying this I am condemning myself. For in 1923, I, like Charlton, had edited *Love's Labour's Lost* and like him had therefore come to know it in no superficial fashion. We had both as it were eaten its paper and drunk its ink; and yet because we had never seen it upon the stage, or at any rate properly produced, we had missed the whole art and meaning of it. Truly, as Berowne says:

> Why, all delights are vain, but that most vain
> Which with pain purchased, doth inherit pain—
> As painfully to pore upon a book,
> To seek the light of truth, while truth the while
> Doth falsely blind the eyesight of his look.[2]

For two strenuous years I had purchased much delight from poring over the textual and topical and glossarial problems with which it teems, but without ever seeing the play as a play any more than Charlton had.

In 1927 Granville-Barker devoted one of his challenging prefaces to it, in which, after declaring that 'there is life in it', that 'it abounds in beauties of fancy and phrase, as

[1] H. B. Charlton, *Shakespearian Comedy* (1938), pp. 270 ff.
[2] I, i, 72–6.

beautiful today as ever', he made a valiant attempt to show that, with judicious cuts, the play was still worth a producer's pains. I read the preface with great interest, and with all the respect due to its author, but I remained sceptical. For after all, the theatre had long ago given its verdict. The thing, I said to myself, was dead to the stage, quite dead.

And then, nine years after his *Preface* appeared, Granville-Barker was proved to be more right than even he can have dreamed possible. For in the summer of 1936 Mr. Tyrone Guthrie revived the play at the Old Vic, dressed it magnificently, put all his very considerable brains into the production, and revealed it as a first-rate comedy of the pattern kind—so full of fun, of *permanent* wit, of brilliant and entrancing situation, that you hardly noticed the faded jesting and allusion, as you sat spell-bound and drank it all in. It was a thrilling production, Shakespearian criticism of the best kind, because a real piece of restoration. The only thing wrong about it was that the critics, the plodding editors and the dictatorial professors had so infected the public with their bookish notions that no one went to see it. It was played to half empty houses for a fortnight or so, and taken off.

But I went, I saw, I was completely conquered; and I was not alone, for Alfred Pollard, my father in Shakespeare, went with me and was as completely conquered. I have had many memorable and revealing evenings with Shakespeare in the theatre—*Hamlet* in modern dress, *Othello* with Paul Robeson in the title role and Peggy Ashcroft as Desdemona, and so on, but none to equal this. For Mr. Guthrie not only gave me a new play, the existence of which I had never suspected, which indeed had been veiled from men's eyes for three centuries, but he set me at a fresh standpoint of understanding and appreciation from which the whole of Shakespearian comedy might be reviewed in a new light. The occasion had found the man, but the thing could probably not have happened earlier. *Love's Labour's Lost* had to wait until the whirligig of time brought both the pattern-play and a producer who believed in it once again into the English theatre.

I propose, therefore, to spend the rest of this chapter in discussing the play from the point of view of a spectator, not from that of an editor.

The first thing one notices about it in the theatre is its extraordinary vivacity; it was evidently written in the highest possible spirits, by a dramatist who was thoroughly enjoying himself, and knew how to make his audience enjoy themselves thoroughly also. If the actors catch this spirit of merriment and alertness, as they can hardly help doing, the spectators will be carried right off their feet from the outset; so much so that the sixteenth-century allusions will seem little more than pebbles in the eddying, yet never-ceasing ripples of their laughter. The critics insist that none of the characters are quite human—we shall see presently what is to be said about that—but at least they are one and all exceedingly bright and agile. Even 'most Dull, honest Dull', the constable, catches the infection, feels that itching of the toes which all the rest display, so that his last words are

> I'll make one in a dance, or so; or I'll play
> On the tabor to the worthies, and let them dance the hay.[1]

The spirit of the whole is far more like that of a Mozart opera—quite an interesting comparison might be made with *Còsi fan Tutte*—than anything we are accustomed to in modern drama.

But quotation will give a better idea of the pace of the play than mere description.

'Master', exclaims the page Moth, who dances about the portentous but magnificent Armado like a glistening speck of dust in sunlight, 'will you win your love with a French brawl?'

ARM. How meanest thou? brawling in French?
MOTH. No, my complete master—but to jig off a tune at the tongue's

[1] V, i, 148–9.

end, canary to it with your feet, humour it with turning up your eyelids, sigh a note and sing a note, sometime through the throat as if you swallowed love with singing love, sometime through the nose as if you snuffed up love by smelling love, with your hat penthouse-like o'er the shop of your eyes, with your arms crossed on your thin-belly doublet like a rabbit on a spit, or your hands in your pocket like a man after the old painting—and keep not too long in one tune, but a snip and away![1]

Prose—but what rhythm! The speaker's body and feet are constantly on the move; he dances the brawl. 'Snip and away' might be the play's sub-title. Its structure may be mechanical, its plot feeble, its 'apprehension of life' shallow —as the critics allege—but it *goes*, goes with a swing and an impetus which, when seen on the stage, are irresistible. For sheer gaiety none of Shakespeare's other comedies can beat it, not even the golden *As You Like It* or that buck-basket stuffed full of fantastics, *The Merry Wives of Windsor*.

But 'keep not too long in one tune', admonishes Moth, and so introduces us to the next outstanding quality of the play—its constant variety. This too can only be rightly appreciated in the theatre. What one first notices is the varied play of colour, which my eyes first learned to feast upon at the Old Vic performance. But I run ahead. To proceed more orderly, let us first consider pattern and begin with the plot, of which all the commentators speak so scornfully. It is slight, though no slighter than that of some of Shakespeare's other comedies, for it contains much more than has hitherto been allowed, and it constitutes the canvas upon which the rest of the dramatic pattern is woven.

The King of Navarre and three sprightly young friends at his court decide to devote themselves to study for three years. The decision takes the form of the establishment of an academy which will embrace the whole court.

Navarre shall be the wonder of the world.

Such little academes were common enough at the time of the Renaissance. Hundreds of them were set up in the petty

[1] III, i, 8–21.

Italian courts in the fifteenth and sixteenth centuries.[1] And when the King tells us his reason for its establishment:

> Let fame, that all hunt after in their lives,
> Live registered upon our brazen tombs,

he gives utterances to yet another Renaissance commonplace. Had not Cicero written 'Trahimur omnes laudis studio, et optimus quique maxime gloria ducitur'? and was not Milton, forty years later, still declaring that

> Fame is the spur that the clear spirit doth raise
> To scorn delights and live laborious days—

lines that exactly express the theme of *Love's Labour's Lost*, though from how different a standpoint!

We are not told the subject of study—but it is clearly philosophy, and Berowne's talk of star-gazing and the vow 'to sleep but three hours of the night' points to natural philosophy, i.e. science, in its most popular form of astronomy. More stress is laid upon the kind of life the students are to lead, which is obviously stoical. They vow to fast once a week, to sleep but three hours out of the twenty-four, and to shut women out of the court altogether.

The last, of course, is what matters in the play. When it opens, the four men have just taken a solemn oath to observe this strict rule of life, and their oath is the pivot of the plot. 'This oath', says Charlton, 'is patently absurd.' Of course; Shakespeare meant it to be. But it is at once more and less serious than Charlton perceived. More serious, because oaths were frequently taken by Elizabethans and meant much more in their life than they do to us, who except in a court of law seldom if ever bind ourselves in this fashion. Shakespeare's audience derived all the more fun, therefore, from watching the oath-takers becoming forsworn as they try to wriggle out of their solemn undertaking. Less serious, because Shakespeare makes it clear from the outset that the oath must be broken. And the comic idea of the play is the

[1] See for example *The French Academies of the Sixteenth Century* by Frances A. Yates, Warburg Institute, 1947.

absurdity not only of the oath, but also of these academes
which drive their votaries to tie themselves up into knots
of the kind. And this, in turn, is symbolical of the absurdity
of the purely academic view of life in general.

The play falls into two halves (i) the retreat from Philosophy, (ii) the campaign for Love. At the outset, I have said,
the oath has just been taken, and the fellow-students are
about to 'subscribe' their names to the schedule which em-
bodies the terms of their undertaking; such subscription
being a particularly solemn form of oath-taking. As they do
so, Longaville and Dumaine reaffirm their intentions, but
Berowne frankly expresses his scepticism, criticizes the
whole scheme, and reminds the King that he cannot shut
women out of his court, since the Princess of France is due
to arrive with an embassy at any moment. Thus it is obvious
from the beginning that it is impossible to live like stoics in
a real world. And after this the academe rapidly crumbles.
Costard, the unlettered swain, is naturally the first defaulter;
but Armado is another. No sooner do the French ladies
arrive than signs of weakness appear in the four students
themselves. We next have Berowne's confession (all the
more striking because unwilling) that he 'that had been
love's whip' was now love's slave. And the whole movement culminates in the delightful IV, 3 in which each of the
students gives himself away in the ears of the others, Berowne utters his great speech of recantation, and all, con-
fessedly forsworn, determine to pursue their courtship *vi et
armis*.

In the second half of the play, therefore, study is relegated
to a subsidiary place: its claims and absurdities are represented by minor characters (pedant and curate) recently
introduced into the drama (for this purpose). The main
theme is the Love campaign, and the manner in which the
four ladies constantly thwart the advances of the men. It is
an elaborate flirtation (the word was unknown in this sense
to Shakespeare) accompanied by masques, dances and an
interlude. After many checks, the campaign is at last pushed

home and victory seems in sight, when 'at the latest minute of the hour' the cup is dashed from the lovers' lips by the news of the French King's death. The men are compelled to take a second vow and condemned to wait another year. This last defeat is one of the main points of the play as its title *Love's Labour's Lost* indicates. The whole is then rounded off with the delightful mockery of the Cuckoo and the Owl, in which the learned men display their knowledge of life by translating the call of spring into a word of fear and the hoot of the owl into a merry note. There is a purpose behind all this, to which I shall return in my conclusion. For the moment, however, watch the patterning.

In the first place, the play is full of speech pattern. There is of course a great deal of rhyme in *Love's Labour's Lost*— so much so that many have thought it must be Shakespeare's earliest play, on the theory that the passage from rhyme to blank verse is one of the indications of his development in dramatic power. But the rhyme here, as in Dryden and Pope, is part of the wit; it adds just that touch of artificiality required for a pattern-play; it points the jest and gives the grace of an echo to the happy repartee. Without rhyme *Love's Labour's Lost* would lose much of its life and colour. But rhyme is not the only form of verse. When something serious shows through the glitter of the surface, blank verse is used. Thus Berowne, who laughingly defends his black mistress in rhyme, turns to blank verse in his great speech of recantation, while it is noticeable that little but blank verse is spoken after the entry of the messenger of death in V, ii. An analysis of the whole play according to its use of rhyme, blank verse and prose would be instructive. Glance a moment, for instance, at the opening scene. It begins solemnly; the King announcing the oath and the three courtiers giving their respective assents to it. Lines 1–48 therefore are in blank verse. Yet the whole thing is artificial, and, as we are intended to feel, a little comic: therefore the blank verse is end-stopped and the speeches terminate in couplets. Then, when Berowne makes his protestation, and the tone becomes lively, even flippant, the blank verse is dropped and the banter of the men, together with Berowne's mock rhetoric, is conveyed in couplets, quatrains and sonnets: a rhyme-pattern that forms a delightful accompaniment to the dialogue, something like the patter of feet on the floor in a Polish mazurka. And even when Costard and Dull enter at l. 181 and prose begins, the patterning is not at an end, for Shakespeare writes his prose as well as his verse in patterned form in this play.

The structure of *Love's Labour's Lost* is of course a pattern also. The two parts are almost exactly equal in length, Berowne's recantation occurring about half-way through. But perhaps the most remarkable instance of parallelism in the two parts is in regard to the oaths. The oaths of the students at the beginning are offset by the oaths of the lovers at the end—with a significant difference, however. The students swear to follow the pagan stoical life for the sake of fame; the lovers are compelled to take *religious* vows as a penance for perjury and as a means of regeneration. And this system of repetition and echo is not confined to the main plot but is carried out in detail of all sorts throughout the play. For example in I, i, Costard's confession concerning Jaquenetta is followed by Armado's letter—both, though in different fashion, going over the same points. Or again, Armado's soliloquy in I, ii is matched by Berowne's in III, i; both have the same theme (contemptuous confession of Cupid's power) and both end with a promise of poetry. Or yet again, we have Armado's letter to Jaquenetta (franked by remuneration) contrasted with Berowne's letter to Rosaline (franked by a guerdon). Or lastly, take once more the famous recantation scene. Each of the four men in turn comes on to the stage, makes his confession of love and perjury, reads aloud his poem and hides himself as his successor appears. And when all have revealed their secrets in the view of their fellows, one by one they step forth again to denounce the perjurer who has last spoken, until at length Berowne the first comer and original spy springs down from his tree to denounce the lot, only to be himself unmasked by the entry of Costard and Jaquenetta with his incriminating letter to Rosaline. The scene winds itself up and unwinds itself again for all the world as if four boys were dancing and reversing about a maypole.

It would be idle to multiply examples, some of them of the subtlest character, so subtle that like the lesser variations upon a theme in music they are felt rather than perceived; suffice it to say that repetition with variations is one of the mainsprings of the play's structure.

But there is another, for there are two elements in every pattern, balance and contrast as well as repetition and variation. These are secured in *Love's Labour's Lost* chiefly by the grouping of characters, and by the shifting colour effects produced by the regrouping.

The play, we are told, is 'deficient in characterization'. But 'characterization' is not one of the purposes of the play. Occasionally the persons fall into character, but as they do they tend to fall out of the pattern.

The minor characters are intended as types—the traditional types of the *commedia dell' arte*—not as rounded human characters at all, and Berowne tells us as much when he sums them up as the pedant, the braggart, the hedge-priest, the fool and the boy.[1] Charlton indeed declared Costard to be 'the most considerable character' in the play and quotes as evidence Costard's oft-quoted words about Sir Nathaniel Alisander as the latter departs discomforted:

> There, an't shall please you, a foolish mild man—an honest man, look you, and soon dashed. He is a marvellous good neighbour, faith, and a very good bowler; but for Alisander, alas you see how 'tis—a little o'erparted.[2]

On the other hand, Granville-Barker, who had to think about stage-production and casting, comes to a very different conclusion, that Costard is (as Berowne calls him) 'the fool', i.e. the official jester at the court of Navarre. And had it not been for the Alisander passage there would have

[1] V, ii, 539–40.    [2] V, ii, 577–81.

been no doubt about it—the mask slips and accidentally reveals a face. For a moment Costard has stepped out of the stage design and become a man, as a Shakespearian Fool is in other plays.

As to the eight principals—the two groups of student lovers and mocking wenches, who 'resemble each other in a wooden conformity', who 'have all to do the same sort of thing'; they constitute of course the most striking feature of the design and they do so the more effectively in that they provide the main element in the colour scheme.

The Elizabethan actors, saved all the cost of scenery and lighting which swells the bill of modern production, are known to have spent lavishly upon dress; and *Love's Labour's Lost*, which contains a sixteenth-century King and three attendant nobles, all in choice costume of similar though not identical cut and design; a French Princess with her three ladies also brilliantly tricked out in dresses of a quasi-uniform style (for when they mask they must look alike); the foppish old courtier Boyet; and 'fashion's own knight', Don Adriano de Armado, with the page Moth at his heels, must have presented a perfect riot of colour and magnificence, to which the pedant and the curate, the patched fool, the frieze cloth constable and the ragged dairymaid acted as foils.

And the scenes are so arranged that the colour-scheme is constantly changing: the King and his lords are outblazoned by Armado and Moth, who after being contrasted with the simplicity of Dull, Costard and Jaquenetta, are in their turn followed by the dapper Boyet and his bevy of dainty ladies. Next, the two main groups are brought together for the splendour of Navarre to confront the grace of France, and this first meeting is followed, of course, by many others. The encounters of the two groups are like dramatic minuets. In the Muscovite scene, indeed, we get what is obviously intended to represent, in a kind of comic ballet, opposing armies with heralds passing to and fro; the men masked and disguised as Russians, on one side of the stage, and the women, likewise masked and disguised by the interchange of 'fairings',[1] on the other. First Moth advances as 'herald' for the men and after a vain attempt to deliver his 'ambassage' retires in confusion. Then Boyet advances to the men and demands their intentions. This business is particularly effective on the stage, because though the two parties are only a few yards apart, the nimble Boyet runs backwards and forwards between them like a busy herald receiving and delivering messages; until at length the ladies line up, dress themselves by the right, make one pace forwards and speak to the enemy face to face.

So the kaleidoscope goes on, until suddenly, with the effect of a smashing hammer-stroke, there appears a figure clothed in black from head to foot. Death enters and the brilliant 'scene begins to cloud'.

The extraordinary impression left upon the audience by the entrance of the black-clad messenger upon the court revels was the greatest lesson I took away with me from the Guthrie production. It made me see two things—(a) that however gay, however riotous a Shakespearian comedy may be, tragedy is always there, *felt*, if not seen; (b) that for all its surface lightness and frivolity, the play had behind it a serious mind at work, with a purpose.

In conclusion then consider this purpose for a moment.[2] First there is the terrible portrait of a renaissance schoolmaster, self-complacent, self-seeking, irascible, pretentious, intolerant of what he calls 'barbarism', and yet himself knowing nothing but the pitiful rudiments, the husks of learning, which he spends his life thrusting down the throats of his unfortunate pupils. Holofernes moves upon Shakespeare's stage as the eternal type of pedant, the 'living-dead man'[3] who will always be with us, because so long as there

---

[1] V, ii, 2.

[2] What follows is virtually a repetition of a passage from an essay on Shakespeare's Schoolmasters which I gave to the Royal Society of Literature in 1928.

[3] The epithet belongs to another schoolmaster, Dr. Pinch, the pedant in *The Comedy of Errors* (V, i, 242).

is a human race to be educated there will always be many to mistake the letter for the spirit.

It is a pity that *Love's Labour's Lost* is in parts so obscure, so topical. Else it might be commended without hesitation to the attention of all teachers, professors, and educationalists to be read once a year—on Ash Wednesday, shall we say?—for their souls' good. For we have here, not only in the figure of Holofernes, but in the play as a whole, Shakespeare's great onslaught upon the Dark Tower, the fortress of the enemies of life and grace and gaiety—

> The round squat tower, blind as the fool's heart,

the name of which is Pedantry. Against it he hoists the banner of Love, but though he talks much of ladies and their bright eyes, he means by love what Shelley means when he writes, 'The great secret of morals is Love; or a going out of our own nature, and an identification of ourselves with the beautiful which exists in thought, action, or person, not our own',[1] or what Rupert Brooke means when he tells Frederick Keeling that 'his occupation is being in love with the universe'.[2] Love for Shakespeare, in short, is a symbol of that passionate apprehension of Life, which sets all five senses afire and is the great gift of the poet and the artist to his fellows. And Berowne gives us the conclusion of the whole matter at IV, iii, 301 ff.

> Why, universal plodding prisons up
> The nimble spirits in the arteries.
> . . . . . . .
> But love, first learnéd in a lady's eyes,
> Lives not alone immuréd in the brain,
> But with the motion of all elements,
> Courses as swift as thought in every power,
> And gives to every power a double power,
> Above their functions and their offices.
> It adds a precious seeing to the eye—

[1] *Defence of Poetry.*
[2] Edward Marsh, *Collected Poems of Rupert Brooke with a Memoir,* 1918, p. liv.

# Love's Labour's Lost: The Story of a Conversion

A lover's eyes will gaze an eagle blind;
A lover's ear will hear the lowest sound,
When the suspicious heed[1] of theft is stopped;
Love's feeling is more soft and sensible
Than are the tender horns of cockled snails;
Love's tongue proves dainty Bacchus gross in taste.
For valour, is not Love a Hercules,
Still climbing trees in the Hesperides?
Subtle as Sphinx, as sweet and musical
As bright Apollo's lute, strung with his hair;
And when Love speaks, the voice of all the gods
Make heaven drowsy with the harmony.
Never durst poet touch a pen to write,
Unless his ink were temp'red with Love's sighs.

[1] An anon. emendation cited in the (old) Cambridge Shakespeare. The 1598 Q reads 'head'. 'Heed'=what attracts attention; cf. I, i, 82.

# CHAPTER IV

# *The Merry Wives of Windsor*

---

In *Love's Labour's Lost* we had a comedy noteworthy for its theatrical and dramatic pattern, with little incident or action and with character-interest deliberately kept in leash. As a complete contrast it will be convenient next to consider together two comedies, which though probably written some five years apart,[1] are alike in many respects. They make little attempt at witty dialogue but they have plenty of 'blundering', especially *The Merry Wives* with its French doctor Caius, its Welsh schoolmaster Sir Hugh Evans, to say nothing of Mistress Quickly; while in *The Merchant of Venice* we have the Gobbos. Both plays are full of incident and rich in character. Both too show a clear line of descent from an Italian source, and *The Merchant* still retains its Italian atmosphere, though in *The Merry Wives* this has been replaced by the atmosphere of an English country town, which it conveys so successfully that the sense of it is one of the outstanding features of this delightful play.

Both, again, are burgher plays, though here the effect is so different that one hardly recognizes the kinship. The merchants of *The Merchant of Venice* are, as I said, merchant-princes, much superior in wealth and rank, we feel, to the merchants of *Errors*. Portia, the Lady of Belmont, can hold

[1] As we have it, *The Wives* must have been written after *Henry V* since it contains Corporal Nym who does not appear in *Henry IV*.

up her head with queens—is indeed meant to be thought a kind of Queen Elizabeth. Antonio, a 'royal merchant' (III, ii, 240), is obviously one of the principal men of Venice, while his friend and 'most noble kinsman' is the Lord Bassanio. The Fords and Pages of Windsor, on the other hand, are honest well-to-do dealers and shopkeepers—their trade is never mentioned, but when we think of Master John Shakespeare, wool-dealer, glover and general storeman, one of the chief citizens of Stratford-on-Avon and at one time its bailiff or mayor, we get their measure without a doubt.[1] We hear of the court, as of something remote and aloof; it affects their lives, when it is stationed at Windsor, but is out of their element.

I do not propose, here, to discuss the sources of The Merry Wives, still less to enter into the maze labelled with the quaint word 'Garmombles', in which a mysterious German duke mounted upon the horses of mine Host has led many an editor and critic into strange capers.[2] Something, however, must be said about the making of the play, and the legend that it was written in a fortnight, at the command of Queen Elizabeth, who having enjoyed Falstaff in the two parts of Henry IV, and disappointed at not seeing him in Henry V despite the promise by the Epilogue at the conclusion of 2 Henry IV, demanded, it is averred, to see him yet again, and this time in love. The legend does not go back beyond the beginning of the eighteenth century but it looks likely enough, and since its acceptance would explain much, there has been a general inclination to believe it. Indeed, the only incredible thing about it is the 'fortnight' Shakespeare is supposed to have taken in the composition. It is difficult enough to credit Ben Jonson's statement that he wrote Volpone in five weeks, quite impossible to suppose a play like The Merry Wives, full of incident and rich in

[1] Cf. Ch. II, p. 50.
[2] If any feel inclined for a canter after them, they cannot do better than follow Professor Crofts whose Shakespeare and the Post Horses (1937) gives the latest, and I suspect the final, news of the German count.

varied character can have been penned in less than half that time.

But if, as the legend implies, Queen Bess, supposing that a play could be improvised as quickly as one of those masque-like entertainments to which she was so often invited by her noble hosts on progress, only allowed something like a fortnight for the composition of the command performance—probably, as the finale of the play indicates, a performance at Windsor for some ceremony connected with the Order of the Garter—there is one way Shakespeare might have accomplished it without undue strain, viz. by going to work upon a play already in being and adapting it to the purpose.[1] It is true that W. W. Greg, who has given us a masterly edition of the 1602 Quarto which is a memorized report of the full text by the actor who played the part of the Host on the stage, can find no evidence of a pre-Shakespearian play at the back of the Folio version. Yet I find it difficult to understand a number of features except on the assumption that Shakespeare has been obliged, either single-handed or in collaboration, to foist the fat knight into a play in which originally he had no part. This seems evident from the opening scene, in which a great effort is made to link the play on to *Henry IV*, an effort which is scarcely maintained beyond that opening.

It is a promising enough beginning. Here we have Justice Shallow of Gloucestershire once again, furnished with Slender, a new cousin, even more exquisitely foolish than his other cousin, Master Justice Silence, and in a towering rage with Falstaff for deer-stealing in his park. Slender, who may have had an original in the old play, remains as the goose-like wooer of Mistress Anne Page, daughter of one of the citizens of Windsor, and the poaching incident gives Falstaff an opportunity for some of his accustomed effrontery; but nothing more is heard of it after the first scene, and old man Shallow drifts aimlessly through the rest of the play. He has served his turn, which was that of a hyphen between Fal-

[1] See Chapter IX, p. 205.

staff as the Master of Revels and Falstaff as the slave of Venus.

Nor is it difficult, I feel, to dissect out an original self-complacent philanderer from the sham Falstaffian proportions beneath which Shakespeare has hastily—too hastily—endeavoured to conceal him. For after his insolence to Justice Shallow in the first scene, he is only fitfully the Falstaff we can recognize. The gallant of the old play evidently held a pretty conceit of himself, and it sounds odd to hear Falstaff boasting of his own good looks, as he does in the following dialogue:

> MISTRESS QUICKLY. . . . I never knew a woman so dote upon a man; surely, I think you have charms, la . . . yes, in truth.
> FALSTAFF. Not I, I assure thee; setting the attraction of my good parts aside, I have no other charms.[1]

This Falstaff is also a 'scholar', a title bestowed upon him not only by the Host (I, iii, 3), but also by the disguised Ford (II, ii, 168), so that it can hardly be accidental.

But strangest of all to my mind is the tone and style of some of the speeches that come from Falstaff's mouth. Witness these questions he puts to the disguised Ford, when the latter comes to him, pretending that he seeks his assistance in the wooing of his own wife:

> Have you received no promise of satisfaction at her hands? . . .
> Have you importuned her to such a purpose? . . .
> Of what quality was your love, then? . . .
> Would it apply well to the vehemency of your affection, that I should win what you would enjoy? . . . Methinks you prescribe to yourself very preposterously.[2]

Or again:

> Mistress Ford, your sorrow hath eaten up my sufferance; I see you are obsequious in your love, and I profess requital to a hair'sbreadth, not only, Mistress Ford, in the simple office of love, but in all the accoutrement, complement, and ceremony of it.[3]

Compare this stilted talk with that he utters in the scene

---

[1] II, ii, 96 ff.         [2] II, ii, 196 ff.         [3] IV, ii, 1-5.

# The Merry Wives of Windsor

after his immersion in the Thames, which gives us the very Falstaff of *Henry IV*:

FALSTAFF *(calling)*. Bardolph, I say!

BARDOLPH *(runs in)*. Here, sir.

FALSTAFF. Go fetch me a quart of sack—put a toast in't . . . *(Bardolph goes.)* Have I lived to be carried in a basket like a barrow of butcher's offal, and to be thrown in the Thames? Well, if I be served such another trick, I'll have my brains ta'en out, and buttered, and give them to a dog for a new-year's gift. The rogues slighted me into the river with as little remorse as they would have drowned a blind bitch's puppies, fifteen i'th' litter: and you may know by my size, that I have a kind of alacrity in sinking; if the bottom were as deep as hell, I should down. . . . I had been drowned, but that the shore was shelvy and shallow . . . a death that I abhor; for the water swells a man; and what a thing should I have been, when I had been swelled! I should have been a mountain of mummy. *(Bardolph returns.)*

BARDOLPH. Here's Mistress Quickly, sir, to speak with you. *(He sets the cups down.)*

FALSTAFF *(takes one)*. Come, let me pour in some sack to the Thames water; for my belly's as cold as if I had swallowed snowballs for pills to cool the reins. *(He drains the cup.)* Call her in.

BARDOLPH. Come in, woman.

QUICKLY *(entering)*. By your leave . . . I cry you mercy! Give your worship good morrow.

FALSTAFF *(emptying the second cup)*. Take away these chalices. . . . Go brew me a pottle of sack finely.

BARDOLPH. With eggs, sir?

FALSTAFF. Simple of itself; I'll no pullet-sperm in my brewage. . . .[1]

The Falstaff of *The Merry Wives* is a sort of monster like the Mock-Turtle in *Alice in Wonderland*; his body, padded out with cushions, has the proportions of the beast he affects to be; but the calf's head that surmounts it discloses his true nature; while the tongue of this remarkable animal-compound speaks the dialect of both elements.

As for the irregular humorists Bardolph, Pistol and Nym, they are stage-figures introduced to remind the audience of the historical play of which *The Merry Wives* is but a pendant, and possess little life of their own. Bardolph

[1] III, v, 1–31. Stage-directions given here and later are editorial.

dwindles into a tapster in the third scene, and only appears twice (in that capacity) for brief episodes later. To Pistol is given the most famous of all the remarks he utters, an utterance worthy of Don Quixote himself:

> Why, then the world's mine oyster
> Which I with sword will open—

but the rest of him is mere flim-flam. Of the three Nym is perhaps the most interesting with his patter about 'humours', but for historical, not dramatic reasons.[1]

It looks too as if *The Merry Wives* had an earlier strain in it than anything derived from sources contemporary with *Henry IV*. The story of a gallant making love to two women at the same time, confiding his designs to the husband of one of them, and escaping that jealous man's vengeance time after time by one device or other, including concealment in a 'dry-vat full of feathers', is a combination of tales from the collection of Straparola, the Italian follower of Boccaccio. Furthermore the other half of the plot, the tale of Master Fenton, the young gentleman who woos the pretty Anne Page, and is thwarted for a time by her match-making parents, is of the normal stuff of Italian comedy; indeed, it goes back to classical comedy itself.

Even more traditional is the part that Mistress Quickly plays. She is, of course, another hyphen-character with *Henry IV*. But it has often been noticed that she cannot be the same woman as the Hostess of the Boar's Head, Eastcheap, who marries Pistol in *Henry V*. For how came that presiding genius over Falstaff's revels in London to be house-keeper to a French doctor in Windsor? Nor does that exhaust her social functions in the royal borough. No reason is given for her interest in Anne Page; yet all three suitors for that maiden's hand seek her out, bribe her, and secure her services in their cause. She works hard for them all, 'for so', she says, 'I have promised, and I'll be as good as my word'. And this is not the end of it either; for Falstaff also

[1] See footnote on page 92 of this chapter.

employs her, his 'good she-Mercury',[1] as go-between with his two would-be mistresses, they themselves having first engaged her to egg him on. Clearly, she is the *lena* of the comedy, playing the part which the old bawd plays in Plautus and Terence, while the fact that she is described by Sir Hugh Evans as 'in the manner of' the doctor's 'nurse, or his dry nurse' suggests that she came under Shakespeare's hands through some Italian source, inasmuch as the classical *lena* became a nurse in the more respectable Italian drama.[2] That Nurse is still coarse-mouthed like Juliet's to whom Mistress Quickly is cousin-german. And yet, though the two Quicklys are different women, they speak with the same voice. They *had* to, because Shakespeare was obliged to foster the illusion of their identity in order to keep open his line of communication with *Henry IV* and so help to conceal the trick of blowing-out a rather commonplace self-complacent philanderer to look like the great Sir John Falstaff.

Nevertheless how extraordinarily successful the whole transformation was! There are textual untidinesses and loose ends here and there which give proof of the haste with which the transaction was carried through—or, as Greg thinks, of successive revisions.[3] But if the re-writing only took a fortnight, the eighteenth-century critic Gildon is justified in acclaiming it 'a prodigious thing, when all is so well contrived, and carried on without the least confusion'. The plot, of course, with its two strands, was ex hypothesi already there, together with the ranting Host, and, I suspect, the French doctor and the Welsh parson. That a Frenchman, apothecary or doctor, comes from the old play is suggested by the name Dr. Caius, which is obviously an attempt to give him a Windsor countenance, since Dr. Caius, second founder of my own college, who died in 1573, had been physician to their majesties Edward VI, Mary, and (for a

---

[1] II, ii, 75.
[2] Cf. Bond, *Early Plays from the Italian*, Introductory essay, pp. xl–xli.
[3] See Chambers, *William Shakespeare*, i, 431 ff.

short while at the beginning of her reign) Queen Elizabeth herself. But the disguise was ill adjusted, since Keys (Caius) was pure English.[1]

Yet, much as I believe he owed to his unknown predecessor, Shakespeare's own contribution to the play was no small one. Besides Falstaff and the fantastics just mentioned he added Justice Shallow, his cousin Slender, and the three 'irregular humourists' Bardolph, Pistol and Nym from the *Henry IV* and *Henry V* underplots, to say nothing of disguising a garrulous old nurse of the original as Mistress Quickly. In a word he gave us a gallery of 'humorous' portraits without rival even in the comedies of Ben Jonson.

Again, by a dozen or more deft touches he contrives to bathe the play in an atmosphere redolent of the countryside. For example, we hear that Master Slender had 'fought with a warrener', of a fallow greyhound in a coursing match on the Cotswolds, of Master Page with 'a good hawk for the bush' up betimes in the morning to go 'a-birding', of Mistress Anne 'at a farm-house a-feasting', we guess upon curds and cream, while Anne herself, when faced with the prospect of mating with the French doctor, expresses herself in forthright country speech:

> I had rather be set quick i' th' earth
> And bowled to death with turnips.[2]

Or take this:

FORD. Buck? I would I could wash myself of the buck! Buck, buck, buck! Ay, buck; I warrant you, buck—and of the season too it shall appear.... Gentlemen, I have dreamed to-night. I'll tell you my dream.... Here, here, here be my keys. Ascend my chambers,

---

[1] Cf. A. D. McNair (*The Caian*, vol. xxviii): 'We are entitled to infer that John Caius was well enough known twenty-five years after his death for his name to suggest to a London audience a distinguished physician, but not so well known that the appearance of his namesake in the guise of a Frenchman would be regarded as an unpardonable incongruity.'

To which I venture to add the conjecture that the name was originally Lopez, that of the Portuguese Jew who spoke, and wrote, broken English, who *was* the Queen's physician, but whose death on the gallows in 1594 would make his name inappropriate in a comedy.

[2] III, iv, 87–8.

# The Merry Wives of Windsor

search, seek, find out: I'll warrant we'll unkennel the fox. . . .
Let me stop this way first. . . . So, now untapis![1]

But Shakespeare, as Hazlitt remarked, 'is the only writer
who was as great in describing weakness as strength', and
his chief contribution to this play, when all is said, is his
unique comic spirit, the spirit of laughter without bitterness,
without malice, without even a trace of contempt. Let us
then look at one or two of the antics which he found when
he came to the play or himself imported into it, and watch
him at work falling in love with them and making us fall in
love in our turn. And we will begin by carving the goose.

Master Slender is a *gull* (lit. = a gosling), one of the stock
figures in Elizabethan drama. He is the witless counterpart,
among the gentry, of the fool natural among clowns. Most
stage-gulls are merely stupid puppets, for the utterance of
inconsequent rubbish, laughing-stocks for the ridicule of all
beholders. Like the rest of his kind, Slender is an imbecile
and a poltroon. We get a picture of him from a talk his
man Simple has with Mistress Quickly:

QUICKLY. Peter Simple, you say your name is?
SIMPLE. Ay . . . for fault of a better.
QUICKLY. And Master Slender's your master?
SIMPLE. Ay, forsooth.
QUICKLY. Does he not wear a great round beard, like a glover's
    paring-knife? [There speaks the son of John Shakespeare, glover
    and wool merchant.]
SIMPLE. No, forsooth; he hath but a little whey-face; with a little
    yellow beard—a cane-coloured beard.
QUICKLY. A softly-sprighted [= gentle-spirited] man, is he not?
SIMPLE. Ay, forsooth: but he is as tall a man of his hands as any is
    between this and his head: he hath fought with a warrener!
    [Not a very fearsome antagonist, rabbits being gentle beasts!]
QUICKLY. How say you?—O, I should remember him: does he not
    hold up his head, as it were, and strut in his gait?
SIMPLE. Yes, indeed, does he.
QUICKLY. Well, heaven send Anne Page no worse fortune![2]

[1] III, iii, 150–6. *Untapis*: a hunting term = Come out of hiding! Cf. *Second
Part of the Return from Parnassus* (1602), 2.5.830, 'At the unkennelling, untapezing
or earthing of the fox' (cited O.E.D.). The F. reads 'uncope'. I owe the emendation to Dr. Alice Walker.                                    [2] I, iv, 13 ff.

But there is a great deal more in Slender than this. He has pride, pride in his uncle, the great Justice Shallow, 'A gentleman born, master parson', he boasts, 'who writes himself "Armigero", in any bill, warrant, quittance, or obligation —"Armigero!" '[1] And pride in his own gentle birth. 'Go sirrah', he bids his servant Simple,

> 'for all you are my man, go wait upon my cousin Shallow. . . . A justice of peace sometime may be beholding to his friend, for a man: I keep but three men and a boy yet, till my mother be dead; but what though? yet I live like a poor gentleman born.'[2]

This last is enough by itself, to endear him to us, had he said nothing else in the play. In simple candour he has uttered the secret thoughts of many an heir that waits for his parents' shoes.

How human too is the strutting in his gait when he first encounters the destined lady! He will show her that he is not like other folk, and refuses to follow them in to dinner. He brags of his 'playing at sword and dagger with a master of fence' and of his delight in bear-baiting:

SLENDER. Why do your dogs bark so? be there bears i' th' town?

ANNE. I think there are, sir; I heard them talked of.

SLENDER. I love the sport well; but I shall as soon quarrel at it[3] as any man in England. *You* are afraid, if you see the bear loose, are you not?

ANNE. Ay, indeed, sir.

SLENDER. That's meat and drink to *me*, now. I have seen Sackerson loose twenty times, and have taken him by the chain; but I warrant you, the women have so cried and shrieked at it, that it passed: but women, indeed, cannot abide 'em; they are very ill-favoured rough things.[4]

That should put her in her place, and show him for the he-man he is! And so, his little triumph over, she soon has him in to his dinner—and hers.

The ordeal of his life comes when he is put to the wooing of her. He has wit enough to realize something of what belongs to love, and has marked Anne Page before his uncle

[1] I, i, 7-9.     [2] I, i, 254-9.
[3] Take exception to it—on principle, as a religious man should.
[4] I, i, 270-81.

# The Merry Wives of Windsor

proposes the match: 'Mistress Anne Page?' he recollects, 'she has brown hair, and speaks small like a woman.' And when she appears before him, he longs for poetry like the approved lover—'I had rather than forty shillings I had my Book of Songs and Sonnets here'—an old-fashioned taste.

He gives her, too, what other men would call his heart: of that there can be no doubt. So love-struck is he, indeed, that he remains unconscious of all that happens between Sir Hugh Evans and Dr. Caius in Frogmore fields, and can only sigh at intervals, 'O, sweet Anne Page!', when he can be heard between their shouts. And yet, when he has to put the question, he is utterly at a loss, do what his uncle can to help him through with it:

SHALLOW. She's coming; to her, coz. . . . O boy, thou hadst a father!

SLENDER. I had a father, Mistress Anne. My uncle can tell you good jests of him; pray you, uncle, tell Mistress Anne the jest, how my father stole two geese out of a pen, good uncle.

SHALLOW. Mistress Anne, my cousin loves you.

SLENDER. Ay, that I do—as well as I love any woman in Gloucestershire.

SHALLOW. He will maintain you like a gentlewoman.

SLENDER. Ay, that I will, come cut-and-long-tail—under the degree of a squire. [That is, I will welcome guests of all sorts provided they are not too grand and expensive.]

SHALLOW. He will make you a hundred and fifty pounds jointure.

ANNE. Good Master Shallow, let him woo for himself.

SHALLOW. Marry, I thank you for it; I thank you for that good comfort. . . . She calls you, coz. I'll leave you. (*He goes aside.*)

ANNE. Now, Master Slender.

SLENDER. Now, good Mistress Anne.

ANNE. What is your will?

SLENDER. My will! od's heartlings! that's a pretty jest, indeed. I ne'er made my will yet, I thank heaven! I am not such a sickly creature, I give heaven praise.

ANNE. I mean, Master Slender, what would you with me?

SLENDER. Truly, for mine own part, I would little or nothing with you. . . . Your father and my uncle hath made motions: if it be my luck, so; if not, happy man be his dole! They can tell you how things go, better than I can; you may ask your father; here he comes.[1]

[1] III, iv, 36-67.

It is a scene at which that hard-faced woman, Queen Elizabeth, must have laughed until the tears ran down her cheeks, as Shakespeare intended she should.

But did Shakespeare laugh when he wrote it? And may he not have guessed that some at least in the audience would find pity as well as laughter in their heart for his idiot boy, with the 'little whey-face' and the 'little yellow beard'? 'A goose to say grace over', as 'Q' says, and the grace is, 'There, but for the grace of God, might go the wisest of us all.'

It is the same story with the other human oddities—we cannot help loving them, because their author so obviously did. Their chief comic function, as already noted, is to 'hack our English'. There is for instance the Welsh parson, who when Anne Page is mentioned as a likely bride for Master Slender, delivers himself after this fashion:

'It is that fery person for all the 'orld, as just as you will desire, and seven hundred pounds of moneys, and gold, and silver, is her grand-sire, upon his death's bed—Got deliver to a joyful resurrections!—give, when she is able to overtake seventeen years old.'[1]

There is the French doctor, who murders the language in his own way: there is mine Host with his staccato manner of speech; there are Pistol and Nym, the former well described by Professor Willcock as 'a walking scarecrow of worn-out shreds and patches', the other a purveyor of the new-fangled jargon of the humours; there are Justice Shallow and nephew Slender, misusing the Queen's English in different fashions; lastly there is Mistress Quickly, who anticipates the malapropisms of Mrs. Malaprop. To quote Professor Willcock once again, the end of Elizabeth's reign was 'a period of unparalleled linguistic awareness. . . . Verbal fashions chased each other through the court, and the smallness of the Elizabethan world gave them currency in all classes of society. . . . Words mattered; they were savoured, bandied to and fro, followed up from jest to jest.'[2] In such

[1] I, i, 45–9.
[2] G. D. Willcock, op. cit., pp. 6–8.

a world the corrupters of language were almost as welcome as the affecters; there was more fun to be got out of them.[1]

Evans's own peculiarities of speech are the more ludicrous that he is himself a schoolmaster, and a whole scene is devoted to a lesson in Latin grammar in which Master William Page is the victim. The name of the boy is, one likes to feel, significant. Little William Shakespeare had no doubt undergone similar examinations in his time, and been dismissed, if not with a threat of a birching, at least with a commendation upon his 'good sprag memory'.

But Evans is much more than a stupid old Welsh pedant. He has the vivacity which possesses all the characters in this rollicking play. And Shakespeare commends him to us by the little human touches which he confers upon him: How fond, for example, he is of his meals! 'The dinner is on the table', announces Mistress Anne at the end of I, i. 'My father desires your worships' company.' 'I will wait upon him, fair Mistress Anne', pronounces Shallow pompously. 'Od's plessed-will', exclaims Sir Hugh, briskly hurrying in; 'I will not be absence at the grace.' He is out again, before the repast is over, in order to dispatch Simple with a letter to Mistress Quickly. But he cuts his instructions short, because of what lies within, and so concludes: 'Be gone. I will make an end of my dinner; there's pippins and seese to come.' And when he is most ridiculous he is most human—as he waits trembling in Frogmore fields for his furious adversary and tries to pluck up heart by singing.

As for Mistress Quickly of *The Merry Wives*, she is surely one of the most precious characters in all Shakespeare, and would long ago have been recognized as such, had not the whole play (together with the personages in it) been over-shadowed and obscured by the silly debate about the degradation of Falstaff.

The banker Walter Bagehot, who is one of Shakespeare's

[1] On p. 203, vol. viii, of Malone's *Shakespeare* will be found an interesting discussion by Johnson and others of the use on the stage of provincial and foreign pronunciation.

best critics, has a fine appreciation of the Mistress Quickly in *Henry IV*. What he fastens upon is her 'confused and undulating style of narration', common to most members of 'the illogical classes' in Shakespeare (Juliet's Nurse, Dogberry, and the rest), a style of the common people of London and Warwickshire. 'He would', Bagehot writes, 'never have interrupted Mrs. Quickly; he saw that her mind was going to and fro over the subject; he saw that it was coming right, and this was enough for him'.[1] For, as he says elsewhere,

> Shakespeare was too wise not to know that for most of the purposes of human life stupidity is a most valuable element. He had nothing of the impatience which sharp logical minds habitually feel when they come across those who do not apprehend their quick and precise deductions.[2]

The mind of Mrs. Quickly in *The Merry Wives* possesses the same delightfully meandering quality, but inasmuch as it has more scope for exhibition than in *Henry IV*, it is able to display another, and still more interesting, feature. She is quite incapable of framing moral judgments or drawing moral distinctions. With a keen sense of the benison of the creature comforts—'we'll have a posset for't soon at night, in faith at the latter end of a sea-coal fire' gives us her idea of bliss—she had that standard and no other in her estimates of other people. Her servant, John Rugby, she tells us, is

> an honest, willing, kind fellow, as ever servant shall come in house withal; and, I warrant you, no tell-tale nor no breed-bate; his worst fault is, that he is given to prayer: he is something peevish that way; but nobody but has his fault.[3]

Not that she is against prayer in itself, for those who can afford time for it: 'Let me tell you in your ear', she says to Falstaff of Mrs. Page,

> she's as fartuous a civil modest wife, and one, I tell you, that will not miss you morning nor evening prayer, as any is in Windsor, whoe'er be the other: and she bade me tell your worship that her husband is

---

[1] Bagehot, *Literary Studies* (Everyman Library, vol. i, 131).
[2] Bagehot, op. cit., i, 128.
[3] I, iv, 7 ff.

seldom from home, but she hopes there will come a time. . . . But Mistress Page would desire you to send her your little page, of all loves: her husband has a marvellous infection to the little page: and, truly, Master Page is an honest man: never a wife in Windsor leads a better life than she does: do what she will, say what she will, take all, pay all, go to bed when she list, rise when she list, all is as she will: and truly she deserves it; for if there be a kind woman in Windsor, she is one.[1]

'Kindness', and a love of comfort especially when expressed in concrete form, are the only virtues she can understand. 'Now heaven send thee good fortune!' she exclaims as Fenton goes out after pressing money into her hand. 'A kind heart he hath: a woman would run through fire and water for such a kind heart.'[2]

In short, from the standpoint of the Charity Organization Society and social reform generally, she is without moral fibre, a speck of dirt in the body politic, fit only for a 'clean-up'. Nor would Ben Jonson have shown her any tolerance; we have only to look at his Doll Common to see what he would have made of her. In the large chamber of Shakespeare's imagination, however, there was a warm corner for her and all her kind, warm enough to stir her blood and give her life and motion, for the delight of man as long as the English language, that she so deliciously mishandled, endures. And what a comment unexpressed, unconscious, but none the less pungent, she is on human society, now as well as then! For what are her muddled ideas about right and wrong but a reflection of the conflict between the ideals and the conduct of her betters? The gift of hypocrisy is beyond her, because she lacks the wit to draw the curtain of convention across the facts of life. She speaks as she finds.

Bergson defined comedy as a criticism in the name of society of characters which show 'a special lack of adaptability' to social conventions and intercourse. Shakespearian comedy is rather a criticism of society itself and its conventions from the point of view of beings who through lack of

[1] II, ii, 91–113.    [2] III, iv, 101–3.

intellect or education or adaptability or because they are
outcasts like Shylock, are not recognized as full members of
society. It has in fact a much closer affinity with the novels
of Dostoevsky (e.g. *The Idiot*) than with the plays of Molière
or Ibsen, possessing as it does tragic implications. Yet there is
nothing whatever tragic about *The Merry Wives*. The
jealousy of Master Ford supplies the only serious note in it,
and that is not taken seriously by anyone but himself. It is
even more consistently light-hearted than the gay *Love's
Labour's Lost*, since it contains no messenger of Death to
convert hilarity into sobriety at the close of the play. From
first to last, all is merry, as the title promises; and though the
judicial Dr. Johnson pronounces 'the conduct' of the drama
to be 'deficient', he is nevertheless compelled to add that

> its general power, that power by which all works of genius shall
> finally be tried, is such, that perhaps it never yet had reader or
> spectator who did not think it too soon at the end.[1]

Yet the play represents the nearest Shakespeare came to
writing a comedy after the fashion of Ben Jonson. It is,
indeed, often classed by critics with *Every Man in his Humour*
and Chapman's *Humourous Day's Mirth*, both of which were
written about the same period. It is all the more interesting,
therefore, to compare just *this* play with the comedies of the
neo-classic school, since the comparison is likely to bring
out Shakespeare's essential differences from them, which I
have already discussed in general terms.

At first sight the similarity is somewhat striking: Like
*Every Man in his Humour*, *The Merry Wives* is, as we have
seen, a comedy of humours, i.e. a collection of whimsical
characters. For example, there is little except mere oddity in
the Host, Pistol, and Nym, and not much more in Evans and
Caius. In fact, I do not know any other of Shakespeare's
plays which contains so many purely stage figures. This may
be due in part to Jonson's influence. It cannot, for example,
be mere coincidence that Falstaff and his cronies are all

labelled 'Irregular Humorists' in the list of characters printed at the end of 2 *Henry IV* in the Folio. The description was clearly intended to recall Jonson's innovation, as was Nym's constantly ejaculated 'And that's the humour of it' in the play we are now dealing with.

But if these things show consciousness of Jonson, it is consciousness of a quizzical nature. For instance, Nym is probably deliberately introduced as a skit either on Jonson himself or on his mannerism. Thus if Shakespeare imitated Jonson he did so as much in mockery, gentle mockery, as in flattery. In any case the similarity between *The Wives* and the plays of Jonson's school is largely a formal one. In outlook and spirit it is totally unlike.

This is true not merely in the attitude of the dramatist towards his characters. Here the difference is well defined by Professor Gayley, who describes Jonson's plays as 'pure comedy of humours by way of ridicule', whereas *The Merry Wives* is a 'comedy of manners or humours, by way of exposition'.[1] Its fantastics are *revealed* to us in all their oddity and their foolishness. And those which do not quite come alive, like the Host and Caius, we take to our hearts because they breathe the same air as Slender and Mistress Quickly. Only Pistol and Nym seem to stand without the charmed circle—and that because I suggest they were meant to be stage-jokes rather than human characters.

Furthermore *The Merry Wives* has a romantic core, which the comedies of Jonson lack. Anne Page and young Fenton keep the love-motive central, and do much to keep the air of the play fresh from beginning to end. Still more do the references to the countryside, already glanced at. It is one of the miracles of the great magician that this play which he made by a fortnight's work, probably upon a drama by some other dramatist, gives us a truer and more

[1] C. M. Gayley, *Representative English Comedies* (1913), ii, 127. Nym at any rate with his tedious patter about 'humour' seems inexplicable if he be not a topical puppet; may perhaps be the 'purge' which Shakespeare was reputed to have administered to Ben Jonson himself.

92

vivid picture of the life and doings of his own Stratford than anything else that has come down to us.

'All is revealed', as Dr. Smart has noted,[1] 'in *The Merry Wives of Windsor*, which might with equal propriety have been called *The Merry Wives of Stratford*. Mr. Ford and Mr. Page are such men as managed their warehouses and cultivated their land on the bank of the Avon, three hundred years ago. Justice Shallow and his cousin Slender come from the country to visit their town acquaintance, and to dine with Page on venison which Shallow has already presented to his host. Page himself has rural taste, likes a day's sport, has his hounds and his hawks, etc.'

All this is very remote from the London which is the scene of so many of Jonson's plays. And the finale in Windsor Park—how entirely un-Jonsonian! It has often been described as mere extravaganza. But it is no more so than the equally effective finale of *A Midsummer Night's Dream*, from which it is clearly in part borrowed. That the fairies here are not 'real fairies' is little to the point. For stage purposes they are 'real', and with their song and dance, their crowns of fire and their coloured ribbons, the choir of boys rounded off the evening of gaiety, at that first command performance, very delightfully. Indeed, it is all gaiety and delight from beginning to end. And the iniquities of Falstaff, once unmasked, confessed, and punished—with nothing more serious than pinching—are so far forgiven that he is invited by honest Master Page to 'a posset at my house, where I will desire thee to laugh at my wife, that now laughs at thee'.[2]

It is a posset-comedy, warm, domestic, exhilarating, a very cordial of merriment and good fellowship.

[1] Smart, *Shakespeare: truth and tradition*, 1928, p. 56.
[2] V, v, 165-7.

# CHAPTER V

# *The Merchant of Venice in 1937*

---

In sooth I know not why I am so sad.

The very first line of the play is ominous—a line uttered by Antonio, a figure of great dignity, much graciousness, and an air quite different from that usually breathed in the world of comedy. So alien is he to that world that when he has to move therein, as he does in the last Act, and not till then, we feel he is quite out of his element. And Shakespeare clearly feels so too, for he keeps him in the background as much as possible and gives him little to say. And in the opening scene he is deliberately contrasted with shallow-pates like Salerio, Solanio, and Gratiano, so that we may have no excuse for doubting his seriousness right from the outset. 'Gratiano', we are told, 'speaks an infinite deal of nothing, more than any man in all Venice. His reasons are as two grains of wheat hid in two bushels of chaff; you shall seek all day ere you find them, and when you have them they are not worth the search'. Thus Shakespeare dismisses the laughing wit-mongers who had formed the staple of his comedy in *Love's Labour's Lost*.

In *The Merchant* he is going to try a new dramatic experiment—to discover how near he can come to the true note and authentic thrill of tragedy without allowing the tragic wave to break and swamp the comic finale.[1] In 1580 or thereabouts, as I pointed out above, Sir Philip Sidney was

---

[1] Cf. Chambers, *Shakespeare: a Survey*, p. 111.

condemning 'mungrel tragy-comedies'. Some fifteen years later Shakespeare set himself to produce the finest specimen of the kind in our language, perhaps in any language. For *The Merchant of Venice* is a great play, let us make no mistake about that. Alas, that it has been staled and hackneyed for so many readers by the treadmill methods of the class-room where the dull brain of the pedagogue perplexes and retards.

It must have been written at much the same time as *Romeo and Juliet*: and it is interesting to compare the two. The first half of *Romeo* with its three great comic characters, so varied in their appeal—Juliet's Nurse, old Capulet, and Mercutio—might be pure comedy; and it is only after the death of Mercutio and Tybalt that the tide turns and heads straight for the gulfs. In *The Merchant* the current takes exactly the opposite course. As just pointed out, the opening scene, dominated by the grave figure of Antonio, might easily be the first scene of a tragedy. And though gay dialogue between Portia and Nerissa follows, we come upon nothing unmistakably comic until the entry of the Gobbos in the middle of Act II; and that note is soon drowned by the onrush of the swiftly-moving events that follow, events connected with Antonio and Shylock which seem to make tragedy well-nigh inevitable. Indeed it is only with the exit of the Jew at the end of the trial that the tension relaxes, we feel safe once more, and know for certain that the story is to be crowned with happiness.

I emphasize the significance of encountering this tragic quality at the gate of the play so to speak, because it seems to have been overlooked by those modern critics who, as we shall presently see, would have Shylock to be a comic character and the supposed tragic elements of the drama to be the invention of Charles Kean and Henry Irving. Whatever you may think about Shylock, Antonio cannot be a comic character; and the existence of Antonio, his appearance at the outset, his function as the Jew's dramatic foil— the Jew's opposite number, to use a convenient piece of modern slang—seem to make it certain that Shylock was at least as seriously conceived as Antonio.

We shall return to the problem of Shylock presently. But first let us glance at the plot of the play and consider in particular the casket-plot, in which he has no part and of which Portia is the central figure. For there are, as we all learned at school, two main plots: the casket-plot and the bond-plot. It is known that two stories 'representing the greediness of worldly choosers and the bloody minds of usurers' had already been combined in one play long before Shakespeare handled them[1]. But as this old play is lost, we cannot tell how much Shakespeare invented himself and how much he simply took over from his unknown predecessor. Anyhow, whoever was responsible for it, the master-stroke was the combination of the two plots by means of the device of disguise; and there is no happier or more striking example of the serviceability of this Elizabethan dramatic convention than the impersonation by the Lady of Belmont of the lawyer called in to give judgment between the merchant and the usurer. That impersonation is the pivot of Shakespeare's play; the only occasion on which his two principal characters, Portia and Shylock, confront each other. Moreover, as everyone knows, in addition to these main plots there is a comic under-plot, that of an exchange of rings which follows on the trial-scene and is the occasion of much laughter at the end of the play.

From the point of view of plot technique, the *Merchant of Venice* is a masterly production. It is a play, too, of wonderful poetry, most wonderful perhaps in the finale, though reaching greater heights of intensity in the mouth of Shylock. And it contains three magnificent scenes: the casket-scene, the trial-scene, and the last and loveliest of all, at Belmont. Let us consider them in turn.

---

[1] The description is given in Gosson's *School of Abuse*, 1579, and the play was evidently derived from *Il Pecorone* by Ser Giovanni, published in 1558 but not translated into English until 1897. See Q's Introduction to *The Merchant of Venice* (New Shakespeare) for particulars.

# The Merchant of Venice in 1937

## The Casket-Scene

To speak of 'the casket-scene' is to betray a modern standpoint and to wrong Shakespeare; for no less than five scenes are concerned with the caskets and four are almost entirely devoted to them. Spectators are inclined to find the whole business just a little silly, and modern producers cut freely into this part of the play, huddling what remains into a couple of brief episodes introducing the Prince of Morocco and the Prince of Arragon, without which the scene when Bassanio makes his choice becomes hardly intelligible. But the casket theme was of a kind well calculated to suit the Elizabethan palate, and I do not doubt that all five scenes were popular in Shakespeare's day. Our records tell us that the first time the *Merchant of Venice* was played before King James I and VI was on Sunday, 10th February 1605; and it seems to have given much pleasure, since the same records inform us that it was performed again two days later, Shrove Tuesday, 'commanded by the King's Majesty'.[1] Probably it was the trial scene which most took the British Solomon's fancy. But the story of the great lady, mistress of much wealth, whom the world sought in marriage; of the strange will devised by her father so as to test the character of successive suitors; the speeches of these suitors, speeches sententious after the true Renaissance fashion; and finally the eloquent discourse of Bassanio himself on the favourite topic of the day, the problem of Judgement by Appearances, and the difference between Seeming and Reality,[2] a topic of which the whole casket-plot is itself an exposition —all this would be very much to men's taste at that period. After all, what is Jonson's *Volpone* with its elaborate machinery of the *captatio* but a satirical treatment of that 'greediness of worldly choosers' which is also Shakespeare's subject?

We can be sure, too, that the mottoes that stood upon the

---

[1] Chambers, *William Shakespeare* (1930), ii, 332.
[2] Moulton, *Shakespeare as a dramatic artist* (1901), p. 52.

three caskets, mottoes which seem to pass almost unnoticed by modern readers and commentators, meant much to the proverb-loving Elizabethans. Morocco thus declares them:

> The first, of gold, who this inscription bears,
> 'Who chooseth me shall gain what many men desire' . . .
> The second, silver, which this promise carries,
> 'Who chooseth me shall get as much as he deserves' . . .
> This third, dull lead, with warning all as blunt,
> 'Who chooseth me must give and hazard all he hath'—

The meaning of the first motto is patent enough, since it has direct reference to the metal of which the casket is composed, namely what Romeo calls 'saint-seducing gold' and later speaks of to the apothecary from whom he purchases his poison,

> There is thy gold, worse poison to men's souls
> Doing more murders in this loathsome world
> Than these poor compounds that thou mayst not sell.
> I sell thee poison; thou hast sold me none.

As to the second, 'Who chooseth me shall get as much as he deserves', we may go to *Hamlet* for comment. Says the Prince to Polonius: 'Good my lord, will you see the players well bestowed; do you hear, let them be well used,' etc. To which Polonius replies, 'My lord, I will use them according to their desert', and Hamlet rejoins, 'God's bodkin, man, much better! use every man after his desert, and who shall 'scape whipping?'

The third motto brings us to the last of the casket-scenes, in which Bassanio makes his choice. It is a scene still fresh and full of delight for us, both on account of all that happens within it and because of the noble verse in which it is written. Yet I think we miss much that Shakespeare intended us to see there.

What, for example, is the *dramatic* setting for Bassanio's choice? His success, to be effective, must seem at once (a) natural, i.e. not just the result of chance, and (b) morally satisfying to the audience. Notice, then, the following points: (1) Shakespeare lets us hear the other two suitors

argue the matter out, and their arguments reveal some flaw
of character or imperfect sense of values which shows them
to be undesirable mates for the Lady of Belmont. (2) But
when he comes to Bassanio, the scene is arranged differently.
We are allowed to hear only the conclusion of his reasoning.
The great speech which begins

> So may the outward shows be least themselves—

tells us that the speaker has already made his choice before
he opens his mouth. (3) In place of the reasoning itself we
are given a song, sung at Portia's command, 'the whilst
Bassanio comments on the caskets to himself'—as the
Quarto, that is Shakespeare's, stage-direction has it. And
have you, my reader, ever examined this song closely? If so,
you may have noticed some interesting things about it.
Here it is:

> Tell me where is Fancy bred,
> Or in the heart, or in the head?
> How begot, how nourishéd?
> ALL. Reply, reply.
>
> It is engend'red in the eyes,
> With gazing fed, and Fancy dies
> In the cradle where it lies.
> Let us all ring Fancy's knell . . .
> I'll begin it—Ding, dong, bell.
> ALL. Ding, dong, bell.

Mark the rhymes first of all: *bred*, *head*, *nourishéd*—and then
medially, *engend'red* and *fed*. Can one think of any apter
rhyme than *lead*? And if the rhymes of the first half of the
song almost cry out the word *lead*, what about the second
half with its talk of Fancy dying 'in the cradle where it lies'
and of the tolling of the funeral bell? Would not that, to an
Elizabethan, suggest lead also, seeing that in those days
corpses were commonly wrapped in lead before interment?
Mind you, I am not proposing, as some have done, that in
her desire for Bassanio's success Portia is playing a trick upon
her dead father and had the song sung in order that her lover

might learn the secret before he makes his choice. 'I could teach you', she had said to him,

> How to choose right, but then I am forsworn,
> So will I never be—

and Portia was a woman of her word. To imagine that she *was* forsworn would so detract from her moral stature as seriously to impair the beauty of the play. What then? The song, I take it, though sung at Portia's command (because she is the lady of the house, and all the music therein) is intended to represent, in distillation, so to speak, the thoughts that are passing through Bassanio's mind as he 'comments on the caskets to himself'. In other words, it is symbolical rather than dramatic, a function which Shakespeare's songs very often perform, as a matter of fact, and perform far more delightfully than the symbolical Dumbshows and Presenters' Expositions with which his rival dramatists commonly sprinkled their plays.[1] And if it be granted that the song gives us the clue to Bassanio's thoughts, the meaning of its words at once becomes plain. The theme is Fancy, by which Shakespeare and his contemporaries understood both what we now call sentimentality and, as the word still signifies, a passing inclination or whim. Originally a contraction of *fantasy*, the meaning of 'illusion', 'error', or 'unreality' yet clung to it, especially when the word was used in connection with Love. *A Midsummer Night's Dream*, for instance, is a dramatic essay on the theme of Fancy, with its tricks and deceptions; and so, after another fashion, as we shall see, is *Twelfth Night*. Fancy, then, is not true love; it springs from the head, that is, from calculation, not from the heart. It is engendered in the eyes; it feeds upon mere appearances; it has no roots in reality, but dies almost as soon as it is born.[2] And what applies in the sphere of love is equally relevant to inclination and choice in other respects—for example in the

---

[1] Cf. *What happens in 'Hamlet'*, pp. 149, 155.

[2] Cf. Richmond Noble, *Shakespeare's Use of Song*, p. 46. He however takes it to be Portia's revelation.

choice between the caskets, two of them glittering in gold
and silver, the third plain lead with no attractions for the
eye whatever but bearing the motto

> Who chooseth me must give and hazard all he hath.

Thus Bassanio quite naturally, as if the song had expressed
his own thought, continues that thought in the opening
words of his speech:

> *So* may the outward shows be least themselves—
> The world is still deceived with ornament—

and then, after further elaboration of the same topic, un-
hesitatingly selects the right casket. His choice is guided not
by any trick of Portia's, but by the genuineness of his own
nature and (which is part of the same thing) by his very real
love for Portia, a love ready to give and hazard all, which
comes out in the plainness (which moves us more than
eloquence) of his simple but direct reply to Portia's lovely
speech of self-surrender:

> Madam, you have bereft me of all words,
> Only my blood speaks to you in my veins.

Yes, the final casket-scene merits far more attention than
it has hitherto received. Its workmanship is more delicate
and its implications deeper than most people realize in these
crude modern times in which we live; for I have little doubt
that 'the judicious' among Shakespeare's own audience took
his points readily enough.

But if Bassanio is Portia's true love—the one genuine
suitor among the throng of self-seeking egoists who prate
of their own worth or claims, as they make their choice at
Belmont—which it was surely Shakespeare's business as a
popular dramatist to represent him, how does this reading
of his character agree with what we learn about him elsewhere in the play? Here we come upon a strange miscon-
ception on the part of some critics. Let me quote two of my
own masters. To begin with Herbert Grierson:

> Of all the suitors who come to Belmont, Bassanio best deserves the
> title of a 'worldly chooser'. The others have apparently as much to

# The Merchant of Venice in 1937

give as to receive; but Bassanio, like Lord Byron when he proposed to marry Miss Milbanke, was a suitor in order to be able to pay his debts and generally settle himself, *se régler*.

Here he echoes Quiller-Couch, who writes:

If one thing is more certain than another, it is that a predatory young gentleman like Bassanio would *not* have chosen the leaden casket.

Finally, he quotes from Bassanio's soliloquy the well-known passage:

> The world is still deceived with ornament.
> In law, what plea so tainted and corrupt,
> But, being seasoned with a gracious voice,
> Obscures the show of evil? In religion,
> What damnéd error, but some sober brow
> Will bless it, and approve it with a text?—

and is moved to interrupt:

'Yes, yes—and what about yourself, my little fellow? What has altered *you*, that you of all men start talking as though you addressed a Young Men's Christian Association?[1]

As Mistress Quickly says to Pistol. 'By my truth, these are very bitter words.' Yet they are quoted by Grierson, who finds 'a strange moral confusion' in *The Merchant of Venice*.[2] In truth, the only confusion in this matter of Bassanio is a critical one in the mind of his modern interpreters. For what are the grounds upon which they condemn him—or rather condemn Shakespeare for making him so badly? Q's exposition of them is too long to meet point by point. But the burden of it is just this: That Bassanio is an extravagant youngster, that he hopes to pay off his debts by marrying Portia, that in order to make the necessary show at Belmont he is forced to borrow still more money from his friend Antonio, and finally that in order to persuade Antonio to put his hand once again into his pocket, he represents his suit to the wealthy Lady of Belmont as more or less of a safe investment, wilfully concealing the fact that his success

[1] Grierson, *Cross Currents in English Literature of the XVIIth Century*, pp. 87 ff.
[2] A. Quiller-Couch, *Shakespeare's Workmanship*, pp. 99 ff., and Introduction to *The Merchant* (New Shakespeare), p. xxv.

stood upon the hazard of being lucky enough to choose the right casket.

It is this last point which gives the whole case away. For consider: in order to get his double plot to work at all, Shakespeare has to make Bassanio borrow money from Antonio to pursue his courtship, since that is the reason why Antonio in his turn borrows money from Shylock. And when one man goes to borrow money from another, even his best friend, he likes to be able to offer him *some* hope of repayment. Bassanio therefore speaks of Portia's wealth and of her obvious interest in himself, saying however (as a young man would) less of his own love for her. All this is surely very natural and it would seem even more natural in Elizabethan days, when most matches were what Q calls 'predatory'; i.e. for business reasons. That Bassanio should stress Portia's wealth, then, so far from reflecting on his character, merely shows him to be acting on principles of common caution; and that he should speak of their mutual attraction shows that, unlike most suitors of the age, he intends a love-match. But what about his deception? What excuse has he for concealing the casket-lottery from his friend? One might answer that the deception is not his but Shakespeare's; that the dramatist is careful to tell the audience nothing about the caskets until the second scene of the play. Bassanio's petition to Antonio and the latter's consent provide enough interest for Scene 1. To have introduced the casket theme into that conversation would have distracted attention from the main point of the borrowing incident and would have raised an awkward issue—the very issue indeed that Q raises. No spectator would notice its absence; and when it is referred to in Scene ii no spectator would remember that it should have been mentioned by Bassanio in Scene i. As a matter of fact I do not believe that anyone before Q has seen that the story involves a small difficulty here. In short, *dramatically* speaking—and Shakespeare was a dramatist, not a novelist or a historian—the difficulty is not there.

So one could argue and the reply to Q would be valid

enough. But no such reply is needed in fact at all, since if one follows the text it becomes clear that Shakespeare intended us to realize that when Bassanio speaks with Antonio in Scene i, he himself knows nothing whatever of the casket lottery or even of the will of Portia's father, for the simple reason that when he last visited Belmont the father was still alive. This is made clear in Scene ii at the first mention of Bassanio. From Portia's complaint that owing to her father's strange will she is allowed no freedom of choice in marriage, from the description of all the suitors who have so far come to Belmont and from the news Nerissa gives that hearing of the caskets they were all packing up to return home unless they can win her 'by some other sort', we gather that Portia's father is only recently deceased, and the contents of his will become known. Thus when Nerissa goes on to ask, 'Do you not remember, Lady, *in your father's time*, a Venetian, a scholar and a soldier, that came hither in company of the Marquis of Montferrat?' Shakespeare leaves no doubt in the mind of those who attend to what he writes that Bassanio had not yet come as a suitor and could have known nothing of the will. *Cadit quaestio!*

And what is true of this matter holds good also for the whole question of Bassanio's character. Whatever he may seem to modern eyes poring over a book, on the *stage* he is always as he was meant to be, an honest young lover. Shakespeare does not develop him very much; he is in the main a lay figure, whose dramatic function is to choose the right casket and to bring out the more important characters with whom he has to do, namely Antonio and Portia. But the references to him by others leave no doubt of his attractiveness. He is announced at his first entry as 'most noble'; and though sly Nerissa in the second Scene knows of course that praise of him will sound welcome in Portia's ears, when she declares that he 'of all men that ever my foolish eyes looked upon, was the best deserving a fair lady', the audience is assuredly expected to accept her words as the truth.

## The Trial-Scene

But 'this flaw in characterization' which Q discovers in Bassanio goes, he says,

'right down through the workmanship of the play, for the evil opposed against these curious Christians is specific: it is Cruelty; and, yet again specifically, the peculiar cruelty of a Jew. To this cruelty an artist at the top of his art would surely have opposed mansuetude, clemency, charity, and specifically Christian charity. Shakespeare misses more than half the point when he makes the intended victims as a class and by habit just as heartless as Shylock without any of Shylock's passionate excuse.'[1]

This passage Sir Herbert Grierson again quotes and endorses, generalizing it in one of his own which begins:

What puzzles one in Shakespeare's plays is that not infrequently while presenting the story and characters so faithfully and vividly that it is difficult for the reader to avoid passing moral judgement on it, Shakespeare himself seems willing not only to omit comment, but to acquiesce in a view that is to us repellent, to accept standards of which his own vivid telling of the story affords the most effective condemnation.[2]

With these statements of the strange case of Shylock and his creator we may turn now to the trial-scene and to the most baffling character-problem, after that of Hamlet, in Shakespeare.

First of all, then, there is no doubt that modern audiences and readers—I stress the word modern—tend to be left at the end of the play with a feeling of frustration or discomfort. The classical expression of this, as will be remembered, is the story told by Heine, himself a Jew, which runs:

When I saw this Play at Drury Lane, there stood behind me a pale, fair Briton, who at the end of the Fourth Act, fell to weeping passionately, several times exclaiming, 'The poor man is wronged!'[3]

She was referring, of course, to the judgment of the court.

---

[1] Introduction to *The Merchant of Venice* (New Shakespeare), p. xxvi.
[2] Grierson, op. cit., pp. 86–7.
[3] Heine, *Sämmtliche Werke*, Philadelphia, 1856, vol. v, p. 324. I quote the translation given in Furness's Variorum edition of the play, p. 449.

But the wrong, be it noted, comes in reality not from Portia or the Duke; for despite Q's words, Shylock, a would-be murderer, is let off remarkably lightly. And though the compulsory conversion is repugnant to our notions, it would have appeared an enforced benefit to the Elizabethan and medieval mind. Some however have argued that Portia's invalidation of the bond on the grounds that while speaking of a pound of flesh it mentions no blood, is a mere quibble; that she does in fact what Bassanio implores her to do, namely

> Wrest once the law to your authority—
> To do a great right, do a little wrong.[1]

Yet her conduct of the case, though it may appear strange in the eyes of modern law, is quite in the manner of Elizabethan trials, and in all likelihood excited no comment whatever from an audience which consisted partly at least of law students. For example, the quasi-legal quibbling of the grave-digger in *Hamlet* on the subject of suicide by drowning—'If the man go to this water and drown himself, it is, will he nill he, he goes, mark you that. But if the water come to him, and drown him, he drowns not himself'—and the rest of it, is an almost exact reproduction of real arguments used at a well-known case of 1554 and probably repeated regularly by counsel on similar occasions later.[2] Portia's law seems reason itself by comparison. No, the wrong to Shylock that we are conscious of is done by Shakespeare and not the court that tries him. The dramatist seems to have excited our interest in and our sympathy for this Jew to such a degree that we find the levity after his exit intolerable and the happiness of the last Act heartless.

It is the fashion among some critics today to say that this feeling is based upon a misunderstanding; that Shakespeare

---

[1] See *The University of Edinburgh Journal*, Summer number, 1939, for another defence of Portia by the Rt. Hon. Lord Normand of Aberdour, who acted as my chairman when the lecture on *The Merchant* was delivered at Edinburgh in 1938.

[2] See note on *Hamlet*, V, i, 10–20 (New Shak.) for the case of Hales v. Petit.

really intended Shylock as a ridiculous villain; that he was so played up to the end of the eighteenth century; and that first Kean and then Irving sentimentalized him; in a word, that our interest and sympathy spring from a humanitarianism which is quite modern and of which Shakespeare himself was totally unconscious.

It is possible, I admit, to sentimentalize Shylock; and I think it has been done. Certainly, if Macready and Irving raised him, in the words of Edmund Booth, 'out of the darkness of his native element of revengeful selfishness into the light of the venerable Hebrew, the martyr, the avenger',[1] they did something which Shakespeare never intended. But a 'comic Jew'? 'a comical villain'? Is not that label equally misguiding? No doubt he was got up to look grotesque; a typical old Jew would be grotesque to an Elizabethan audience, while Shakespeare makes Gratiano the mouthpiece of the ordinary citizen's attitude.

There are, however, good reasons, I think, why we ought to regard Shylock as a tragic and not a comical figure:

(i) If he is merely comical, the play assuredly loses a great deal dramatically, and it is a sound principle to view with suspicion any critical interpretation which involves dramatic loss—Shakespeare may generally be relied upon to make the greatest possible capital out of his material.

(ii) *The Merchant of Venice* is not the only play of the period containing a detailed study of Jewish character. Marlowe's *Jew of Malta* preceded it, had been (and still was) an exceedingly popular play on the London stage, and belonged to the Admiral's Men, the rival company to Shakespeare's. Shakespeare's Jew would, therefore, inevitably be compared with Marlowe's, and Shakespeare would have striven to the utmost to excel his predecessor. What kind of character, then, was the Barabas of Marlowe? He was, like all Marlowe's heroes, 'conceived of on a gigantic scale . . . a very terrible and powerful alien, endowed with all the

[1] Quoted in E. E. Stoll, *Shakespeare Studies*, p. 256.

resources of wealth and unencumbered by any Christian scruples'.[1] Is it likely that Shakespeare would have set up a ludicrous Shylock to outbid this Barabas? Surely he would have desired, especially with Burbadge at his elbow also desiring to outdo Edward Alleyn, to create a figure equally terrible, but human and convincing at the same time, which Marlowe's Jew never succeeds in being?

(iii) And my third reason is that a ridiculous villain is un-Shakespearian. Can you find such a villain in any other of his plays? Is Iago, or Macbeth, or Edmund, or even Richard III in this sense comical? But these, it may be said, come from the tragedies, and therefore do not count. Very well, where in the comedies is he to be seen? There are plenty of such villains in Ben Jonson. The Jonsonian comedies are full of them; they are his chief stock-in-trade. Indeed, that is one of the main differences between his conception of comedy and Shakespeare's. Villainy is never comic with Shakespeare; and Shylock is not to be fitted into the formulae of Bergson or George Meredith. He does not belong to what is called 'pure comedy' at all.

Yet, if he is not comical, he is not a mere villain of melodrama like Barabas either. He is a 'tragic' villain, i.e. he is so represented that we feel him to be a man, a terrible and gigantic man enough, but with 'hands, organs, dimensions, senses, affections, passions—fed with the same food, hurt by the same weapons, subject to the same diseases, healed by the same means, warmed and cooled by the same winter and summer, as a Christian is'. Shylock is a far greater character than Barabas, not because he is less blood-thirsty —his lust for blood is more awful because more convincing —but because he is one of ourselves. And, as he goes out, what we ought to exclaim is not (with Heine's fair Briton), 'The man is wronged', but 'There, but for the grace of God, go I', as I suggested should be our comment upon a very different character in *The Merry Wives*.

It is, of course, just this common humanity, which Shake-

[1] H. S. Bennett, *Introduction*, p. 9, *Jew of Malta*.

speare brings out and insists upon in stroke after stroke, that the Christians of Venice deny (like the Nazis of modern Germany). And if Shylock is a villain, an awful and appalling human being, who made him such? People like Antonio. Antonio, we are told by one of his friends, is the perfect Christian gentleman,

> The kindest man,
> The best-conditioned and unwearied spirit
> In doing courtesies;[1]

yet, when the Jew reminds him

> You call me misbeliever, cut-throat dog,
> And spit upon my Jewish gaberdine . . .
> You that did void your rheum upon my beard,
> And foot me as you spurn a stranger cur,

he raps out:

> I am as like to call thee so again,
> To spit on thee again, to spurn thee too.

But Shakespeare, we are told, shared the prejudices of his age against Jews; he would himself have applauded Antonio's action, might even have imitated it. Shylock excites our modern sympathies because Shakespeare allowed his imagination to run away with him. The humanity of the Jew was an unconscious by-product of his dramatic genius.[2]

For myself, I think we have heard more than enough of the vegetable Shakespeare, of the impersonal, almost witless, imaginative growth, exfoliating plays and poems without premeditation or reflection, as a gourd-vine produces pumpkins. No doubt, as with all the great novelists and poets, once the theme seized upon him, it was liable to take him in charge, so that he could never tell at the beginning exactly how a play might work out. Yet, as he fell under the spell, he must have retained consciousness of his direction, and when all was done, he surely, if he had a mind at all, saw his achievement as a whole and assessed it at its proper

---

[1] III, ii, 293.
[2] Cf. Bradley, *Shakespearean Tragedy*, p. 21, and Charlton, Ch. VI ('Shakespeare's Jew').

worth. Shylock may have taken him to some extent by surprise, but Shylock was the child of *his* imagination and *his* intellect, and it seems to me absurd to suppose that the sympathies of such a father can have been wholly on the side of the spitting Antonio.

Nothing is more difficult than to pin a dramatist (and Shakespeare above all dramatists) down to definite opinions and a definite point of view. And though it is hard to associate the author of *The Tempest*, most humanly compassionate of all dramatic poems, with the standpoint of Herr Julius Streicher, many years lie between that play and *The Merchant*, and Shakespeare may conceivably, like Prospero, have been converted in the interval.

In this instance, however, we are able to put the matter to the test, by comparison with another early play on a similar theme. There lies in the British Museum, as all the world is now aware, a MS. play-book on *Sir Thomas More*, one scene in which is acknowledged by most competent authorities to be of Shakespeare's composition and actually in his own hand. It is a crowd scene, representing a riot of the 'prentices of London, who on May Day, 1517, rose against the aliens resident in the city, sacked their houses, stole their goods, and generally behaved very much as the Nazis behaved in the streets of the cities in Germany. With this difference, however, that what was done in Germany under the authority, or with at least the full approval, of the government, was in Tudor England a rising against the powers that be, who suppressed it with due severity.

In the scene I speak of, this point is forcibly brought out in a long speech to the crowd by the Sheriff of London, who was according to the play at that date Sir Thomas More himself. More insists that the 'prentices are rebels, rebels against the King, and since the King is God's deputy on earth, rebels against God Himself. But the portion of the speech relevant to our present purpose is that which pleads with the rioters to put themselves in the place of the foreigners they have attacked. More bids them

# The Merchant of Venice in 1937

> Imagine that you see the wretched strangers,
> Their babies at their backs, and their poor luggage,
> Plodding to th'ports and coasts for transportation.

It might have been written yesterday, might it not?

> Imagine all this,

he continues—and here we have prophecy—

> What had you got? I'll tell you: you had taught
> How insolence and strong hand should prevail,
> How order should be quelled; and by this pattern
> Not one of you should live an aged man;
> For other ruffians, as their fancies wrought,
> With self-same hand, self reasons, and self right,
> Would shark on *you*, and men like ravening fishes
> Would feed on one another.

For you are rebels, rebels against the King, who will surely punish you. But suppose the king is merciful enough to do no worse than banish you, what then?

> What country by the nature of your error
> Should give you harbour? . . .
>                                   Would *you* be pleased
> To find a nation of such barbarous temper
> That breaking out in hideous violence,
> Would not afford you an abode on earth,
> Whet their detested knives against your throats,
> Spurn you like dogs, and like as if that God
> Owed[1] not nor made not you, nor that the elements
> Were not all appropriate to your comforts,
> But chartered unto them? What would *you* think
> To be thus used? This is the strangers' case
> And this your Momtanish[2] inhumanity.[3]

Not merely are the situations of the Jews in Shakespeare's Venice and the strangers in Sir Thomas More's London closely similar, but we can be pretty safe I think in identifying the views expressed by More with those of the dramatist who writes his speech.

[1] I.e., 'owned'.
[2] I.e., 'unchristian', literally 'Mohammedan'. But the word may be 'mountainish'.
[3] ll. 74–140.

Observe too the parallels in phrase and thought. In 'spurn you like dogs' we have the very words of *The Merchant*, while Shylock's great outburst on the subject of Jewish humanity, with its particular assertion that the Jew is 'warmed and cooled by the same winter and summer as a Christian is', finds a clear echo in More's declaration that the 'elements' were 'appropriate to the comforts' of all mankind, not 'chartered' by Englishmen, to the exclusion of the foreigners they disliked.

But what More makes explicit, is not explicit in *The Merchant*. The Jew is allowed no defendant in the court to plead for him as a fellow human being and a defenceless alien. There is no one to speak for him except himself. In the light of the parallels from the *Book of Sir Thomas More* I have no doubt at all that Shylock was intended by Shakespeare to be a comment upon the treatment of Jewry throughout the Christian dispensation.

Why does he not say so? Why did he not even, as Q says he should, oppose to the cruelty of Shylock, clemency, charity, and specifically Christian charity? Imagine the author of *The Tempest* and of More's great speech to the pogrom-rioters, living in Nuremberg a few years ago and ordered by the Nazi party to compose a play upon the subject of some Jew who had conspired against the life of Herr Hitler. Could he speak out? Would he not depict the ferocious assassin in all his dire ferocity, and yet contrive to *imply*, for those who had ears to hear, that there was another side to the question?

This is no rhetorical flourish. The actual position of Shakespeare when he wrote *The Merchant* was not unlike that I depict in imagination. Shortly before the play was first staged, the London crowds, from whom he drew his audience, had watched in their thousands, and with howls of gleeful execration, a venerable old Hebrew, Dr. Lopez, falsely accused of attempting to poison the Queen, done to death with the hideous ritual of hanging and disembowelling before their blood-lustful eyes. There is even I believe an allusion to the event in the play itself. You remember that strange image which Shakespeare places in the railing mouth of Gratiano:

> thy currish spirit
> Governed a wolf, who hanged for human slaughter,
> Even from the gallows did his fell soul fleet,
> And whilst thou layest in thy unhallowed dam,
> Infused itself in thee.

What does it mean? A wolf hanged for human slaughter, who ever heard of such a thing? This wolf was no quadruped, it was a Jewish animal, in other words it was Lopez himself, who is commonly called Lopus or Lupus in the literature of the time.

And there was still more involved. Not only would the groundlings in the audience at the play be inflamed with anti-Semitism at the time, the great ones who might be found among the judicious spectators were in a like mood. Lopez had unhappily incurred the hatred of the all-powerful Earl of Essex, who was the main instrument in bringing him to the gallows; and the earl's bosom friend was another young lord, the Earl of Southampton, Shakespeare's own patron and in all likelihood his intimate.

Such were the perilous circumstances in which the compassionate Shakespeare was compelled to write his Jew play. I say compelled, for the rival company to his own had revived Marlowe's *Jew of Malta* for the occasion, and were drawing large houses, while his friends at court would doubtless look to him for a Jew-baiting spectacle in the theatre. Well, he gave them what they asked, he gave them an appalling Shylock and the coarse-grained storm-trooper Gratiano to express their sentiments about him; he even represents the best man in the story spurning him like a dog and bespitting him—would not his friends the earls have done the same?

But he did more, by making Shylock a suffering human being, he revealed 'the momtanish inhumanity' of the behaviour of Christians towards the Hebrew race, and in the speech on Mercy, at the very centre and climax of the play, he revealed his own standpoint. Portia's speech, one of the greatest sermons in all literature, an expression of religious thought worthy to set beside St. Paul's hymn in praise of Love, is of course addressed to the Jew. But I find it incredible that Shakespeare intended it for Jews alone. The very fact that it is based throughout upon the Lord's Prayer, which would mean nothing to a Hebrew, suggests that it was composed to knock at Christian hearts.

When Q accuses Shakespeare of not setting up the ideal of 'clemency, charity and specifically Christian charity', to oppose that of Cruelty and Revenge, he strangely forgets 'the quality of Mercy'. And Shylock, as I have said, is let off very lightly. He loses the money he had made by usury—that was only right and proper. He is compelled to become a Christian—that was only an enforced benefit. But he was not hanged, drawn and quartered as Dr. Lopez was—much to Gratiano's disgust.

Shylock is a terrible old man. But he is the inevitable product of centuries of racial persecution. Shakespeare does not draw this moral. He merely exposes the situation. He is neither for nor against Shylock. Shakespeare never takes sides. Yet surely if he were alive today he would see in Mercy, mercy in the widest sense, which embraces understanding and forgiveness, the only possible solution of our racial hatreds and enmities.

### Belmont

But the exit of Shylock is not the end of the play. The cloud which had been gathering since the opening scene and looked so black for Antonio, instead of breaking, passes over, leaving him unharmed and even the villain himself with only a light punishment. And so the tension is relaxed for the audience. The trial is followed by an amusing interview between the disguised women and their lovers, together with the surrender of the rings, which promises further fun to come.

Is the incident, as I asked earlier, too trivial, too light to counterbalance the stress of emotion from which we have just emerged? Only if our sympathies have been with Shylock the man, rather than Jewry; and as I said, we misapprehend Shakespeare the dramatist if they are. Certainly, Shakespeare knew that the audience for which he wrote would have no sympathy with Shylock; and it is just because he knew that, that he could afford to exhibit his humanity.

Yet the crisis of the trial scene was unusually serious for a comedy. That he knew also; and realized that all his efforts would be needed to send his spectators home in the mood he wished to leave with them. And so, we have the scene at Belmont—the gayest, happiest, most blessed scene in all Shakespeare. Suddenly we are caught away from Venice, from its scorns, its hatreds and revenges, and transported to a world of magic in which men and women live like gods, without care, without toil, without folly, and without strife—except such folly and strife as lovers use one with another. Belmont is not heaven, because there is much talk of marrying and giving in marriage; and withal a roguish touch of Boccaccio now and again. Rather it is Elysium, a Renaissance Elysium, a garden full of music under the soft Italian night, with a gracious and stately mansion in the background.

Shakespeare paints the scene with all his wonderful artistry. Observe, for instance, the part the moon plays in it, how she rides in and out of the shifting clouds as the action goes forward—at one moment it is bright as day, at the next

> The moon sleeps with Endymion

so that Lorenzo cannot see Portia's face.

Music and the moon are the twin themes of this final movement:

> Sweet soul, let's in, and there expect their coming.
> And yet no matter: why should we go in?
> My friend Stephano, signify, I pray you,

# The Merchant of Venice in 1937

> Within the house, your mistress is at hand,
> And bring your music forth into the air. . . .
> How sweet the moonlight sleeps upon this bank!
> Here will we sit, and let the sounds of music
> Creep in our ears—soft stillness and the night
> Become the touches of sweet harmony. . . .
> Sit, Jessica. Look how the floor of heaven
> Is thick inlaid with patens of bright gold.
> There's not the smallest orb which thou behold'st
> But in his motion like an angel sings,
> Still quiring to the young-eyed cherubins;
> Such harmony is in immortal souls!
> But while this muddy vesture of decay
> Doth grossly close it in, we cannot hear it. . . .
>
> The man that hath no music in himself,
> Nor is not moved with concord of sweet sounds,
> Is fit for treasons, stratagems, and spoils,
> The motions of his spirit are dull as night,
> And his affections dark as Erebus:
> Let no such man be trusted. . . . Mark the music.

After Mercy—Harmony!

Grossly closed in by our muddy vesture of decay, it is difficult—perhaps impossible—for us poor mortals to hear it, and missing it we, Jew or Christian, grow 'fit for treasons, stratagems, and spoils', and our 'affections dark as Erebus', the Erebus which Shylock and Jew-baiter alike inherit; but the music is there all the while.

Some day, one blessed day we shall not live to see, perhaps the world may come to Belmont and be moved not with internecine hatred and racial scorn, but 'with concord of sweet sounds'.

And if there be any reader to ask what connexion there can be between music and politics, between our woeful discords and the 'touches of sweet harmony', I do not need to refer him to the *Republic* of Plato, but to a disciple of Plato who had never read his book. I mean Shakespeare himself, who in *Henry V* (I, ii, 180-3) tells us that

> government, though high and low, and lower,
> Put into parts, doth keep in one consent,

116

> Congreeing in a full and natural close,
> Like music.

Is the world capable of such music? That is *the* political problem of our time and, if we cannot solve it, he prophesies in *Troilus and Cressida*, I, iii, 110–24:

> Hark, what discord follows! . . .
> Force should be right; or rather right and wrong,
> Between whose endless jar justice resides,
> Should lose their names, and so should justice too.
> Thus everything includes itself in power,
> Power into will, will into appetite;
> And appetite, an universal wolf,
> So doubly seconded with will and power,
> Must make perforce an universal prey,
> And last eat up himself!

The prophecy seems nearer fulfilment in 1962 than it did in 1938.

The impending dissolution of the universe, though in other terms than ours, was never far from the mind of Shakespeare and his contemporaries; and Prospero supplies a calmer because more contemplative account of it in his famous epilogue after the masque in *The Tempest*. The Prospero however who gave us the vision he called *The Merchant of Venice* had no wish to trouble us at Belmont with thoughts of doomsday or any apocalyptic imaginings. And even our memories of cruel Venice begin to fade when we hear Lancelot winding his mock postman's horn in and out among the trees to announce to Lorenzo and Jessica and to us, the audience, that the travellers are about to return home. And presently, when we return home, or shut our books, the characters themselves begin to fade and melt into thin air, as we realize that Bassanio the young lover, his bosom friend Antonio, Portia the great lady and learned judge, yes, even the fierce Jew himself, rushing with uplifted knife upon his victim—all are spirits, the creatures of dramatic art.

Yet if we are to go home happy, the characters all but Shylock must first of all be given happiness. How was this to be accomplished for Antonio, who though saved from the knife was still a ruined merchant? It was Portia who saved him; it was given to her to restore his fortune. But mark how she does it.

> Antonio, you are welcome,
> And I have better news in store for you
> Than you expect; unseal this letter soon,
> There you shall find three of your argosies
> Are richly come to harbour suddenly.
> You shall not know by what strange accident
> I chanced on this letter.

That three of Antonio's argosies should be 'richly come to harbour suddenly' would be unbelievable if Shakespeare had allowed us a moment to ponder it, yet not more difficult of credence than the 'strange accident' by which Portia chanced upon the letter that told it. It is all a little piece of Shakespearian legerdemain, of which we shall have another example on page 203. When we edited the play together in 1926 Q and I were delighted to catch Shakespeare out over it, the more so that we fancied we were the first to do so. And I cannot conclude this little essay of my own more happily than by quoting the conclusion of the Introduction by Q, the more so that I have dared to wrestle with him on an earlier page. 'You shall not know', says Portia, and Q replies, 'No, nor anyone else'—and he then goes on to point out that Shakespeare had already made at least one attempt to rid Antonio of his burden before this. But let him speak for himself:

Upon Lorenzo's and Jessica's lovely duet there breaks a footfall. Lorenzo, startled by it, demands:

LORENZO. Who comes so fast in silence of the night?
STEPHANO. A friend.
LORENZO. A friend! what friend? your name, I pray you, friend?
STEPHANO. Stephano is my name, and I bring word
    My mistress will before the break of day
    Be here at Belmont—she doth stray about
    By holy crosses, where she kneels and prays
    For happy wedlock hours.

# The Merchant of Venice in 1937

LORENZO.                    Who comes with her?
STEPHANO. None, but a holy hermit, and her maid.

'Nothing', continues Q, 'loose in literature—in play or in poem—ever caught Dr. Johnson napping. "I do not perceive", says Johnson, in his unfaltering accent, "the use of this hermit, of whom nothing is seen or heard afterwards. The Poet had first planned his fable some other way; and inadvertently, when he changed his scheme, retained something of the original design".'

And while all this has been passing, the moon has sunk and every thicket around Belmont has begun to thrill and sing of dawn. Portia lifts a hand:

> It is almost morning,
> Let us go in.

And so the comedy comes home. 'Pack, clouds away! and welcome, day!'

# CHAPTER VI

✴

# *Much Ado about Nothing*

---

W e reach the crown of Shakespeare's achievement in comedy with the three great plays which belong to the turn of the century.

They were written at what must have been a time of great pressure for Shakespeare—perhaps the busiest period of his life. He had just secured a resounding success with Falstaff and the two *Henry IV* plays, a success which had made his name a household word in London in 1598, and his company would be urging him to strike while the iron was hot. *Henry V*, the sequel of these plays, was under way, and was ready in 1599, but it was only the completion of a task. For what Shakespeare's mind was clearly beginning to turn towards was tragedy. *Julius Caesar*, also in 1599, followed hard at the heels of *Henry V*, while beckoning him round the corner, so to speak, and perhaps already finished in first draft, were *Troilus and Cressida* and that herculean dramatic labour, *Hamlet*; and somewhere among these (the exact date is uncertain), Shakespeare had to find a spare fortnight for preparing the copy for the command performance of *The Merry Wives*.

Taking these four years, 1598–1601, together, we have the two parts of *Henry IV*, *Henry V*, *The Merry Wives*, *Julius Caesar*, *Troilus and Cressida*, and *Hamlet*—all completed and put on to the stage. Six plays, including Falstaff at one end and Hamlet at the other!—and all, not only written, but to be rehearsed, produced and acted; for Shakespeare was producer and actor too. And yet we have to add still another three, the three greatest Shakespearian comedies: *Much Ado about Nothing, As You Like It* and *Twelfth Night*, the first generally dated 1598, and the other two 1599–1600.

Such productivity seems incredible; it is, I think, un-paralleled. But I draw attention to it, not to invoke admiration for the miracle, but to remind the reader that he who wrought it was a man. We must not be surprised to discover signs of haste in the plays we are now to examine. We shall be able to credit the miracle more easily if we suppose that not all these nine plays were created out of the author's inner consciousness, but that some, perhaps most, were based upon plays already existing in the possession of Shakespeare's company, his own earlier plays or those of others. We know this was the case with *Henry V* and *Hamlet*; we may suspect it for *The Merry Wives*; we must at least allow for its possibility in the three comedies.

On this matter, the titles may tell us something; *Much Ado about Nothing, As You Like It, Twelfth Night, or What You Will*—they are, as Sir Edmund Chambers remarks, 'floutingly vague',[1] with a take-it-or-leave-it air about them. They show a dramatist very sure of his public; they exhibit a certain careless indifference, real or assumed, on his part, towards the dishes he sets before them; they may conceal a pricking of the artistic conscience for scamped work. But if these plays are at times careless, and at others perfunctory, they are written by a dramatist at the very height of his powers, both as a poet and as a craftsman of the theatre— and that dramatist Shakespeare!

*Much Ado* follows the two *Henry IV* plays; *The Merchant of Venice* immediately precedes them, and there are affinities between the comedy of Messina and that of Venice. *Much Ado* may be called a tragi-comedy—as in *The Merchant*, the clouds gather in the fourth Act and look like breaking into tragedy, only to pass away in the fifth. But the 'stress of

[1] *William Shakespeare*, i, 272.

emotion' is less intense; and the villain who is the instrument of the threatened disaster and is moved, like Shylock, by revenge, is far less dominant. Shylock is one of the great characters of the world; who ever talks or thinks about Don John the Bastard?

If in general shape, however, *Ado* pairs off with *The Merchant*, it has its likenesses with other plays. The whole Beatrice-Benedick plot with its brilliant flyting is clearly a development of the *Love's Labour's Lost* manner, so clearly that many critics have supposed that *Ado* is simply a revision of *Love's Labour's Won*, the lost twin of *Love's Labour's Lost* which Meres mentions as Shakespeare's in 1598. Certainly Benedick is a more mature Berowne, while the part Beatrice plays has points of similarity with that of Rosaline in the earlier drama.

Shakespeare, I have suggested, had at his disposal and in his mind a heterogeneous collection of dramatic types, devices and species, medieval, classical, Italo-renaissance— like costumes in the tiring-wardrobe of his theatre—and these he could combine and re-combine into an almost infinite variety of patterns. But always, or generally, he imposes upon the pattern or patterns he takes over from others, a pattern of his own, peculiar to the play he is writing. This we shall find he does in *Ado*.

The play has two main plots: (i) the Hero-Claudio plot, belonging to the tragi-comedy type of *The Merchant*; and (ii) the Beatrice-Benedick plot, belonging to the comedy of wit, exemplified in *Love's Labour's Lost*. The dramatic dovetailing is carried out with Shakespeare's usual tact in such matters, but most critics appear to agree that, as we find them declaring in the case of the casket-plot and the bond-plot of *The Merchant*, there is to their thinking some dissonance of tone. Sir Edmund Chambers, for example, premising that Beatrice and Benedick are creatures of 'pure comedy', while the story of Hero, Claudio and Don John is 'melodrama', writes:

Benedick and Beatrice may be structurally subordinate to Claudio and Hero. This does not prevent them from being a very living man and a very living woman, and as such infinitely more interesting than the rather colourless lay figures of the melodrama. . . . The plane of comedy . . . is far nearer to real life than is the plane of melodrama. The triumph of comedy in *Much Ado about Nothing* means therefore that the things which happen between Claudio and Hero have to stand the test of a much closer comparison with the standard of reality than they were designed to bear. . . . Before Beatrice's fiery-souled espousal of her cousin's cause, the conventions of melodrama crumble and Claudio stands revealed as the worm that he is, and that it should have been the dramatist's main business to prevent the audience from discovering him to be. The whole of the serious matter of the last Act fails to convince. Don Pedro and Claudio could not, outside the plane of melodrama, have been guilty of the insult of staying on in Leonato's house and entering into recriminations with him. Claudio could not have complacently accepted the proposal to substitute a cousin for the bride he had wronged. Hero could not have been willing to be resumed by the man who had thrown her off on the unconfirmed suggestion of a fault. Such proceedings belong to the chiaroscuro of melodrama; in the honest daylight which Benedick and Beatrice bring with them, they are garish.[1]

Here indeed is much ado! And, since Sir Edmund is only the spokesman of many, scarcely about nothing.

It would take too long in this chapter to answer all his points, though I think a reply might be found for every one. I must deal with them in general terms only, thus:

(i) I do not think that the 'garishness' which Sir Edmund sees in reading the play in his study is visible on the stage. On the contrary, *Much Ado*, when I first saw it acted, took me almost as much by surprise as Guthrie's *Love's Labour's Lost* had done. And, having seen it now several times and played by companies of very different calibre—amateur, first-rate companies, and second-rate ones—I have come to the conclusion (a) that *Much Ado* is a capital stage-play, indeed a better one than either *As You Like It* or *Twelfth Night*; and (b) that the Hero-Claudio plot, on the whole, is quite as effective as the Beatrice-Benedick one, which is to

[1] Chambers, *Shakespeare: a Survey*, pp. 134–5.

# Much Ado about Nothing

some extent cumbered with dead wood in the sets-of-wit between the two mockers.

But these are only personal impressions, and carry no weight. Speaking, then, by the book, the criticisms of the Hero–Claudio story appear to be based partly upon mis-apprehension, partly upon forgetfulness of different social customs which reigned in Shakespeare's day, and partly upon failure to observe the pattern of the play.

Let me take up these matters in order. Surely, Shakespeare never intended Claudio to be a hero, any more than he does Bertram in *All's Well*, who is in many ways Claudio over again, or that other Claudio in *Measure for Measure*, who is also cast in the same mould. All three are young noblemen, with plenty of physical courage (at least two of them have), an attractive presence, and very little judgment or experience. Claudio's youth is much insisted upon—'he hath borne himself beyond the promise of his age, doing in the figure of a lamb the feats of a lion'; to Don John he is 'a proper squire' and a 'very forward March-chick'; Leonato speaks of

His May of youth and bloom of lustihood

and his inexperience of the ways of woman is surely proved by the fact that Don Pedro no sooner hears that his mind is on Hero, than he offers to do the courtship for him. He is no 'worm', only a rather foolish boy.

As for his belief in Borachio's story of Hero's infidelity, there are several things about it which are generally over-looked:

(i) Claudio is not only very youthful but of an abnormally jealous disposition. A youthful Leontes, he gratefully accepts the Prince's offer to woo Hero in his name; but the suggestion is no sooner put to him that Don Pedro is really trying to steal the young lady for himself than he believes it and goes off and sulks. 'Alas, poor hurt fowl,' exclaims Benedick, 'now will he creep into sedges.' It is true that Benedick also thinks Don Pedro has been courting Hero on his own

124

account; but he knows nothing of his offer to act as Claudio's proxy. Claudio's suspicions of his Prince are unpardonable —and having doubted the good faith of a friend well known to him, he will hardly continue to believe in that of a girl, whom he scarcely knows at all, and this in the face of what seems to be ocular proof of her treachery.

(ii) Shakespeare deals a little carelessly with the incident of Borachio and Margaret at Hero's window, which was probably more consistent and clearer at some earlier stage of the play's history.[1] But both Claudio and Don Pedro watch a strange man climbing into Hero's bedroom and received lovingly by a woman dressed in Hero's clothes. They could not see her features in the dark, but they had every excuse for assuming her to be that which she pretended.

(iii) If Leonato, Hero's father, is at Claudio's revelation in the church ready at first to believe her guilty, is it surprising that Don Pedro and Claudio have done so? Women were easier of access in those days, and morals generally were looser. Critics have been too ready to assume that the household of Leonato was a Victorian one.

A fairly recent editor of *Ado* has declared:

> There is scarcely a rag of credibility in a story that causes a king and a count to conduct themselves like a pair of ill-bred and over-stimulated brawlers.[2]

Surely this is the very ecstasy of misinterpretation.

Sir Edmund Chambers is at once more subtle and more cautious. But his objection to the proceedings of the last Act seems to me no less misguided. Don Pedro is a king; he has done Governor Leonato, who is not even of noble birth, the signal honour of accepting his hospitality. Is he to move into meaner quarters because the old man's daughter is not as honest as she might be? Would any monarch of the period

[1] See below, pp. 126-7, 138-9 and my 'Note on the Copy' in the New Shakespeare, *Much Ado*, pp. 104 ff.

[2] G. Sampson, p. lxviii of *Much Ado* (Pitt Press Shakespeare).

have done so? So far from regarding the continuance of his stay as an 'insult' he would think of it as a favour. And if he stayed on, Claudio would have to do likewise. Shakespeare does not say all this; he didn't need to, for it would never have occurred to him that his spectators might question it.

Similarly, Claudio had done Leonato honour by asking the hand of his daughter; he, a count, was a great match for a gentleman's house. The least he can do, then, in restitution, when he discovers that his suspicions are baseless, is to agree to marry the cousin of the supposedly dead girl, in order that Leonato may not lose his match. Marriage in those days was first a matter of business, and only secondarily (if at all) a matter of love. The mood in which Claudio goes to this second marriage is evident in V, iv, 38: 'I'll hold my mind,' he declares, 'were she an Ethiope.' He is sacrificing himself for the old man's sake. The story of Hero and Claudio is no more melodrama than that of Ophelia and Hamlet, to which as a matter of fact it bears some resemblance.

Finally, a word may be said in defence of Don John, not as a man but as a dramatic character. Here again there may be some obscurity owing to revision. But his villainy is surely not of the melodramatic kind of Richard Crookback, who was a villain only because, as he says,

I am determinéd to prove a villain.

Nor does the melancholy of the bastard suffice to account for it. The matter is not, I say, as clear as it might be, but he tells us that Claudio, 'that young start-up, hath all the glory of my overthrow' (I, iii, 62), and when we remember the glory that Claudio had won in the late 'action', of which we hear at the opening of the play, is it not at least plausible to suppose that Don John had been fighting against his brother, Don Pedro, in that action, and being overthrown had perforce become 'reconciled to the prince' (I, i, 148)? To suppose so would, at any rate, go far to explain his actions, and make a man of him, instead of the 'thorough-paced villain of the deliberate Machiavellian type dear to the Elizabethan imagination'[1] as Sir Edmund Chambers labels him.

But though I think the tone and significance of the Hero-plot have been badly misjudged by modern criticism, I am not claiming it as more important than Beatrice and Bene-dick. Their plot is simple, so simple as hardly to be a plot at all, while the story of Hero is an intricate one. But in dramatic perspective there is no doubt which is the more prominent. From the very outset Beatrice and Benedick take the centre of the stage, and though 'structurally sub-ordinate to Claudio and Hero' in the sense that the story of the latter determines their actions and explains their move-ments, they are actually the outstanding figures of the play.

And they are more interesting and more alive than the younger lovers, not because they belong to 'pure comedy' and the others to 'melodrama', but because Shakespeare intended them so to be and gave them far more to say. Apart from the scene where Beatrice lies hid in the pleached arbour, a scene in which Hero of necessity leads the dia-logue, the latter has less than fifty lines to speak in the whole play. She does not even speak a word when she is formally betrothed to Claudio in Act 2—it is Beatrice who covers her natural shyness with 'Speak, cousin, or if you cannot, stop his mouth with a kiss, and let him not speak neither.' (II, i, 290-1.) Similarly, though Claudio has of course more to say than Hero, because the action demands that he should, he does not even play second fiddle to Benedick. For between the two stands Don Pedro, who woos for his young favourite; and so leads him by the hand throughout the play, that we cannot overlook the latter's subordinate position.

All this is, without question, quite deliberate on Shake-speare's part. In *The Merchant* he had two plots, a love-story and a revenge-story, of almost equal weight. They were cleverly linked together, but he only just kept the balance, and so saved the play. In *Much Ado*, the comedy that fol-

[1] Chambers, op. cit., p. 129.

lowed, he ran no such risks. Once again, he had two plots—
this time combining love and revenge into one, and revert-
ing to *Love's Labour's Lost* for the other. But he kept the
former in strict subordination to the latter, and so created
what was, in my opinion, structurally a more shapely
play.

Furthermore, he imposed, as I have said, his own pattern,
a special pattern peculiar to *Much Ado*, upon the texture of
plot and character. *The Merchant of Venice*, for all its excitement and its beauty, does not really hang well together, and,
apart from the grey thread of the melancholy Antonio, no
pattern runs through it.

*Much Ado*, on the other hand, possesses a very definite
pattern of its own, at once pretty and amusing; and though
no modern critic, I believe, has ever noticed it, that does not
prove that generations of spectators have not unconsciously
derived much pleasure from it. Indeed, in my view, it contributes very materially to the life and interest of the play,
though it does so more certainly in the theatre than in the
study.

When one watches *Much Ado* on the stage, does one not
feel somehow as if one were looking on at an elaborate
game of Hide and Seek? Shakespeare himself suggests it at
one point, when he makes Claudio describe Benedick lurk-
ing in the arbour as 'the hid-fox'. Whether the children's
game of 'Hide-fox' in Shakespeare's day was exactly the
same as the modern Hide and Seek, I do not know. In any
case, he is thinking in *Much Ado* of it rather from the point
of view of the hidden person than of those who seek. The
hid-fox lurks unseen and listens to the other children as they
move about and talk—sometimes of him.

In a word, the pattern is partly made by eavesdropping,
of which there are no fewer than half a dozen instances in
the play.

(i) A serving-man in a 'thick-pleached alley' of the orchard overhears the Prince and Claudio talking of the
intended courtship of Hero, and misapprehending what he

# Much Ado about Nothing

has heard, reports to Antonio, the brother of Leonato, that Don Pedro proposes to win her for himself.

(ii) Next Borachio, Don John's spy, from behind the arras in a room overhears the Prince and Claudio still discussing the same project and reports likewise to his master, this time however getting the facts correctly.

These two eavesdroppings we are told of but do not see on the stage—they introduce the theme as it were, to use a musical term. The next two are enacted before our eyes, viz.:

(iii) and (iv) Benedick and Beatrice are in turn lured into the pleached arbour in the orchard in order that they may overhear their friends in talk and so come to imagine that each is in love with the other.

(v) This time not seen on the stage, Claudio and Don Pedro are similarly led to believe Hero unfaithful by eavesdropping outside her bedroom window.

(vi) Lastly, the Watch overhear the scoundrels Conrade and Borachio talking under a penthouse, and after much misunderstanding and delay, this leads to the discovery of the plot against Hero's honour.

Closely connected with this eavesdropping motif, though not identical with it, is a subsidiary design of the familiar disguise variety. Thus Borachio gains access to the room in which he spies upon the Prince and Claudio, disguised as a fumigator. There is a masked dance in Act II, very similar to that in *Love's Labour's Lost*, in the course of which Don Pedro, pretending to be Claudio, woos Hero, and after which Don John, addressing Claudio as if he were Benedick, persuades him that the Prince is acting treacherously. Margaret again disguises herself as Hero for the scene at the bedroom window. And finally Hero herself, masked once more, poses as Leonato's niece in the last scene.

Eavesdropping and misinterpretation, disguise and deceit —sometimes for evil ends, but generally in fun and with a comic upshot—such are the designs in the dramatic pattern of *Much Ado*. It is simple enough, once the matter is explained: it is dependent upon stage-effects rather than upon poetic construction, and Shakespeare was to improve in subtlety upon it later. But this spying and hoodwinking give the play its special atmosphere, an atmosphere which is reproduced for tragic purposes, though by similar devices, in *Hamlet*.

In *Much Ado about Nothing*, however, it is all a game. The children skip in and out of their pleached alleys and arbours, and the hid-fox is fitted with his pennyworth. Shy little Hero gets put into the corner unjustly for a while; jealous young Claudio misdoubts her, insults her, repents and hangs his little verses upon her empty monument; the melancholy Don John does his worst and then flees.

But our main interest lies neither in this background nor in the patterned framework; what we remember when the play is done are three figures which stand out in front of it all, and for the exhibition of whom most of what I have been hitherto speaking of was designed by the dramatist— I mean Beatrice, Benedick and the immortal constable, Master Dogberry. The rest of this chapter belongs to them by right.

The first thing to note about them is that they all talk prose; in this dramatic composition poetry belongs to the romance which forms the background, prose to the foreground. The Constables would talk prose in any case; it is their element as it is that of Bottom and Lancelot Gobbo. It is a new thing however in Shakespearian comedy for characters who sit above the salt, as it were, to speak anything but verse. But Shakespeare had been at school since he wrote *The Merchant of Venice*, he had learnt to write the raciest, supplest, most delicately articulate prose in English dramatic literature, a prose that speaks itself and is so constructed that it is as easily committed to memory as blank verse, and is therefore perfectly adapted to the theatre, I mean, of course, the prose of Falstaff, and the Falstaff scenes. For an example of the rhythm of it, take part of his *Apologia pro vita sua*:

If sack and sugar be a fault, God help the wicked! if to be old and merry be a sin, then many an old host that I know is damned; if to be fat be to be hated, then Pharaoh's lean kine are to be loved. No, my good lord; banish Peto, banish Bardolph, banish Poins; but for sweet Jack Falstaff, kind Jack Falstaff, true Jack Falstaff, valiant Jack Falstaff, and therefore more valiant, being, as he is, old Jack Falstaff, banish not him thy Harry's company; banish plump Jack, and banish all the world.

(1 *Henry IV*, II, iv, 461–70)

Having forged a steel of that temper, Shakespeare was not the man to lay it lightly aside. He fashioned a couple of bright rapiers from it and placed them in the hands of Benedick and Beatrice for the duel of sex.

There can be little doubt that Benedick was played by Richard Burbadge, the leading actor in Shakespeare's company. We may see him also in Berowne, the Bastard of *King John*, Petruchio the shrew-tamer, Mercutio, the taciturn Bolingbroke, and probably Henry V. To judge from the description of Cœur-de-Lion's bastard son, Burbadge possessed a large frame and a roistering manner; and we have records of his taking vigorous action in private life.[1] In any case, all these characters possess much in common and were clearly modelled upon the same actor. They are bluff soldiermen, rough wooers or whimsical rudesbies in turn, or two of these combined.

There is nothing, therefore, very new in the character of Benedick, who may be described, I have said, as a Berowne with a touch of Petruchio about him. What is new is his speech, to which I have just referred, and the fact that his love civilizes him, for when he comes to the business of courting he does it with a grace far beyond anything within the scope of Berowne, or even Henry V.

The case of Beatrice is different. We have found a shadowy foretaste of her in the mocking wenches of *Love's Labour's Lost*, and at times we may be reminded of Petruchio's shrew,[2] but to all intents and purposes she is a new creation, some-

[1] See Chambers, *Elizabethan Stage*, ii, 307.    [2] See p. 138.

thing Shakespeare had never before dreamt of, but a something that was to be imitated time and again down the
centuries. There is no one in the Histories in the least like
her, not even Lady Hotspur, and which character in the
Comedies so far written can be set beside her? None except
Portia, and Portia, though not lacking in a sprightly wit, is
of a different cast—at once tenderer and wiser, and yet less
completely realized.

Beatrice is the first woman in our literature, perhaps in
the literature of Europe, who not only has a brain but
delights in the constant employment of it. She is not without
beauty; if Benedick in his scornful days is to be believed, she
exceeded Hero 'as much in beauty, as the first of May doth
the last day of December'. But it never occurs to her to use
that in her dealings with men. On the contrary: 'I had
rather hear my dog bark at a crow than a man swear he
loves me.' She does not want to catch men at all; what
interests her in them is not their person but their intelligence,
of which she generally holds a poor opinion. She knows
enough about marriage to dread it.

> For hear me, Hero—wooing, wedding, and repenting, is as a
> Scotch jig, a measure, and a cinque-pace; the first suit is hot and
> hasty like a Scotch jig, and full as fantastical; the wedding mannerly-
> modest, as a measure, full of state and ancientry; and then comes
> Repentance, and with his bad legs falls into the cinque-pace faster
> and faster, till he sink into his grave.[1]

It is a sorry sequence—though many a twentieth-century
Marriage Guidance Council would endorse it—and so she
is at God upon her knees every morning and evening for the
blessing of having no husband, and 'will even take sixpence
in earnest of the bearward, and lead his apes into hell'
(II, i, 36–7)—the fate of old maids who could not lead
children into heaven.

'Well, then,' asks her uncle ironically, 'go you into hell?'
'No,' retorts Beatrice,

[1] II, i, 65–71.

'but to the gate, and there will the devil meet me like an old cuckold, with horns on his head, and say, "Get you to heaven, Beatrice, get you to heaven—here's no place for you maids." So deliver I up my apes, and away to St. Peter: for the heavens, he shows me where the bachelors sit, and there live we as merry as the day is long.'[1]

How Sir Thomas More would have delighted in that speech!

Her heaven is with the bachelors, because she sets her wits against theirs and beats them at their own game. In our last conflict' she reports of Benedick before he appears,

four of his five wits went halting off, and now is the whole man governed with one. (I, i, 61–3.)

This is not intended, of course, to be taken seriously, and is only uttered that it may be reported to Benedick again; but it shows that her chief delight in life was—not hunting men for capture, but shooting at them her barbed arrows and watching them quiver, as she smites between the joints of the harness.

And she delights especially in Benedick, because he is as impatient as she is with all this sex-business, and in their wit-skirmishes can give as good as he gets, or rather as good as 'a piece of valiant dust . . . a clod of wayward marl'[2] can be expected to give.

For note that Benedick, brave face as he puts upon it, always comes a little halting off from one of their encounters. The trouble is that his male vanity cannot quite concede to her the equal rights which the conditions of the game demand and so he never wounds *her* and *she* always gets past his guard. 'She told me', he complains,[3]

that I was the prince's jester, that I was duller than a great thaw—huddling jest upon jest with such impossible conveyance upon me, that I stood like a man at a mark, with a whole army shooting at me. . . . She speaks poniards, and every word stabs.

And he acknowledges his defeat in what follows:

DON PEDRO. Look, here she comes. *Enter Beatrice.*

BENEDICK. Will your grace command me to any service to the

---

[1] II, i, 39–45.    [2] II, i, 56–7.    [3] II, i, 225 ff.

world's end? I will go on the slightest errand now to the Antipodes that you can devise to send me on: I will fetch you a toothpicker now from the furthest inch of Asia: bring you the length of Prester John's foot: fetch you a hair off the great Cham's beard: do you any embassage to the Pigmies—rather than hold three words' conference with this harpy. You have no employment for me?

DON PEDRO. None, but to desire your good company.

BENEDICK. O God, sir, here's a dish I love not—I cannot endure my Lady Tongue. *Exit.*

This is not all banter; it conceals a real wound. The hurt fowl creeps into his sedges. His vanity is touched to the quick partly because his heart is already engaged without knowing it.

The Prince, who is too high a mark for shooting at, and whose heart is free, sees her more clearly than Benedick does. He offers to find a husband for her.[2]

BEATRICE. I would rather have one of your father's getting; hath your grace ne'er a brother like you? Your father got excellent husbands if a maid could come by them.

DON PEDRO. Will you have *me*, lady?

BEATRICE. No, my lord, unless I might have another for working-days—your grace is too costly to wear every day. . . . But I beseech your grace pardon me, I was born to speak all mirth and no matter.

DON PEDRO. Your silence most offends me, and to be merry best becomes *you*, for out o'question you were born in a merry hour.

BEATRICE. No, sure, my lord, my mother cried—but then, there was a star danced, and under that was I born.

And presently, after she goes out, the Prince remarks to her uncle:

DON PEDRO. By my troth, a pleasant-spirited [i.e. jocose] lady.

LEONATA. There's little of the melancholy element in her, my lord. She is never sad [i.e. serious] but when she sleeps, and not even sad then: for I have heard my daughter say, she hath often dreamt of unhappiness and waked herself with laughing.

This light-hearted merriment, this apparent indifference to suitors, might be qualities of a coquette. And if that be

---

[1] II, i, 244-56.    [2] II, i, 301 ff.

not too hard a word for Rosalind, we find them again in her, and even more so in Cleopatra, and Congreve's delightful transformation of Cleopatra, Millament. But for Beatrice's intellectual gifts, for her sheer pleasure in talking men's talk on terms of equality, and without the undertones of sentiment, we have to wait until modern times for parallels—for the women of George Meredith, and George Bernard Shaw.

Her merriment is without a spark of malice, and she is quite unconscious of the depth of the wounds she inflicts—

> Deals she an unkindness, 'tis but her rapid measure,
> Even as in a dance.

She notes, and rejoices in, Benedick's wincings; but she thinks it is only annoyance at being worsted in word-play.

> He'll but break a comparison or two on me, which peradventure, not marked or not laughed at, strikes him into melancholy—and then there's a partridge wing saved, for the fool will eat no supper that night.[1]

Yet, though without malice, she in her turn has her little vanities. Her very blindness to the pain she gives is proof of them. When, therefore, she hears herself taxed by Hero in these terms:

> But nature never framed a woman's heart
> Of prouder stuff than that of Beatrice:
> Disdain and scorn ride sparkling in her eyes,
> Misprizing what they look on, and her wit
> Values itself so highly, that to her
> All matter else seems weak: she cannot love,
> Nor take no shape nor project of affection,
> She is so self-endeared—[2]

there is just enough truth in the calumny, deliberate caricature though it be, to make her feel mighty uncomfortable. Intellectual pride might easily have been her undoing, but for the revelation of the 'pleached arbour'. And no woman on earth, however much she may profess to scorn love, will endure being told she is incapable of it.

[1] II, i, 135-9.     [2] III, i, 49-56.

# Much Ado about Nothing

Benedick is also accused of pride by his orchard critics, but what touches him is not that, so much as the salve to his wounded vanity when he learns that she has been half-dying for love of him all the time. And so, both are brought to realize the love which had been implicit in their intellectual attraction from the beginning.

The garden-scenes are first-rate sport, of the kind Shakespeare excelled in. But the device, after all, is simple enough; and far more skill is shown in the dramatic setting of the declaration which follows. It was indeed a master-stroke to combine this with the defamation of Hero, so that the two plots intersect, as it were, at their most crucial points. The situation calls out the full manhood and womanhood of each: we feel, for the first time in the play, that they are deeply serious; and Beatrice's sudden appeal to him to avenge her cousin's honour comes upon us with an almost overwhelming force, after the previous scenes of gaiety; with an effect indeed not unlike that produced by the news of the French King's death towards the end of *Love's Labour's Lost*.

BENEDICK. Lady Beatrice, have you wept all this while?
BEATRICE. Yea, and I will weep a while longer.
BENEDICK. I will not desire that.
BEATRICE. You have no reason, I do it freely.
BENEDICK. Surely I do believe your fair cousin is wronged.
BEATRICE. Ah, how much might the man deserve of me that would right her!
BENEDICK. Is there any way to show such friendship?
BEATRICE. A very even way, but no such friend.
BENEDICK. May a man do it?
BEATRICE. It is a man's office, but not yours.
BENEDICK. I do love nothing in the world so well as you—is not that strange?
BEATRICE. As strange as the thing I know not. It were as possible for me to say I loved nothing so well as you—but believe me not —and yet I lie not—I confess nothing, nor I deny nothing—I am sorry for my cousin.
BENEDICK. By my sword Beatrice, thou lovest me.
BEATRICE. Do not swear and eat it.

BENEDICK. I will swear by it that you love me, and I will make him eat it that says I love not you.

BEATRICE. Will you not eat your word?

BENEDICK. With no sauce that can be devised to it—I protest I love thee.

BEATRICE. Why then God forgive me—

BENEDICK. What offence sweet Beatrice?

BEATRICE. You have stayed me in a happy hour, I was about to protest I loved you.

BENEDICK. And do it with all thy heart.

BEATRICE. I love you with so much of my heart, that none is left to protest.

BENEDICK. Come bid me do anything for thee.

BEATRICE. Kill Claudio.

BENEDICK. Ha! not for the wide world.

BEATRICE. You kill me to deny it—farewell.

BENEDICK. Tarry sweet Beatrice.          *He stays her.*[1]

I referred in my second chapter to the quartet, two men and two ladies, who are found in varying combinations and relationships in most of Shakespeare's comedies, and I mentioned that the conflicting claims of love and friendship often determined their grouping. Here we have the leading lady bidding her lover kill his 'sworn brother' in order to vindicate the honour of her cousin. We have travelled a long way from the finale of *The Two Gentlemen* in which the leading man is prepared to hand over his lady to the friend who has just attempted to violate her before his eyes, in order to prove his unselfish devotion to friendship. The journey has been from Convention to Life, from an attempt to give dramatic form to an ideal accepted from others to one which succeeds in combining dramatic illusion with a situation which is felt by dramatist and audience to be real.

How long did Shakespeare take over *Ado*? If *The Merry Wives* occupied two weeks, *Ado* can hardly have taken two months. The source of the plot, the main Hero-Claudio plot, is well known, viz. a novella by Bandello probably read in the French version by Belleforest in his *Histoires Tragiques* which also contained the Hamlet story. But

[1] IV, i, 254 ff.

clearly, I think, Shakespeare was not concerned with this in 1598. He was working over an old play, his own or some other's. There are a number of little clues in the text pointing to revision which it is unnecessary to speak of here. It is enough perhaps to note two points:

(i) In the stage-directions of the 1600 Q, but not elsewhere in the text, Hero is provided with a mother called Innogen, a name which crops up again in *Cymbeline* in the form of I*m*ogen.

(ii) I find it impossible to read III, i (the scene in which Hero persuades the hidden Beatrice that Benedick is in love with her) without being convinced that the verse is older than that of most of the rest of the verse in the play. And what a strange Beatrice it is who emerges from the arbour at the end of the scene:

> What fire is in mine ears? Can this be true?
> Stand I condemned for pride and scorn so much?
> Contempt, farewell! and maiden pride, adieu!
> No glory lives behind the back of such. . . .
> And Benedick, love on, I will requite thee,
> Taming my wild heart to thy loving hand:
> If thou dost love, my kindness shall incite thee
> To bind our loves up in a holy band:
> For others say thou dost deserve, and I
> Believe it better than reportingly.[1]

'Taming my wild heart to thy loving hand'! The Beatrice *we know* is incapable of such a thought even in soliloquy: it is some primitive puppet who speaks, perhaps a sister to the Shrew Katherine after her taming. And—'No glory lives behind the back of such'! What a line! It is inconceivable for Shakespeare in 1598. Indeed, I find it hard to believe he can ever have been capable of it. The speech is patently from a drama of the early nineties; what Shakespeare did in 1597 therefore was to revise an old play. And in his rehandling he tightened up and abbreviated the original Hero-Claudio story so as to push it into the background in order

---

[1] III, i, 107–16.

to bring forward Beatrice and Benedick, rewriting and greatly expanding their dialogue or almost all of it. It is possible that he rewrote and expanded the Dogberry scenes at the same time, for it is at least conceivable that the original Dogberry was a small part, one corresponding with the part of Constable Dull in *Love's Labour's Lost*. But this contingency is connected with the theory that the unrevised *Ado* can be equated with *Love's Labour's Won*.[1]

But however long the reshaping may have taken, Shakespeare produced an excellent theatre piece in the process which gave something for everyone at the Globe.

(i) It provided excellent parts for the leading men—Dogberry for Kempe,[2] Benedick for Burbadge, and Beatrice for the leading boy:

(ii) it had a good story with strong situations, which all parts of the audience could appreciate;

(iii) the Beatrice and Benedick scenes would appeal to the noble patrons in the 'lords' room, the gentlemen and the critics:

(iv) and Dogberry would fit the groundlings with far more than their pennyworth.

I once tried Dogberry upon a typical Elizabethan audience: I had been asked to lecture on Shakespeare to 288 male prisoners in Lincoln gaol, but learning from the chaplain that 60 per cent of them were illiterate, instead of a lecture I read them the Dogberry scenes, and at once had the whole prison roaring with laughter over the antics of the constable. The medieval crowd had likewise roared over the antics of the Devil—that universal constable. They knew the Devil might (many of them knew he *must*) get them in the end; but it was some satisfaction to be able to watch him bamboozled in play. Shakespeare knew that his rascals on the floor of the Globe would get the same kind of satisfaction from Dogberry, Verges and the rest.

[1] See above, p. 122.
[2] That Kempe played Dogberry is proved by Q 1, which at more than one point reads 'Kempe' for 'Dogberry' in the stage-directions.

'O, that I had been writ down an ass!' (IV, ii, 84-5). How the pothouses after the play must have rung with the laughter over that jest!

But Shakespeare did not write only for Burbadge, the gallants, and the groundlings; he wrote for himself and his artistic conscience. For he *had* a conscience, though Ben Jonson didn't think so, because it was so different from his own. Shakespeare's conscience was not of the kind that set up before it an ideal of artistic perfection, derived from previous masterpieces, or what students thought were the laws previous masters had observed, and strove to attain it. Shakespeare's was of a more adventurous type. He was always trying new things, new forms, new possibilities, and having once begun on a new line, to better his experiment. And when he felt he had gone as far as he could in a certain direction, he tried a new tack. *Romeo and Juliet* marks a final stage—he never tried to better that, though *Antony and Cleopatra* was in a sense (a maturer sense) a return; *Richard II* marks another stage; and Falstaff (in *Henry IV*) was yet a third, though his creator had to fake a spurious image of him in *The Merry Wives* and kill him definitely off in *Henry V* before he could escape from him.

Was his artistic conscience satisfied with *Ado*? He was surely pleased with one thing—the Beatrice-Benedick business, and that he had succeeded in fitting it into his romantic pattern. But the rest—it is not good enough!

I fancy he underlined *Nothing* in the title. He felt there was an emptiness in the play. He could do better than this, much better. As an afternoon's entertainment *Ado* makes, I said, a shapelier stage-play than *As You Like It*, but *As You Like It* is in every way riper and more golden; the harvest was still to come.

# CHAPTER VII

# *As You Like It*

---

A<small>s</small> *You Like It* was probably produced in 1599, and that London at any rate was liking it very much in 1600 is suggested by an order in the Stationers' Register of August 4th of that year that 'As you like yt, a booke', was 'to be staied', which suggests that the pirates were after it, hoping to secure some kind of surreptitious text, 'maimed and deformed', to palm off upon the reading public.

Is it still 'as we like it', I sometimes wonder. We pay it lip service, and unite to impose it upon the boys and girls of our schools. But do we grown-ups read it ourselves, and do we enjoy it when we see it in the theatre? Speaking for myself, until the other day I had never witnessed a performance of it which gave me much pleasure, and I am sure that most boys and girls who have to study it (generally for examinations! What *would* Shakespeare have thought about that— and said about it!—could he have known?) are frankly bored with it.

At one time I was an inspector of schools, and whenever I found *As You Like It* being taken in class, I made it my business to get the master or mistress out of the room, so as to have a private talk with the victims. And once I had won their confidence, they were ready enough with their opinions, which were downright, as those of young people are apt to be. They generally boiled down to this: the boys liked the wrestling-match, and the girls liked some of the songs—but for the rest, well, whatever *was* it all about? And

As You Like It

I came away from these visits with the conviction, not only that the pupils did not know what it was all about, but that their pastors and masters did not know either—otherwise, they could not have compelled them to 'take' the play at school. I suspect, too, that the actors and producers, responsible for most of the performances of the play I have seen, understood it just as little, otherwise they could not have made it so dull. But I may have been unlucky in my experiences. That I had been was proved by the entrancing and convincingly Shakespearian Rosalind of Vanessa Redgrave which I witnessed at Stratford in September 1961 not very long before sending off this book to the publisher. The wrestling was good too. We are getting along!

What, then, *is* it all about? Perhaps it will help us to answer this question, if we first ask ourselves what the Elizabethans thought it was all about—for they clearly enjoyed it, and Shakespeare knew they would, or he would not have dared to give it the title he did.

The wrestling and the songs were, of course, popular then as now. Much more popular indeed, since we may be certain that the bouts of Charles, the duke's champion, and Orlando were carried through in the most thorough, sportsmanlike, and realistic fashion. Not then the feeble scuffle between two spindle-legged and pot-bellied actors which often disgraces our modern stage, but a proper display, according to the rules, and offering real excitement, as wrestling should. For this match had no doubt been well advertised in the bills stuck on posts about the city; the 'prentice-boys will have paid their pennies expressly to see a man thrown in what at least appeared to be earnest; and if, as I suspect, the brawny Burbadge played Orlando and was matched by a Charles who looked equally brawny, the audience did not go home without the sport they came for. Interest in physical contests was as universal as in modern London and far more intelligent, while the players in the London theatre laid themselves out to perform their stage-contests as convincingly as possible.

142

As for the songs, they too were more masculine, being sung by men and boys, while we may be sure too, that the hunting-song in IV, ii—a scene of under twenty lines in the book—was enacted with great effect and elaboration, inasmuch as the slayer of the deer was, according to ancient custom, clad in the skin and the horns, and hoisted upon the shoulders of the company, who 'sang him home'. ' 'Tis no matter', remarks Jaques, 'how it be in tune, so it make noise enough.' And a fine healthy noise it must have been!

There are no fewer than five songs in *As You Like It*—if we include the little mocking dance-song of Touchstone, as he flouts Sir Oliver Martext (III, iii, 92 ff.); and they are well spaced out through the play, so as to recur at more or less regular intervals. At times, they are introduced without much relevance to the immediate dramatic context. This, for example, is the casual way in which *It was a Lover and his Lass*, one of the best-known songs in Shakespeare, is introduced: 'Here come two of the banished duke's pages', Audrey suddenly remarks to Touchstone. Whereat two boys run up, of whom we have not previously heard, nor shall hear again, and the following dialogue takes place:

1 PAGE. Well met, honest gentleman.
TOUCH. By my troth, well met. Come, sit, sit, and a song.
2 PAGE. We are for you: sit i' th'middle.
1 PAGE. Shall we clap into 't roundly, without hawking or spitting or saying we are hoarse, which are the only prologues to a bad voice?
2 PAGE. I'faith, i'faith; and both in a tune, like two gipsies on a horse. (V, iii, 6 ff.)

The song is then sung, after which Touchstone rallies the boys a little on their voices, and goes out with Audrey.

Then there is Touchstone himself. There had been no successor to Lancelot Gobbo in *Much Ado*. The Clown's place had been taken by Master Constable Dogberry, who as we know from the text of Q1 was played by Will Kempe, Shakespeare's colleague and impersonator of his clowns and fools since 1594, if not before. In 1598 or early in 1599,

Kempe for some reason parted with the Chamberlain's company and was succeeded by Robert Armin—undoubtedly a great event in Shakespeare's dramatic development. What Shakespeare thought of this new player may be seen from the fact that he created for him Touchstone, and Feste, and Lavache in *All's Well*, and the Fool in *Lear*. Has any other comic actor in history ever had such a compliment paid him?

To the audience who came to *As You Like It* in 1599, however, Armin was probably a comparatively unknown player, who had to win his way—perhaps in the teeth of opposition from Will Kempe's favourers. We can hardly doubt (in view of the parts Shakespeare later entrusted him with) that he triumphed. Kempe had chiefly played clownish servants, such as Launce or Peter, fan-bearer to the Nurse in *Romeo and Juliet*, or low-class characters, such as Christopher Sly or Dogberry, and when the plays in which these occurred were revived no doubt Armin played them also. But he was evidently a much subtler comic man than Kempe, and Shakespeare accordingly created a subtler kind of character for him, viz. the professional or court fool, who now figures so largely in the dramas.

Touchstone was not actually the earliest of these, since we get a faint adumbration of him in Launce of *The Two Gentlemen* and something less faint in Lancelot Gobbo,[1] while (if Granville-Barker be right) Costard of *Love's Labour's Lost* was also intended to be a court fool.[2] But Touchstone is the first that really counts, and if you can imagine *As You Like It* without him you will see how much he counted, while compare Lancelot Gobbo with Touchstone, and the superiority of the new type is at once obvious. The humour of Lancelot Gobbo consists, in the main, of two elements: first, a comic misuse of words—an old trick, already becoming a little stale by the time *The Two Gentlemen* was written—a trick which Shakespeare's clowns share with his old women, Juliet's Nurse and Mistress Quickly;

[1] See above, p. 48.  [2] See also p. 47.

144

and of which Dogberry marks the culmination; and second,
a very shrewd notion of where his own interests lay, made
comic because combined with an air of extreme stupidity.

The humour of Touchstone is at once more elaborate,
deliberate and cultivated than that of Lancelot Gobbo. He
pretends to have been a courtier:

> I have trod a measure—I have flattered a lady—I have been politic
> with my friend, smooth with mine enemy—I have undone three
> tailors—I have had four quarrels, and like to have fought one.[1]

Such pretensions are far beyond the scope of Lancelot
Gobbo. Touchstone is capable of extempore rhyme, affects
to have written poetry, and can deliver himself on the subject; he has heard of Ovid and of his banishment; he delights in moralizing, and still more in argument.

There was, then, plenty to attract and please the groundlings in *As You Like It*. They might feel that the story was
rather thin, as indeed it was, but they had food for laughter
in the melancholy Jaques, and found much entertainment in
the goings-on of the tall boy who played the heroine. For if
Shakespeare has a new comic man to play his fools, he could
hardly have written any one of the three great comedies,
*Ado*, *As You Like It*, *Twelfth Night*, if he had not at that time
also had a boy of more than usual charm and cleverness to
create Beatrice, Rosalind and Viola.

Nor must we forget that a large proportion of the
groundlings were 'prentice-boys, who had an interest in
women's parts that their successors in our theatre lack. They
could watch and admire one of themselves, so to speak,
going through a performance of much skill. One would
give much for half an hour's talk with a few of these lads.
Some of them, perhaps, despised the antics of the boy-
players as effeminate; but such would be more likely to be
found at the Cock-pit or the Bear-garden than at the
theatre. Regular frequenters of the Globe would possess, I
suspect, a very shrewd judgment on the points of acting
technique. Shakespeare's theatre was entirely without that

[1] V, iv, 43–6.

money-making asset of modern times, female glamour—or what is vulgarly known as sex appeal—and so had to draw its public by other means, the means which now attracts the large football crowd—or such of it as is not taken to the match by betting—I mean the interest in personal skill. Indeed, if *The* induction to Beaumont and Fletcher's *Knight of the Burning Pestle* is evidence, the 'prentices were stimulated by what they saw in the public theatres to indulge in amateur performances at home; and though Ralph, the grocer's assistant, affected 'couraging parts', or 'huffing parts', like that of Hotspur, others might be expected to play the women.

*As You Like It*, however, was written not for the groundlings (though Shakespeare never forgot them) but for the young gentlemen in the audience—for noblemen like Southampton and his friend Rutland, who are recorded in this very year[1] to have been busy 'in going to plays every day', or like William Herbert, the 'Mr. W. H.' of the *Sonnets* as I believe, now nineteen years old, who was to become Earl of Pembroke two years later and three years later still entertained James I at Wilton with a private performance of *As You Like It* itself;[2] or just for students of the Inns of Court, like Jack Donne and others, who

> Of study and play make strange hermaphrodites.

What then did they find in this play for their delight? They found something which was at once an exquisite essay in the pastoral manner, and a sly criticism of it.

When *As You Like It* first appeared, the pastoral vogue had been in the ascendency for a score or more years, and was to last for some time yet. The publication of Sidney's *Arcadia* in 1590 had given it a new stimulus, but the writing of that book—'a trifle and that triflingly handled' as its author styled it—was only a striking incident in a long story. In a time when chivalry seemed upon its death-bed, when

---

[1] See G. B. Harrison, *Elizabethan Journal*, 13th October, 1599.
[2] See E. K. Chambers, *William Shakespeare*, ii, 329.

rapid change and the thronging claims of a new world were everywhere thrusting into the background the noblest ideals and traditions of the past, without any clear promise of a worthy succession, it was natural that minds of a reflective and imaginative cast should seek refuge and refreshment in the contemplation of an age of innocence and scenes of rustic life and love, tinged with a gentle melancholy and surrounded by the ideal landscape which forms the background to so many of the Italian pictures of the Renaissance, and is as we have seen the background also of most of the Happy Comedies.

> There were hilles which garnished their proud heights with stately trees: humble valleis, whose base estate seemed comforted with refreshing of silver rivers: medows enameld with al sorts of ey-pleasing floures: thickets, which being lined with most pleasant shade, were witnessed so to by the cherefull deposition of many wel-tuned birds; each pasture stored with sheep feeding with sober security, while the prety lambs with bleting oratory craved the dams comfort: here a shepeards boy piping, as though he should never be old: there a yong sheperdesse knitting, and withal singing, & it seemed that her voice comforted her hands to work & her hands kept time to her voices musick.[1]

Such is the first and loveliest glimpse Sidney gives us of his Arcadia.

But the following, which forms the opening paragraph of the third book of Montemayor's *Diana*, in the English translation by Bartholomew Young, published in 1598, is to my mind even lovelier:

> With great content the faire Nymphes with their companie were going on their way thorow the middes of a thicke wood, and now the sunne being readie to set, they entred into a faire valley, in the mids of which ran a swift brooke, beset on either side with thicke Sallows and Sicamours, amongst the which were many other kindes of lesse trees, which twyning about the greater, and the golden and coloured flowers of the one, wouen (as it were) with the greene bowes of the other, represented a goodly sight and delight to the eie. The Nymphes and Shepherds tooke a pathway betweene the brooke

[1] *The Countess of Pembroke's Arcadia*, 1590, ed. by A. Feuillerat, 1912, p. 13.

and the faire arbours, who had not gone farre, when they came to a large greene meadow, wherein was a very faire great moate of cleere water, from whence the brooke did spring, that with great force ranne thorow the valley. In the middes of that moate was an Iland, wherein grew some greene trees, amongst the which stoode a Sheepe-cote, and about the same a flocke of sheepe went feeding of the greene and tender grasse. The Nymphes thinking this a fit place to passe away the night, which was neere at hand, vpon a fine causey of stones most artificiallie (as it seemed) laide in order, they passed all ouer into the iland, and went directly to the cote which they sawe before them. But *Polydora* going in first (for she was a little before the rest) was scarce entred in, when she came foorth as fast againe, and looking towards her companie, did put her finger vpon her mouth, in token that they should come softly on & without any noise, which the Nymphes & the Shepherdes perceiuing, with the least they could, came into the cote, and looking into it, espied a bed in a corner, not made of any other thing, then of the greene bowes of those Sicamours, that were growing about it, and of the greene grasse, that did growe about the water brinkes. Vpon the which they sawe a Shepherdesse lying a sleepe, whose beautie stroke them with no lesse admiration, then if on a sudden they had seene faire *Diana* before their eies. She had on a light skie coloured petticoate, and vnder that a gorget of so passing fine net-worke, that they might at pleasure behold the delicate proportion of her snow white brest, and comely feature of her euen body, for the vpper part (being of the same colour with the rest) hung so loose about her, that they might take a perfect view of her fine and daintie waste. Her yellowe haire in brightnes surpassing the sunnie beames, were loose and hanging downe without any order. But neuer did frizeling and adorned peri-wigge of any Lady in stately court beautifie in such sort, as the carelesse disorder that these had; and her white legge, being bare by negligence of her harmlesse sleepe, laie seemely out of her petticoate, but not so much, that the lookers on might perceiue any part, but what with modestie they might well beholde. And by manie teares that (sleeping yet) went trickling downe her faire and rosie cheekes, her sleepe (it seemed) should not hinder her sorrowfull imaginations. The Nymphes and Shepherds were so amazed at her beautie, and at her inward sorrow, which by outward signes they well coniec-tured did trouble her waking soule, that they knew not what to saie, but were forced to shed teares for pittie of those, which they sawe the Shepherdesse powre foorth.

Clearly Sidney's picture owes something to Monte-

mayor's[1] and both represent the ideal world of rural content-
ment which combined the legend of the golden age with
the pastoralism of Theocritus and Virgil. In every period of
confusion and revolutionary change, the soul of man casts
back or forwards to this land of the heart's desire. Thus the
breakdown of the *ancien régime* at the end of the eighteenth
century gave us Rousseau and his dream of a natural society,
Wordsworth and his deification of mountain, stream and
peasant, while William Morris's prose romances provided a
similar literature of 'escape' for late nineteenth-century
England, oppressed with the devastation of the industrial
revolution.

And just as Morris and his fellow artists begat the
aesthetic movement, so the pastoral poets and novelists of
Elizabeth's reign fathered the pastoral craze at court. Love-
making and the singing of songs to the rebeck, the bagpipe
or the recorder, which were the chief occupations of Arcadian shepherds and shepherdesses, were enough by themselves to attract the courtier and the maid-in-waiting to the
fashion, while pastoral themes were highly appropriate to
the masques and other theatrical entertainments with which
Queen Elizabeth expected to be greeted when visiting her
great subjects on her progresses during the summer months,
and James I's Queen Anne spent most of her time watching
or herself acting in. The maiden monarch was of course
identified with the goddess Diana, queen of the woods, and
attended by her train of nymphs, while the courtiers became
her shepherds, Sir Walter Ralegh, for example, assuming
the title of 'Shepherd of the Ocean'. Pastoralism grew to be
a solemn game, in which the whole court took part.

Sidney's *Arcadia* was the first pastoral romance produced
in this country; but it is indebted to two previous romances
written on the Continent—Sanazzaro's *Arcadia* published in
Italy in 1504, and the *Diana* of Montemayor, which appeared in Spain in 1552 and is quoted above. The latter

[1] Young's translation was dedicated to Lady Rich (Sidney's 'Stella' and
Essex's sister). See Chapter II, p. 41.

was one of the most popular books of the age, and was well known to Shakespeare. As pointed out in Chapter II, he took the plot of *The Two Gentlemen of Verona* directly or indirectly from it, while his familiarity with it is also attested by Rosalind's reference to Diana weeping in the fountain at IV, i, 148, an allusion which must have been unintelligible except to those who knew the story. It is therefore probably significant that the first English translation, by Bartholomew Young, appeared (as I have said) in 1598, a year before the production of *As You Like It*, which certainly owed much of its general atmosphere to it, though not the details of its plot, as *The Two Gentlemen* and *Twelfth Night* did. Tears came easily to the lovelorn shepherds and shepherdesses in this Spanish romance. But to none more frequently than to Diana herself, who spends most of the time gazing into a pool in a grove of sycamores and augmenting it with her silent tears. Young's translation had been in existence for sixteen years before its publication and as I suggested earlier Shakespeare may already have had access to it in manuscript.[1] Anyhow, Montemayor seems to have been almost as important a source for his comedies as Holinshed was for the Histories and North's Plutarch for the Roman plays.

Modern literary historians laugh at the book, but if one can judge from Young's translation, it was well worthy of the admiration given it in an age which delighted in Sidney's *Arcadia* and Spenser's *Faerie Queene*, both of which are much indebted to it, while it is easy to see how passages like that quoted above might inspire Shakespeare to create his own forest of Arden.

Yet, as everyone knows, Shakespeare took the *story* of *As You Like It* from a little pastoral novel by Thomas Lodge, entitled *Rosalynde, or Euphues' Golden Legacy*, and published in 1590. This slender tale is however the least important part of the play; it gets it going and finishes it off. But all the middle portion is taken up with encounters and talk, songs

[1] See p. 41.

and jests, in the forest of Arden, which Shakespeare sets before the eyes of our imagination by a hundred little touches. The forest makes the play, and the forest is a blend of two elements: (i) the delightful scenery of Montemayor, and (ii) Shakespeare's memories of the Warwickshire scenery round about his native home—his own forest of Arden, in fact.

His success in the creation of this atmosphere, of this 'golden world' in which his characters 'fleet the time carelessly' for so many scenes, is all the greater when we call to mind that he wrote for the bare Elizabethan stage. And yet, it was just the bareness of that stage which put him to his task and challenged him. Shakespeare's scenery is in the verse he writes. His earliest success of the kind is *A Midsummer Night's Dream*, and we found him bettering that in the last Act of *The Merchant*. *As You Like It* goes one better still, in atmospheric effect, to be excelled only by the night of *Macbeth*, the storm of *Lear*, and the music-laden air of Prospero's island.

But, while the forest is a triumph of dramatic scene-painting and the play as a whole the very distillation of pastoral romance, the more judicious among Shakespeare's audience would not miss the vein of mockery that runs throughout.

First of all, Arden takes a good deal of getting to. Rosalind, Celia and Touchstone reach it utterly dead-beat; old Adam cannot walk a step further, so that Orlando is forced to carry him in his arms; Oliver, Orlando's brother, arrives footsore, in rags, and so dog-tired that when he falls asleep even a snake coiling about his throat is not able to wake him. Moreover, though eternal summer reigns in the lands of pastoral romance, our first glimpse of Arden is in wintertime. The exiled Duke is bravely making the best of it, and welcoming

> the icy fang
> And churlish chiding of the winter's wind,
> Which, when it bites and blows upon my body,
> Even till I shrink with cold, I smile and say

'This is no flattery: these are counsellors
That feelingly persuade me what I am.'
Sweet are the uses of adversity.[1]

And the emphasis upon winter and its trials is continued in
the song, 'Under the greenwood tree' with its refrain of

No enemy
But winter and rough weather[2]

and the later 'Blow, blow thou winter wind', the second
verse of which begins

Freeze, freeze, thou bitter sky.[3]

Only in the fifth Act does spring arrive with 'It was a lover
and his lass'.

And in the third place, there is a touch of irony about most
of the characters. The exiled Duke and his co-mates are
slightly ridiculous in their enforced stoicism, and were intended, I have little doubt, to recall the attitude of so many
of Elizabeth's courtiers, like Ralegh and Essex, who when
they fell out of the Queen's favour, as they not infrequently
did, retired to their own estates in the provinces and sulked
in voluntary or involuntary exile.

This peeps out clearly enough in Jaques's scornful parody
of 'Under the greenwood tree':

If it do come to pass,
That any man turn ass . . .
Leaving his wealth and ease,
A stubborn will to please,
Ducdame, ducdame, ducdame:
Here shall he see,
Gross fools as he,
An if he will come to me.

And what follows is equally pointed:

AMIENS. What's that 'ducdame'?
JAQUES. 'Tis a Greek invocation, to call fools into a circle. . . . I'll
go sleep, if I can: if I cannot, I'll rail against all the first-born of
Egypt.[4]

[1] II, i, 6–12.          [2] II, v, 1–8.
[3] II, vii, 174 ff.      [4] II, v, 48 ff.

As You Like It

Many editors have asked with Amiens, 'What's that "duc-dame"?' And the answer, first given by Dr. John Sampson, the Librarian of Liverpool University, showed it to be a corruption of a Romany word meaning 'I foretell, or I can tell fortunes', which as the call of a gipsy at fairs or public gatherings, is a 'Greek' (= sharper's) invocation to call fools into a ring. In short Jaques implies that the members of the banished court are like so many amateur gipsies, forced to lead this uncomfortable life by the stubborn will of the Duke, who as the elder brother is 'the first-born of Egypt'.

The presence of such a character as Jaques, for whom there is no parallel in Lodge or Montemayor, is also highly significant. Jaques is Shakespeare's misanthrope—though a very different one from Molière's Alceste. We are not told why he has accompanied the Duke into exile, but it is clear that while he rails at his fellow-exiles for being fools, he despises the world so much that he prefers the country to the court. It is for instance noteworthy that he does not return to court with the Duke at the end of the play, but joins the 'convertite' brother usurper. His famous 'All the world's a stage', which used to be given to boys and girls to learn as a set piece in the old days, and may be still so given for all I know, is of course sheer cynicism.

Some have supposed that he was intended to represent Ben Jonson—that he was in fact the 'purge' which Shakespeare is known to have given his fellow playwright, a purge no one has been able to trace with any certainty. The fact that he is an old man is, I think, against this theory, and I find a more likely caricature in Nym. But Jaques may certainly be taken as in some ways standing for the Jonsonian point of view—the critical standpoint I spoke of earlier. If so, it is noteworthy that while Shakespeare employs him for ironical comment upon pastoral affectation, he does not allow him to pass uncriticized himself.

The crucial scene here is II, vii, in which Jaques, after encountering Touchstone, declares that he is 'ambitious for a motley coat' (l. 43).

Invest me in my motley; give me leave
To speak my mind, and I will through and through
Cleanse the foul body of th' infected world,
If they will patiently receive my medicine. (ll. 58–61.)

It is the very ideal of the neo-classical comedy which in 1599 Jonson was busy founding. But mark the Duke's rejoinder:

DUKE. Fie on thee! I can tell what thou wouldst do.
JAQUES. What, for a counter, would I do but good?
DUKE. Most mischievous foul sin, in chiding sin:
    For thou thyself hast been a libertine,
    As sensual as the brutish sting itself,
    And all th' embosséd sores and headed evils,
    That thou with licence of free foot hast caught,
    Wouldst thou disgorge into the general world. (ll. 62–9.)

Is this what Shakespeare himself thought about the 'comical satires' of Ben Jonson and others? It may have been. By exposing to men's view the seamy side of London life in order to vent their virtuous indignation upon it, they dragged to light what might have been better left in obscurity, and familiarized the many, those of tender years as well as those of experience, with vices and moral infection hitherto known only to the few.

That is always the danger of the satirist. Social and moral pestilence is the material in which he deals, the food on which his art is sustained. And he must ever be seeking for fresh material, so that he becomes a sort of public scavenger, poking about the middens which are to be found in the back premises of any society. And when he has found them he disgorges them 'into the general world'—and the more successful his art, the wider the infection spreads.

And like all satirists Jaques is also a sentimentalist. His famous tears of sensibility over the wounded stag, tears which anticipate those of Laurence Sterne over the dead donkey, are the product of a cultivated pathos, of his pose of misanthropy. Meredith has deftly exposed this kind of thing to the oblique light of his comic spirit in

### Whimper of Sympathy

Hawk or shrike has done this deed
Of downy feathers: rueful sight!
Sweet sentimentalist, invite
Your bosom's power to intercede.
So hard it seems that one must bleed
Because another needs must bite!
All round we find cold Nature slight
The feelings of the totter-knee'd.

Whether Jaques was connected in Shakespeare's mind with Ben Jonson or not, the Duke's retort proves that his cynicism is not to be taken as Shakespeare's. Jaques is, in short, an important figure to be reckoned with in our estimate of the standpoint of Shakespearian comedy. For he is not only one of the leading characters of the play, with critical comments illuminating the absurdities of other characters, but also himself a comic creation, and is put into his proper place both by the severe censure of the Duke and by the merry commonsense of Rosalind.

JAQUES. Yes, I have gained my experience.
ROSALIND. And your experience makes you sad! I had rather have
    a fool to make me merry than experience to make me sad—and
    to travel for it too! . . .
    Farewell, Monsieur Traveller.[1]

Yet Jaques, who can suck melancholy out of a song, as a weasel sucks eggs, laughs at least once in the play. For the fool can make even him merry. The incident is not shown upon the stage; but Jaques reports it to the Duke at great length in the beginning of II, vii, from which I have already quoted:

'Good morrow, fool', quoth I: 'No sir', quoth he,
'Call me not fool till heaven hath sent me fortune.'
And then he drew a dial from his poke,
And looking on it with lack-lustre eye,
Says very wisely, 'It is ten o'clock.
Thus we may see', quoth he, 'how the world wags:
'Tis but an hour ago since it was nine,

[1] IV, i, 24 ff.

And after one hour more 'twill be eleven,
And so from hour to hour we ripe and ripe,
And then from hour to hour we rot and rot—
And thereby hangs a tale.'—When I did hear
The motley fool thus moral on the time,
My lungs began to crow like chanticleer,
That fools should be so deep-contemplative;
And I did laugh, sans intermission,
An hour by his dial.[1]

Familiar words, familiar as 'All the world's a stage'—and like them as often misunderstood. Jaques laughs at the melancholy Touchstone; it does not occur to him that the Fool, who has not a true note of melancholy in him, is really laughing at him—is shooting at his melancholy from behind the stalking-horse of his wit.

Touchstone mocks Jaques as he mocks all the other characters he encounters in Arden. He is the second critic of the pastoral world and like Jaques an addition by Shakespeare to the characters Lodge gave him. He is the realist of the play, or one of the two realists (for Rosalind is another). As his name implies, he *tests* all that the world takes for gold, especially the gold of the golden world of pastoralism. And he had made up his mind about Arden directly he arrives:

ROSALIND. O Jupiter! how weary are my spirits!
TOUCH. I care not for my spirits, if my legs were not weary.

And again,

ROSALIND. Well, this is the forest of Arden!
TOUCH. Ay, now I am in Arden, the more fool I. When I was at home, I was in a better place, but travellers must be content.[2]

Mr. Aldous Huxley has an essay upon travel somewhere entitled 'Why not stay at home?' which is little more than an expansion of that.

But what raised most laughter, no doubt, with Shakespeare's original audience was Touchstone's lording it as a courtier, a gentleman and a philosopher, over the simple

---

[1] II, vii, 18-33.  [2] II, iv, 1-3, 14-17.

rustics of Arden—he 'the roynish[1] clown'! His long discussion with Corin, the old shepherd, on the comparative
merits of life in the court and life in the country leaves little
to be said in defence of either state. But the humour of it is
in the superior airs which the Fool puts on—as of a thinker
and a wit, leaving the poor simpleton before him damned,
'like an ill-roasted egg all on one side'.

Or mark how he puts down William, his rival for the
hand of Audrey:

*Enter William.*

TOUCH. It is meat and drink to me to see a clown. By my troth, we
that have good wits have much to answer for; we shall be flouting;
we cannot hold. . . . You do love this maid?

WILLIAM. I do, sir.

TOUCH. Give me your hand. . . . Art thou learned?

WILLIAM. No, sir.

TOUCH. Then, learn this of me—to have, is to have; for it is a figure
in rhetoric that drink, being poured out of a cup into a glass, by
filling the one doth empty the other; for all your writers do consent that ipse is he: now, you are not ipse, for I am he.

WILLIAM. Which he, sir?

TOUCH. He, sir, that must marry this woman. . . . Therefore, you
clown, abandon (which is in the vulgar 'leave') the society (which
in the boorish is 'company') of this female (which in the common
is 'woman'); which together is, 'abandon the society of this
female', or, clown, thou perishest.[2]

So far from misusing the language, like Gobbo and the
clowns which Kempe had played, Touchstone is a master
of it. He can parody the rhetorical jargon of the affected
courtier. What I have just quoted is in the very style of
Armado. Thus Touchstone, who had an eye for affectation
of all kinds, mocks at the court which seems heaven to those
who have never been there and at the country life which
seems a golden world to those who are of the court.

If Corin is ill roasted on one side, the Duke and Jaques
are equally ill roasted on the other. And when Touchstone
finds himself in the Duke's court at the end of the play, he

[1] Scurvy.    [2] V, i, 10-53.

not only assumes the courtier's style with a ludicrous grace all his own, but delivers himself fo the most brilliant burlesque of the preliminaries to a court duel which the literature of the period affords.[1]

Yet we must never forget, what Armin did not for a moment allow his audience to forget, that Touchstone is a *Fool*. 'And in his brain', as Jaques tells us,

> Which is as dry [i.e. stupid] as the remainder biscuit
> After a voyage, he hath strange places crammed
> With observation, the which he vents
> In mangled forms.[2]

He possessed, in the educational jargon of our time, a better *background* than Launcelot Gobbo; but he was just as much the 'natural'. His stiff mechanical gait, his drawling speech, his wooden face (all the more so for the flashes of intelligence, released as it were by a hidden spring, which passed across it), together with the motley of his profession, combined to mark him off from the other characters as something less than human.

In the shimmering air of Romance which the inhabitants of Arden breathe, love (as I said) is the main industry, love the course of which 'never did run smooth'. Touchstone must perforce press in amongst the rest of the country folk 'to swear or to forswear, according as marriage binds and blood breaks', and his pairing off with Audrey, the half-witted goatherd, is at once a parody of the love-making of the others and a symptom of his own nature.

For he is 'a material fool', and this materialism, gross as it is, is itself a touchstone; it helps to keep the balance of the play and its atmosphere sane. For as he himself had originally put it:

> As the ox hath his bow, sir, the horse his curb, and the falcon her bells, so man hath his desires.[3]

What Dull and Costard supply in *Love's Labour's Lost*, Touchstone gives to *As You Like It*. They, who had not

---

[1] V, iv, 65-85.    [2] II, vii, 39-42.    [3] III, iii, 75-6.

'ate paper as it were' and 'not drunk ink', who were only 'animals, only sensible in the duller parts'; and he, with Audrey upon his arm—'A poor virgin, sir, an ill-favoured thing, sir, but mine own—a poor humour of mine, sir, to take that that no man else will'—contribute the rich, rank, scent of Mother Earth to the synthetic airs of Learning's academe and Love in Arcadia.

The comparison with *Love's Labour's Lost* suggests a reference to the structure of the play and the matter of its stage production.

As I remarked at the beginning of this chapter, *As You Like It* has not often been very successful on the modern stage. And the fault I am convinced is not Shakespeare's but the modern producers'.

Unlike *Ado* and *Twelfth Night*, it does not act itself, i.e. it is without those ludicrous situations, like the scenes in which Malvolio reads Maria's letter or Benedick and Beatrice lurk in the pleached arbour, scenes which are foolproof and cannot fail with an audience, however stupidly put on. But *As You Like It* belongs to the same type of comedy as *Love's Labour's Lost*. It is made up of encounters between opposed points of view and of the talk that results therefrom. In other words it is a pattern play and demands brains in the true performing of it.

Clearly it requires a different technique of production from that employed in *Love's Labour's Lost*, though the two plays have much in common. So much indeed that I often wonder whether *As You Like It*, and not *Ado*, was the *Love's Labour's Won* which Meres mentions in 1598 among Shakespeare's plays though no one since has been able to identify it. Each is a burlesque upon a prevailing affectation and the characters are in many ways strikingly parallel: the exiled Duke and his co-mates are matched by the King and his fellow stoics, Touchstone and Audrey by Costard and Jaquenetta, the melancholy Jaques by the melancholy Armado, Sir Oliver Martext by Sir Nathaniel—even Le Beau by Boyet.

Though far riper in wit and deeper in wisdom than its predecessor, it lacks the mobility, that ballet-like quality which keeps all the characters agog in *Love's Labour's Lost*. The lands of Arcadia and Arden are by their nature calm and leisurely. In a golden world where the denizens fleet time carelessly they do not need that itching of the toes and incessant movement which marks out the inhabitants of sprightly Navarre. There is much sitting and eating and sleeping in *As You Like It*: even the songs are a little melancholy, except 'It was a Lover', and that is sung by pages seated on the ground.

Yet the design is there, to be discovered with a little scrutiny and to be brought out by the discerning producer. There are for example the different types of love—a pattern which runs throughout and is often accompanied by patterned speech. Shakespeare found the conventional lovers of Arcadia in Lodge—the scornful Phoebe and the forlorn Silvius (whom Lodge calls Montanus), but he made much more out of them and uses them skilfully as foils to the genuine passion of Rosalind and Orlando; a third type is, of course, provided by Touchstone and Audrey.

Then again the idealized shepherds and shepherdesses are contrasted with the genuine yokels Audrey and William. And yet again there is much deliberately contrived encounter between characters representing diverse or opposed attitudes of mind. Thus Corin and Touchstone discuss the life of a shepherd: Jaques and Orlando discuss love; Rosalind and Jaques discuss melancholy; and Orlando and Rosalind (disguised as Ganymede) discuss love and marriage and the ways of womankind.

But it is time I came to the heart of the matter and that which keeps the play alive today: in despite of literary fashion gone out of mind and of all the sins of producers, *As You Like It* is much more than an essay in pastoralism and quizzical side glances and comments upon it. It is much more than a lovely poem on the theme of the forest of Arden.

All that has been said so far is but the framework and background to one of the most lifelike and enchanting characters in Shakespeare. And the play can never grow stale to the stage because it is every actress's ambition to play Rosalind, as it is every actor's to play Hamlet.

Rosalind's doublet and hose possess many advantages. They enable her to play the 'boy' as well as the 'lady' of the play; the audience is led to expect 'saucy lackey' talk (III, ii, 293) and she gives it them. They complicate the plot by causing Phoebe to fall in love with her. Above all they give opportunity for entertaining scenes with Orlando in which he woos his lady in pretence and she pretends to mock at love to the man she is deeply in love with.

Yet they also set Shakespeare a serious dramatic problem. For inasmuch as the audience knew that the Rosalind who played the boy was in reality a boy playing a girl pretending to be a boy, it was a doubly difficult task to win from them that willing suspension of disbelief which we call dramatic illusion. It was nevertheless the magnitude of this difficulty, I believe, which gave us the Rosalind the world rejoices in. For in order to plant her womanhood firmly in the minds of the spectators Shakespeare had to show it to them as convincingly and attractively as he could before she reaches Arden and to insist upon it whenever she and Celia are alone in the forest. Thus while Beatrice 'dwindles into a wife' at the end of *Ado*, Rosalind's pride is humbled by love in the very second scene of *As You Like It*, while with the frankness which is one of her endearing traits she is speaking of Orlando as the prospective father of her child in the third (l. 11). It is love at first sight, and the episode, in which everything and yet nothing is said on either side, is managed with exquisite tact. As it should bring Rosalind in all her delicious freshness before my reader's imagination, I will end with it:

CELIA.                    . . . Sir, you have well deserved.
  If you do keep your promises in love

But justly as you have exceeded promise,
Your mistress shall be happy.
ROSALIND (*takes a chain from her neck*). Gentleman,
    Wear this for me . . . one out of suits with fortune,
    That could give more, but that her hand lacks means. . .
    Shall we go, coz? (*She turns and walks away.*)
CELIA (*follows*). Ay; fare you well, fair gentleman.
ORLANDO. Can I not say, 'I thank you'? My better parts
    Are all thrown down, and that which here stands up
    Is but a quintain, a mere lifeless block.
ROSALIND. He calls us back; my pride fell with my fortunes—
    I'll ask him what he would . . . (*She turns again.*) Did you call, sir?
    Sir, you have wrestled well and overthrown
    More than your enemies.
CELIA (*plucks her sleeve*). Will you go, coz?[1]

The heart of either has been humbled to the ground by the other—such is true love at first sight.

*As You Like It* is Shakespeare's Arcadia, his escape-play; it is also Shakespeare's criticism of Arcadia and escape literature. But Rosalind makes it more than either of these: for she is his ideal woman.

Beatrice, I said in my last chapter, was the first woman in our literature who delights to use her brain. Rosalind has brains and a quick wit too; but her more conspicuous qualities are the gallantry and gaiety of her spirits and the clarity of her vision. In Beatrice we may see a foretaste of the late Victorian women of emancipated intelligence whom Meredith loved to depict. In Rosalind we have a prophetic adumbration of the gallant girls of our own time, full of the spirit of adventure, ready to take ship or aeroplane for 'the farthest inch of Asia' at a moment's notice and yet passionately devoted to the service of mankind, in which service they are not at all averse to include that of a particular husband if a suitable one offers.

[1] I, ii, 230–43.

# CHAPTER VIII

★

# *Twelfth Night*

---

ave you ever found a little bird imprisoned in your
room some early spring morning? It has made its
way in through the open window, and puzzled by
the glass has exhausted itself in vain efforts to escape. There
it crouches, with its iridescent wings all a-quiver and its
tiny heart, full of song and gaiety under the free sky, now
panting with terror and faint with exertion. To help it, to
give it life and liberty, song and soaring, once more, you
must take it in your hand, and put it out; and you are then
yourself fearful, lest you should with clumsy fingers crush
its loveliness and mar its delicate perfection. In some such
mood does the critic address himself to the handling of this
most exquisite of all Shakespeare's comedies.

> Our meddling intellect
> Misshapes the beauteous forms of things;
> We murder to dissect.

And yet of course the play—so long as the English tongue is
intelligible to man—lies as far out of reach of injury or
decay as Keats's *Grecian Urn*. It dawns afresh upon every
generation, and remains for ever

> in midst of other woe
> Than ours, a friend to man.

No, *Twelfth Night* has nothing to fear from the critics. It is
those who listen to criticism of it who may suffer loss
through misrepresentation and the consequent distortion of

their vision. But since you, my reader, have this book of criticism in your hand and are presumably preparing to continue it for one more chapter, the risk must be run. For insurance, however, may I beg you to follow this piece of advice? When you come to the end, forget everything I have said, take your copy of *Twelfth Night* down from its shelf, and submit yourself once again to the magic and the music of it. And if then anything come to mind without distaste of what is here said, it may be only a single phrase, my labour will not have been in vain and your time not entirely misspent.

The earliest recorded performance of *Twelfth Night* took place in one of the London colleges of law called the Middle Temple, on February 1602—360 years ago. The association with the Inns of Court is significant, since there are a number of little points in the play which suggest such an audience— an audience of law-students. But, if so, it was probably originally written for one of the other Inns, inasmuch as it clearly followed close upon *As You Like It*, and there are literary and historical clues which point to 1600. Some have supposed that it was first produced in the late autumn of 1599, under the title of *What You Will*, which corresponds with *As You Like It* and *Much Ado about Nothing*; and that it was then given again at court before the Queen on Twelfth Night, 1600.

As there is nothing about Twelfth Night in the play, the title seems to have been derived from the fact that it was performed on that day—the greatest feast-day in the year in London, the culmination of the Christmas festivities. We may suppose that it had to be renamed because it would have been hardly polite to present a play at Court with an off-hand label like 'What You Will'. Yet, though the actual feast is not mentioned in the text, the play is pre-eminently one for a feast of some kind. It is full of merriment and high jinks, to say nothing of the drinking-scenes, while the spirit of the whole is embodied in the Fool, whose name Feste is the contemporary French for 'fête'.

The text, too, though unusually straightforward for a Shakespearian play, shows some signs of slight revision, as if it had had to be adapted for different occasions. The most striking of these is one which suggests that originally the songs in the play were sung, not by Feste as now, but by Viola. She tells the Captain in the second scene:

> I'll serve this duke [i.e. Orsino].
> Thou shalt present me as an eunuch to him.
> It may be worth thy pains; for I can sing
> And speak to him in many sorts of music. (ll. 54 ff.)

While at the opening of II, iv, we actually find Orsino bidding Cesario (i.e. Viola) to sing

> That old and antic song we heard last night—

though the song is sung by Feste immediately after, and though Feste does not belong to Orsino's household at all, but Olivia's. At first sight it looks as if the voice of the boy who took Viola had become 'cracked i'th'ring' since the play was originally put on, and that Armin who took Feste had to step into the breach. But Armin, who as Sir Andrew declares, 'has an excellent breast', sings 'O, mistress mine' in II, iii, which can never at any stage of the play's evolution have fallen to Viola's part, and that suggests revision to take advantage of his singing powers, the quality of which had not seemingly been realized when he played Touchstone, since the only singing the Fool is given in *As You Like It* is his part with the two boys in 'It was a lover and his lass'.[1]

Apart from all this, *Twelfth Night* like *As You Like It* casts back to Shakespeare's early plays and has points of affinity both with *The Comedy of Errors* and with *The Two Gentlemen of Verona*. We find outselves in Illyria, once again by the shores of the Mediterranean, the sea of Plautus and

[1] See C. J. Sisson, *New Readings in Shakespeare* (1956), i, 188–91, for a topical interpretation of 'The Lady of the Strachy', etc. (II, v, 39 f.) which, if it became accepted, would imply a revision, or at least an interpolation, later than 1616, the year of Shakespeare's death. An astonishing reflection on the text of the First Folio, to say the least of it.

# Twelfth Night

Terence, of Ariosto and Grazzini,[1] and though there are no actual merchants in the play, we have a couple of sea-captains, one of them a 'notable pirate', while (as in *Errors*) a wreck separates twin children, this time boy and girl, whose presence in the play, unknown to each other, leads to much confusion. Even details, e.g. that one of the twins is tied to a mast, are the same, while Sebastian, like Antipholus of Syracuse, sees the sights of the town upon arrival and names as his rendezvous an inn, in *Errors* 'the Centaur where we host', in *Twelfth Night* 'the Elephant' (is this the modern Elephant and Castle?) 'in the south suburbs'.

On the other hand, *Twelfth Night* has much in common with *The Two Gentlemen*. In both a forlorn lady, disguised as a page, serves the man she loves in the courtship of another woman; and in both the lady finds her rival falling in love with herself. Here, however, Shakespeare is doing more than merely repeating himself; he is again drawing upon a common source for both plays, viz. the story of Felix and Felismena, told in Jorge de Montemayor's *Diana*. Furthermore, the love-sick Orsino belongs wholly to the romantic tradition, while the devotion of Antonio, the sea-captain, for Sebastian recalls that of Valentine for Proteus in *The Two Gentlemen* and of Antonio, the merchant of Venice, for his Bassanio. Again, while Olivia is a very different character from Portia, her household has some correspondence with that at Belmont. So much for the texture of the canvas upon which Shakespeare painted. What matters to us now is the completed picture.

Notice first of all then to what rich and delicate ends he here turns the device of disguise originally used in *The Two Gentlemen* but repeated with variations in every comedy since then. Like the heroine of *As You Like It*, the heroine of *Twelfth Night* is dressed as a girl in the second scene, but becomes a boy for the rest of the play. Yet Viola makes a very different boy from Rosalind; there is nothing of the 'saucey lackey' about her; she never even assumes the

[1] See Bond, *Early Plays from the Italian* (1911), pp. xix-xxvi.

swagger of the man except in the scuffle with Maria in the first interview with Olivia. On the contrary, the whole charm of the part is the gentle girlhood that breathes behind the male doublet. And if there be any who, with Meredith, tend to despise Shakespeare's 'incredible imbroglio', let them imagine *Twelfth Night* without disguise and ask how Shakespeare could have got his effects in any other way. The scenes between Viola and Orsino (II, iv, 80–124) and between Viola and Olivia (I, v, 222–98; III, i, 94–166), depend entirely upon the disguise, and they are the subtlest and loveliest scenes in the play. Their emotional quality, as of fine-spun silk, is shot with cross-lights and shifting colour. The Duke, sick with hopeless passion for Olivia, discussing Love with the disguised Viola, sick with passion for him,[1] compose a situation in which tenderness, beauty and 'the slim feasting smile' of the comic muse are perfectly blended.

One passage to remind the reader of it. The Duke sends Cesario a second time to urge his suit with Olivia:

VIOLA. But if she cannot love you, sir?
DUKE. I cannot be so answered.
VIOLA.                    Sooth, but you must.
    Say that some lady, as perhaps there is,
    Hath for your love as great a pang of heart
    As you have for Olivia: you cannot love her;
    You tell her so; must she not then be answered?
DUKE. There is no woman's sides
    Can bide the beating of so strong a passion
    As love doth give my heart; no woman's heart
    So big, to hold so much; they lack retention.
    Alas, their love may be called appetite—
    No motion of the liver, but the palate—
    That suffers surfeit, cloyment and revolt;
    But mine is all as hungry as the sea,
    And can digest as much. Make no compare
    Between that love a woman can bear me
    And that I owe Olivia.
VIOLA.                    Ay, but I know—

[1] In the passionate service of Pyrocles by Zelmane disguised as a page Sidney gave Shakespeare a hint for this in *Arcadia*, 1590, Lib. 2, pp. 290 ff.

DUKE. What dost thou know?
VIOLA. Too well what love women to men may owe:
  In faith they are as true of heart as we.
  My father had a daughter loved a man,
  As it might be, perhaps, were I a woman,
  I should your lordship.
DUKE.             And what's her history?
VIOLA. A blank, my lord: she never told her love,
  But let concealment like a worm i' th'bud
  Feed on her damask cheek; she pined in thought,
  And with a green and yellow melancholy
  She sat like Patience on a monument,
  Smiling at grief. Was not this love, indeed?
  We men may say more, swear more—but indeed
  Our shows are more than will; for still we prove
  Much in our vows, but little in our love.
DUKE. But died thy sister of her love, my boy?
VIOLA. I am all the daughters of my father's house,
  And all the brothers too . . . and yet I know not . . .
  Sir, shall I to this lady?
DUKE (*starts and rouses*). Ay, that's the theme.
  To her in haste; give her this jewel; say,
  My love can give no place, bide no delay. (*They go*.[1]

Scarcely less poignantly humorous are the scenes in which Olivia, courted for Orsino by Viola, falls in love with the messenger. And both situations have the same root—the contrast between Love and Fancy—Love, genuine, tender and appealing, embodied in the wistful figure of the slender Cesario—and Fancy in the persons of Orsino, the melancholy egoist, and Olivia, the wilful recluse.

    Tell me where is Fancy bred,
    Or in the heart or in the head?
    How begot, how nourishéd?
        Reply, reply.
    It is engend'red in the eyes,
    With gazing fed; and Fancy dies
    In the cradle where it lies.
        Let us all ring Fancy's knell:
        I'll begin it,—Ding, dong, bell.

[1] II, iv, 87–124.

Such we found was Shakespeare's comment upon Sentimentalism (a word not then invented) in *The Merchant of Venice*. In *Twelfth Night* he devotes a whole play to the subject.

Orsino is the sentimentalist in love with Love. He has steeped himself, we may imagine, in Petrarch; he prefers worshipping at a distance, and wooing by proxy; he likes to stab himself with the thought of the cruelty of his adored. It is not Olivia's person he desires—he readily makes shift with Viola at the end, when Olivia proves to be the bride of another. It is the dream of her that fills him with melancholy satisfaction. Viola will make him a good wife, because she wants *him* and is the soul of loyalty and devotion. But will he make her a good husband? It is significant that in his last words he hails her as

> Orsino's mistress and his *fancy*'s queen.

She is Laura still, as Olivia had been. But can one marry Laura and retain the Fancy? Your sentimentalist is seldom contented with

> A creature not too bright and good
> For human nature's daily food.

The opening scene of the play gives us, indeed, all we need to know about Orsino.

> If music be the food of love, play on,
> Give me excess of it; that, surfeiting,
> The appetite may sicken and so die . . .
> That strain again! it had a dying fall;
> O, it came o'er my ear like the sweet south[1]
> That breathes upon a bank of violets;
> Stealing and giving odour. [*music*] Enough, no more!
> 'Tis not so sweet now as it was before.
> O spirit of love, how quick and fresh art thou,
> That, notwithstanding thy capacity
> Receiveth as the sea, nought enters there,

---

[1] Pope's emendation of F 'sound'; Steevens cites *Arcadia*, 1590, Lib. i, p. 7. 'Her breath is more sweet than a gentle south-west wind which comes creeping over flowrie fieldes . . . in the extreeme heate of summer.' This renders Pope's 'south' almost certain.

Of what validity and pitch soe'er,
But falls into abatement and low price,
Even in a minute . . . So full of shapes is fancy,
That it alone is high fantastical. (ll. 1–15.)

Lovely lines—one of the loveliest openings in all Shakespeare's plays. Yet the loveliness must not be allowed to
hide the meaning from us, which has been almost universally misunderstood. Orsino is generally supposed to be
wishing that his love may die of a surfeit and so cease to
trouble him. But this, as a matter of fact, is the last thing
he would desire. He is acclaiming the tyranny of love,
which accepts all offerings but at the same time makes them
seem worthless. He does not value music for itself but as the
temporary food for his love, which is 'all as hungry as the
sea, And can digest as much'.[1] He has to keep feeding Love,
as best he can; and when Love's appetite for this or that
dies, he must turn to something else, as indeed he does in
the last words of the scene, which concludes:

Away before me to sweet beds of flowers—
Love-thoughts lie rich when canopied with bowers.

His constancy is but the excuse for a variety of emotional
self-indulgence. For, as Feste exclaims upon him, 'Now, the
melancholy god protect thee, and the tailor make thy
doublet of changeable taffeta, for thy mind is a very opal.'[2]
He is the epicurean lover, ever seeking, not the satisfaction
of his desires, but their perpetuation. Olivia, Viola, womankind in general, are a means not an end. They exist, not as
objects to be attained, but as stimulants, stimulants which
induce that intoxicating mood of yearning, melancholy and
despair in which his spirit delights.

Orsino's is the lover's melancholy; Jaques despises love,
and has a melancholy of his own 'compounded of many
simples'. Yet they are variant specimens of the same breed;
and their affinity comes out best in their attitude towards
music. For Orsino like Jaques can 'suck melancholy out of a
song as a weasel sucks eggs'.

[1] II, iv, 100–1.    [2] II, iv, 73 ff.

Orsino and Jaques are two studies in sentimentalism. And Olivia is another. True, she has lost father and brother, both deeply beloved, within a twelve-month. But she cannot 'let the dead bury their dead', and decides, like Victoria, the Widow of Windsor, to feed upon her sorrow. We are told:

> The element itself, till seven years hence,
> Shall not behold her face at ample view;
> But like a cloistress she will veiléd walk,
> And water once a day her chamber round
> With eye-offending brine; all this to season
> A brother's dead love, which she would keep fresh
> And lasting, in her sad remembrance.[1]

It is an attitude which Orsino, of course, much admires, even while he complains of her cruelty towards himself. It takes the Fool to tell her the rude truth:

CLOWN. Good madonna, give me leave to prove you a fool.
OLIVIA. Can you do it?
CLOWN. Dexteriously, good madonna.
OLIVIA. Make your proof.
CLOWN. I must catechize you for it, madonna. Good my mouse of virtue, answer me.
OLIVIA. Well, sir, for want of other idleness, I'll bide your proof.
CLOWN. Good madonna, why mourn'st thou?
OLIVIA. Good fool, for my brother's death.
CLOWN. I think his soul is in hell, madonna.
OLIVIA. I know his soul is in heaven, fool.
CLOWN. The more fool, madonna, to mourn for your brother's soul, being in heaven . . . Take away the fool, gentlemen![2]

Olivia is a gentler Constance, to whom King Philip shrewdly remarks, after one of her outbursts of sorrow for Prince Arthur,

> You are as fond of grief as of your child.

Olivia is as fond of grief as of her brother, and in her extravagant vow of seven years' seclusion, and her abjuring 'the company and sight of men', she reminds us of the students in *Love's Labour's Lost*, who vow to observe a three years' seclusion in their little academe from the society of women.

[1] I, i, 25–31.      [2] I, v, 55–70.

Such vows, with which men bind themselves in their self-conceit, and in defiance of nature, cannot last, and hers endures no longer than theirs. No sooner does a young man (as she takes Viola to be) appear before her than she falls head over ears in love, and it is with delicate irony that Shakespeare makes her plight her troth with Viola's twin in the very chantry that she had erected to her brother's memory—a point, I think, usually overlooked by readers and spectators. Another subtle point, often likewise overlooked, is that, as Malvolio informs us, Olivia's seal is an intaglio of Lucrece, the classical type of chastity. Clearly, she had elaborated her dedicated life into a system.

These two sentimentalists, the opal-minded lover of Love and the cypress-clad lover of Sorrow, make, as it were, the poles of the Illyrian world. They sit apart, he in his palace, she in hers, each in an isolation exquisitely ridiculous—and Viola passes from one to the other. Viola acts as foil to both, and as touchstone to their unrealities. For Viola, like Rosalind, carries fresh air with her wherever she goes; she is compact of sweetness and common sense; and when she loves, she loves flesh and blood. Thus true Love, hiding herself behind her disguise, and eating her heart out in simple humility of spirit, links the houses of the two Fancymongers. It is a pretty pattern.

But there's more in it even than that. There is Malvolio, the chief character in the underplot, or anti-masque; the comic underplot which reflects in a kind of distorting mirror the emotional situation of the main plot. For Malvolio is a dreamer, after his kind; like Orsino he aspires for the hand of Olivia; and like both Orsino and Olivia he mistakes dreams for realities. When Maria tells Sir Toby that 'he has been yonder i' the sun practising behaviour to his own shadow',[1] she goes near to the heart of this shadow-dance of a play—Orsino, Olivia and Malvolio all, in different fashion, practise behaviour to their own shadows. And when Olivia[2] tells Malvolio that he is 'sick of self-love', she

[1] II, v, 17–18.  [2] I, v, 88.

puts her finger on one of the roots of her own sickness and
of Orsino's. They are all three egoists, though they wear
their egoism with a difference.

The Elizabethans would have called them three melan-
cholics. The melancholy of Malvolio is a fantastic ambition.
He is not, of course, in love with Olivia. He dreams of
becoming her husband, as a means of becoming the lord
of her house; and his distempered imagination is constantly
presenting him with visions of himself in that exalted position. 'Having been three months married to her', he muses
in the garden,

> sitting in my state, calling my officers about me, in my branched
> velvet gown; having come from a day-bed, where I have left Olivia
> sleeping. And then to have the humour of state: and after a demure
> travel of regard, telling them I know my place, as I would they
> should do theirs, to ask for my kinsman Toby. Seven of my people,
> with an obedient start, make out for him: I frown the while, and
> perchance wind up my watch, or play with my [*touches his steward's
> chain an instant, and then starts*] some rich jewel.[1]

Differences of rank meant so much to the men of that
time—so incalculably much more than they do to us—that
the dreams of Malvolio would have seemed to them preposterous to a degree which we are unable to appreciate.
And in a play by anyone but Shakespeare he would appear
to a twentieth-century audience a rather stupid butt, upon
which an amusing practical joke is played by Maria, and
that is all. But in Shakespeare's hands his dream blossoms
into a monstrous beauty, expressed in all the magnificent
magniloquence of post-Falstaffian prose, a beauty which
rivals in its fashion that of Shylock's rhetoric or even
Falstaff's itself. As with Shylock, so with Malvolio: Shakespeare let himself go, to the risk of wrenching the drama
out of frame.

Malvolio is the most interesting—I was going to say, the
largest-souled—character in the play. Lytton Strachey's

[1] II, v, 44–61. The stage direction, surely right, was suggested by Brinsley
Nicholson.

earliest, and I think his best, book—the masterly little *Land-marks in French Literature*—contains a comparison between the characters of Malvolio and Tartuffe which is worth quoting in this connexion:

> The narrowed and selective nature of Molière's treatment of charac-ter presents an illuminating contrast when compared with the elaborately detailed method of such a master of the romantic style as Shakespeare. The English dramatist shows his persons to us in the round; innumerable facets flash out quality after quality; the subtlest and most elusive shades of temperament are indicated; until at last the whole being takes shape before us, endowed with what seems to be the very complexity and mystery of life itself. Entirely different is the great Frenchman's way. Instead of expanding, he deliberately narrows his view; he seizes upon two or three salient qualities in a character and then uses all his art to impress them indelibly upon our minds. His Harpagon is a miser, and he is old—and that is all we know about him: how singularly limited a presentment, compared with that of Shakespeare's bitter, proud, avaricious, and almost pathetic Jew! Tartuffe, perhaps the greatest of all Molière's charac-ters, presents a less complex figure even than such a slight sketch as Shakespeare's Malvolio. Who would have foreseen Malvolio's ex-quisitely preposterous address to Jove? In Tartuffe there are no such surprises; he displays three qualities, and three only—religious hypo-crisy, lasciviousness, and the love of power; and there is not a word he utters which is not impregnated with one or all of these. . . .
>
> His [Molière's] method is narrow, but it is deep. He rushes to the essentials of a human being—tears out his vitals, as it were—and, with a few repeated master-strokes, transfixes the naked soul. . . . Nor is it only by its vividness that his portraiture excels. At its best it rises into the region of sublimity, giving us new visions of the grandeur to which the human spirit can attain.[1]

I have quoted this much, not only because I think Strachey's distinction between the methods of Shakespeare and Molière both useful and penetrating, but also because I consider that, different as their methods are, Shakespeare and Molière achieve similar results in their creation of Malvolio and Tartuffe. Both characters, however we may laugh at the one's absurdity and detest the other's vices, raise us ʻinto

[1] Lytton Strachey, *Landmarks in French Literature* (Home University Library). pp. 82–4.

the region of sublimity'. And just because this is so, some readers and spectators find the treatment meted out to Malvolio in the dark-house scenes intolerable.

There is no evidence that Shakespeare himself felt any tenderness for Malvolio, as he obviously did for some of his other fantastics, e.g. for Mistress Quickly or Master Slender, for Armado or even the odious Parolles. The character is drawn as coldly and as objectively as that of Holofernes, or as that of Jaques, with which as a matter of fact Malvolio has some affinity.

The letter-scene in the garden is a thing of sheer delight, and Malvolio's behaviour is so 'exquisitely preposterous' that our laughter goes wholly against him. But when we come to the mad scene, we begin to feel that the jest has been 'refined even to pain', and our sympathies veer towards the victim, despite the excellent fooling of Feste with his two voices. Here we must recollect that madness has long ceased to be comic to us, as it was to the Elizabethans, who flocked to Bedlam for amusement as Londoners now flock to the monkey-house at the Zoo. But this does not excuse Shakespeare, if excuse be needed.

It is more to the point to stress the significance of Malvolio's appearance in the final scene. There he is allowed to say his say in his own defence in a letter to his mistress and an indignant speech, both couched in language of great dignity, without a touch of cringing or a false note of any kind, so that we feel that, awaked from his dream, he is after all a man of spirit and self-respect. But his thirst for revenge somewhat alienates us again.

Moreover Olivia knows him well, and values him as an admirable steward; had, indeed, declared when she thinks he is really mad, 'I would not have him miscarry for the half of my dowry.' Once the whole plot against him has been exposed, she pities him and implicitly condemns the jest as a sorry one. 'Alas, poor fool! how have they baffled thee' bursts from her lips at the end of Fabian's explanation, while after Malvolio's exit she declares, 'He hath been most notoriously abused.' These words, coming as they do at the very end of the play, prove I think that Shakespeare intended us to realize that Malvolio had a case, and that while he has himself no affection for him, he acknowledges that less than justice had been meted out to him.

To speak dramatically, having made excellent use of him as the butt for his comic scene in the garden, he later deliberately adjusted the balance of our sympathies in his favour.[1] There are some to whom a dramatic issue left indecisive is anathema; they think Shakespeare must take sides, must exhibit his sympathy with this character or that, with this attitude or that. If so—surely, the less dramatist he! As we saw in Chapter V, Shakespeare takes sides neither for nor against Shylock, he shows us the issue, forces us indeed to contemplate it in all its hideous reality and its apparently hopeless irreconcilability, and leaves it at that. So, in a less intense degree, with Malvolio. For the Malvolio-Sir Toby antithesis stands for a great human issue scarcely less significant than that which concerns Shylock and Antonio. 'Marry, sir', declares Maria to Sir Toby, 'sometimes he is a kind of puritan.' And though she goes on to say, 'The devil a puritan that he is, or anything constantly but a time-pleaser, an affectioned ass'[2], Shakespeare has dropped his hint, which is supported by Fabian's hint later that Malvolio is an opponent of bear-baiting (a sport against which the puritans, all honour to them for it, waged a constant war).[3] Malvolio is not a typical puritan—that was Ben Jonson's way, not Shakespeare's. But he is somewhat of that way of thinking: and he quite obviously stands for order and sobriety in the commonwealth of Olivia's household.

Further, he has the defects of his qualities, the defects that so often afflict the puritan, the revolutionary, the social

[1] It is of course a great part for an actor and Professor Alexander reminds us that Charles Lamb 'could never see Bensley play that character without feeling in it a tragic dignity'. (See *Elia*, 1823, 'On Some of the Old Actors', and Alexander, *Shakespeare's Life and Art*, pp. 64-5.)

[2] II, iii, 146, 153-4.

[3] Cf. Slender's attitude in *The Merry Wives*, I, i, 273-4, and above p. 85.

reformer: viz., absence of humour, intolerance of the innocent pleasures of life, and belief that order, seemliness, and
respectability are the greatest things, if not the only things,
that matter; and, together with all this, a firm conviction
that he, Malvolio, is the true representative of order, the
heaven-directed censor and corrector of the morals and
habits of other people. Not all this, perhaps, is explicit in
the text; but it is all, I think, implied. Certainly, the famous
and unexpected cry of 'Jove, I thank thee!' after the perusal
of the supposed letter from Olivia, suggests just that in-
timacy with the Almighty which persons of his serene self-
assurance are wont to assume.

On the other hand, while Sir Toby is hardly the typical
cavalier, he too, quite obviously, shares the cavalier attitude
towards life, or, shall we say, the somewhat disreputable
side of it, a closer kinsman indeed of Falstaff's than the Sir
John of that family in *The Merry Wives of Windsor*. He is
'sure care's an enemy to life'; he hates 'a false conclusion . . .
as an unfilled can':[1] with him it is always too late to go to
bed at night, and never too early to get drunk in the morning. Yet he has the ruins of gentry about him, together with
the dregs of learning. He speaks Spanish (or is it Italian?) on
one occasion,[2] French on another, and Latin on a third[3]; he
knows more about contemporary physiology than most
modern editors; he talks theology in his cups; and is prepared to discuss 'philosophy' i.e. science, when there is no
drink at hand to discuss.[4] And his boon companions, the
foolish Sir Andrew Aguecheek, and the wiser Feste, together
with Fabian—all enemies of Malvolio—are of the party of
Misrule also. The 'thin-faced'[5] Sir Andrew, is cousin-german
to Slender of *The Merry Wives* and was doubtless played by
the same actor; but he has little of Slender's attractiveness.

---

[1] I, iii, 2–3; II, iii, 7–8.
[2] I, iii, 43, 'Castiliano vulgo' for which Henry Thomas conjectured (T.L.S.,
4/6/33), 'Castiglione voglio' = 'I want some Castiglione', a costly wine,
alternatively known as Lacrima Christi.
[3] II, iii, 3.                    [4] See note on II, iii, 11 in my edition.
[5] V, i, 206.

Fabian calls him Sir Toby's 'manakin' (III, ii, 52), and the name fits excellently, since the knight manipulates him like a puppet. He evidently too delights in his sheer fatuity, though he delights still more in the 'three thousand ducats a year' (I, iii, 22) which he does his best to help him spend. Dramatically, Sir Andrew and Sir Toby are linked together like Siamese twins.

Very different is Feste, the subtlest of all Shakespeare's Fools, about whom I shall have more to say in a minute. Here, I would only note that the scenes involving the Fool and Sir Toby to some extent reflect the old medieval custom of appointing a Lord of Misrule, who was responsible for the revels between Christmas and Twelfth Night at court and other places. Sir Toby is clearly the Lord of Misrule in Olivia's household, and Feste, as I have said above, stands as it were for the very spirit of Christmas revelry. Now the great enemy of all these old customs and festivals, which they were doing their best to suppress throughout the land, were of course the puritans. It is therefore no accident that Shakespeare gives to Sir Toby and Feste the immortal, unanswerable, retort to Malvolio and his kind:

SIR TOBY. Dost thou think because thou art virtuous, there shall be no more cakes and ale?
FESTE. Yes, by Saint Anne, and ginger shall be hot i' th'mouth too.[1]

In the clash between the precise steward and the caterwauling kinsman, you have the puritan-cavalier issue in little, the issue which was beginning to divide England during Shakespeare's lifetime, which led to civil war shortly after his death, and which is even yet undecided. I am not claiming that Shakespeare is also among the prophets, still less that he deliberately set out to illustrate a thesis in his Toby-Malvolio scenes; only that, having a riotous knight and an orderly-minded steward upon his hands, the dramatic conflict between them quite naturally took a form which illustrated the prevailing tendencies of the time. In other words

[1] II, iii, 120–4.

the super-sensitive imagination of a supreme dramatic artist so penetrates to the root of an issue presented to him by his plot that his exposition of it, without his being perhaps in the least conscious of the fact, becomes a comment upon the main problem of his age.

Such things are not unparalleled in modern literature. In the novels of Dostoevsky, for example, you may catch glimpses of the spiritual development of Russia and of Europe for half a century after they were written. In particular, *The Possessed* foreshadows in unmistakable terms the Bolshevik revolution which did not take place for another fifty years.

But it is a little ridiculous to speak of Dostoevsky in relation to *Twelfth Night*. We must not take Malvolio too seriously; for assuredly Shakespeare did not. He is only part of the dramatic composition, the total effect of which is one of gaiety and high festival.

How much, for example, does music mean in this play? More, curiously, than in *As You Like It*, which has twice as many songs. It begins

> If music be the food of love, play on,

and ends with

> When that I was and a little tiny boy,
>  With hey, ho, the wind and the rain;
> A foolish thing was but a toy,
>  For the rain it raineth every day,

while between them lie two of Shakespeare's loveliest songs:

> O, mistress mine, where are you roaming? (II, iii, 41 ff.)

and

> Come away, come away death. (II, iv, 51 ff.)

The music as constantly accompanies Orsino, as the kettle-drums do Claudius in *Hamlet*. And there is all the music of Shakespeare's verse, at its ripest and sweetest, at the turn of the tide between his comedies and his tragedies.

And to the music Feste contributes more than any other character. For 'the Fool has an excellent breast' (II, iii, 21 f.), and though rightly a member of Olivia's household, must be borrowed by Orsino for the supply of his music. He is also, to use a good Elizabethan term, well-languaged. To recall a few of his sayings:

> Foolery does walk about the orb like the sun, it shines everywhere. (III, i, 38 f.)
> A sentence is but a cheveril glove to a good wit—how quickly the wrong side may be turned outward! (III, i, 11–13.)
> No indeed, sir, the Lady Olivia has no folly. She will keep no fool, sir, till she be married, and fools are as like husbands as pilchards are to herrings—the husband's the bigger. I am, indeed not her fool, but her corrupter of words. (III, i, 32–6.)
> 1 am afraid this great lubber, the world, will prove a cockney. (IV, i, 13 f.)
> And thus the whirligig of time brings in his revenges. (V, i, 375 f.)

But perhaps he is most brilliant in the conversation he holds as Sir Topas the curate with the much-abused Malvolio in the dark-house. For a brief extract:

FESTE. Say'st thou that house is dark?

MALVOLIO. As hell, Sir Topas.

FESTE. Why, it hath bay windows transparent as barricadoes, and the clerestories toward the south-north are as lustrous as ebony; and yet complainest thou of obstruction?

MALVOLIO. I am not mad, Sir Topas. I say to you, this house is dark.

FESTE. Madman, thou errest. I say, there is no darkness but ignorance, in which thou art more puzzled than the Egyptians in their fog.

MALVOLIO. I say, this house is as dark as ignorance, though ignorance were as dark as hell; and I say, there was never man thus abused. I am no more mad than you are—make the trial of it in any constant question.

FESTE. What is the opinion of Pythagoras concerning wild fowl?

MALVOLIO. That the soul of our grandam might haply inhabit a bird.

FESTE. What think'st thou of his opinion?

MALVOLIO. I think nobly of his soul, and no way approve his opinion.

FESTE. Fare thee well: remain thou still in darkness. Thou shalt hold th'opinion of Pythagoras ere I will allow of thy wits, and fear to kill a woodcock, lest thou dispossess the soul of thy grandam. Fare thee well.[1]

[1] IV, ii, 35–61.

Besides the music and the merriment which the Fool provides, the play has much excellent entertainment. As well as the delicately ironical scenes, full of lovely poetry, in which Viola confronts first Orsino and then Olivia, there are the scenes, less subtle, but no less entertaining to the groundlings—far more entertaining indeed—namely the drinking-scene, the scene in which Malvolio is gulled with the forged letter, the scene where he appears before Olivia in yellow stockings, the mock-duel between Aguecheek and the disguised Viola, and the scene with Malvolio in the dark house, from which I have just quoted—five scenes of first-rate fun, any one of which might have made the fortunes of the play with the general public.

Mirth and music, laughter and love—love tender and true with an adorable girl to represent it and love high fantastical in three distinct kinds—and all this so cunningly woven into the seamless robe of drama and so craftily dyed in the shifting colours of emotion as to defy analysis—it was a fitting play to celebrate Shakespeare's farewell to happy comedy.

When he came to the making of *Twelfth Night* he had nine comedies to his credit, to say nothing of the comic scenes and characters in *Romeo* and the Falstaff scenes in *Henry IV*; which means that by that time he possessed, at the back of his mind and ready to his hand, a heterogeneous collection of dramatic types, devices and characters, classical, medieval and Italo-Renaissance, which he could combine and recombine into an almost infinite variety of patterns.

All this, fused and transmuted in the crucible of his dramatic and poetic imagination, in the fullness of time produced that gem of his comic art, that condensation of life and (for those who know how to taste of it rightly) elixir of life—*Twelfth Night*. He could never better this—and he never attempted to. He broke the mould—and passed on!

Looking back over the road we have traversed, let us note in conclusion one or two of the general characteristics of

Shakespeare the dramatist that have emerged from this study of the Happy Comedies. First of all is his delight in experiment, in trying out new dramatic forms, new stage patterns, new methods of character-construction, new poetry and new prose. This love of experiment is evident from the very outset. We saw that his early plays, though very varied in shape, conformed individually more rigidly to type than those which came later. *Errors* is almost purely classical comedy: *Two Gentlemen* more purely romantic than any of its successors; *A Midsummer Night's Dream*, still to be considered, at once a fairy play the like of which he did not repeat, and a study in woodland atmosphere; *Love's Labour's Lost* a play of wit and a stage masterpiece of movement and colour. Such were the proto-patterns which are found in part and in varying combinations in almost every one of the later comedies, though always with some new pattern added.

Secondly, though he was ready to borrow from any source that came to his hand, so that like the melancholy of Jaques, his comedies are 'compounded of many simples, extracted from many objects', one thing he always refused to do—he would not be tied to a system. He sat loose to his own theories, if he had any, and put aside those of others. In the course of his development as a writer of happy comedies he encountered at least two theorists: Marlowe at the outset and Ben Jonson towards the end. Marlowe poured scorn upon 'such conceits as clownage keeps in pay'—and Shakespeare made the clown which Marlowe rejected the headstone of his corner. Ben Jonson turned disdainfully aside from the Italian romantic comedy—Shakespeare replied by composing *Much Ado*, *As You Like It*, and *Twelfth Night*.

Yet though he had no system and seemed to live from hand to mouth in the construction of his plays, it is possible to trace definite tendencies in his development as a comic dramatist and a definite ripening of his art as he proceeded.

Let me mention five among others, without going into particulars:

(1) more skilful management of plot;

(2) greater command of character, together with an increasing diversity of types; in the early comedies before *The Merchant* the characters which seem to be most alive are the clowns and the rudesbies like Petruchio, Antipholus of Ephesus, and Berowne, namely those specially fitted to Kempe and Burbadge;

(3) a neater adjustment of character to plot;

(4) an increasing delight in the creation of atmosphere;

(5) lastly, we may note too his progress in the use of the critical elements of comedy. In my first chapter I distinguished Shakespearian comedy from the comedy of Jonson and later comic writers, as human and poetic as contrasted with critical. We have seen, however, that his comedy does not entirely lack critical elements. But they are always implicit and indirect rather than emphatic and forthright as in Ben Jonson. One never feels he is trying to teach, only that he derives ever keener amusement in contemplating the absurdities of the average human being. Indeed, it is always possible to watch and enjoy Shakespeare's comedies without noticing the critical aspects at all. And that was clearly what he intended. He wrote for two publics and mirrored life in his plays on two planes as it were: the surface plane of sheer entertainment, and a criticism of life below the surface for his own satisfaction and for the delight of the 'judicious' among his audience. There is something deeper too. Beneath that inexhaustible spring of geniality and fun, that prodigality of entertaining word-music, that tender and humorous observation of human frailty, that irresistible gusto and delight in every manifestation of life which we call Shakespearian comedy, we may hear, if we attune our ears, the still sad music of humanity. As I said in my first chapter, the tragic Shakespeare is implicit in the comic Shakespeare from the beginning. And after *Twelfth Night* the greatest spirit which ever spoke our tongue turned from the sunlit side of the garden to the other. He had enjoyed life, as few have ever enjoyed it, for ten years; he now set himself to face it.

# CHAPTER IX: A POSTSCRIPT (1961)

# *Variations on the theme of A Midsummer Night's Dream*

---

As stated in the Preface, when drafting in 1937–8 the lectures which form the basis of this book, I omitted *A Midsummer Night's Dream* and *The Taming of the Shrew* for two reasons: (i) that I could not feel sure that either of them was wholly Shakespearian; and (ii) that the course at Liverpool did not allow room for me to deal adequately with more than eight out of the ten Happy Comedies. Except for some general observations on it in Chapter II, I am still leaving *The Taming of the Shrew* out in the cold, partly because I have never myself been able to warm up to it. But *A Midsummer Night's Dream* has always been one of my favourite plays—as whose is it not? If not the loveliest, it is certainly the happiest, of all the Happy Comedies—which a wedding play should be. To have sent this book, then, out into the world without even a bow to Titania and Bottom would have given it a lame entrance indeed.

Moreover, I had already made a preliminary study of *A Midsummer Night's Dream* before these lectures were undertaken at all, in the form of a textual note that appeared in the New Cambridge edition of 1924; and stimulated by Walter de la Mare's adoption and development twelve years later of my disintegrating theories, I made his essay (as I mentioned on page 13) the subject of a contribution to his

Seventy-fifth Birthday Book, published in 1948. At the same time I went on to suggest *The Golden Ass* of Apuleius as an ultimate source of the play. A reprint of that contribution forms Section III of what follows, and I have added now two earlier sections dealing with the play as a whole and in particular with the meaning of Oberon's vision and the tribute to Elizabeth in Act II, Scene 1, which in turn has led on to a discussion of the noble weddings at which *The Dream* may have been performed.

## I. THE PLAY

The play has been justly praised for its ingenuity. It consists in fact of four plots so cleverly intertwined that the working of each is necessary for the working of the others, the cusp, if I may so call it, at which the lines of the tracery meet being Cupid's little magic flower. What is technically the main or central plot is provided by the Lovers who form the usual quartet that we find at the centre of most of the Happy Comedies: two men and two women at cross purposes, Lysander and Hermia being the true-loves, Demetrius the unfaithful man and Helena the forlorn lady. Here however the imbroglio that holds up the happy ending is the result not of confused identity arising from a family resemblance or an assumed disguise, but of supernatural intervention by Puck, who brings it about by the mistaken application of Cupid's flower and in the end resolves it by means of its antidote, Dian's bud. This pivot of the lovers' plot is pivot also of the Fairies', since it is to punish Titania that Oberon sends for Cupid's flower in the first place. Further the plot of the Mechanicals turns on it as well; for it is by dropping the magic juice into her eyes that Oberon causes the fairy queen to fall in love with Bottom, while the plot of Bottom and his fellow mechanicals is linked with the plot that envelops the whole play, the marriage of Duke Theseus, since they meet in the wood to prepare for that marriage. Finally, the marriage itself is doubly linked with the Lovers' plot, first by the Duke's command to Hermia to conform to her fath er'swill and consent to marry Demetrius within the next four days; and secondly by the Lovers, now sorted out, being married themselves at the same time as the Duke. Thus the plot mechanism has a circular as well as a transverse motion.[1] No plot by Ben Jonson is more cunning, and more successfully concealed; for all that the audience is aware of is the inevitable sequence of the events it produces. But while Jonson's plots work towards the confounding or exposure of his chief characters, Shakespeare's find their consummation in happiness. And none of his comic consummations is neater or happier than this. For with supernatural characters at his disposal Shakespeare can make them intervene at any point he chooses. And he is able as well to bring the Fairies back at the end to give us that ravishing epilogue in which they sing the three pairs of married lovers to bed and bestow upon them, and upon us the audience, their blessing.

But if the play ends by celebrating a triple happiness, the dramatic tension which makes the play is an effect, as the title informs us, of midsummer madness, the sort of madness which comes to man on Midsummer Night or St. John's Eve; 'the one season of the year around which Elizabethan superstition gathered most closely'.[2] And quite apart from the disease of love-in-idleness induced by Cupid's flower, nearly all the characters—the whole world indeed —seem to be infected by it; the lovers are distraught with cross-purposes before the play opens; Titania and Oberon give way to an irrational quarrel which in turn sends the weather mad, so that all the seasons are topsy-turvy; and even the self-possessed Duke Theseus is troubled with 'vexation' at having to wait until the new moon for his wedding day. Bottom alone keeps his head; and although that head suffers a symbolical transformation for a few hours, nothing can shake his equanimity. But here Peter Alexander has

---

[1] Cf. Quiller-Couch's analysis of the plot structure quoted later, on p. 214.
[2] Chambers, *Shakespeare: a Survey*, p. 83.

gathered together Shakespeare's hints into so excellent and humorous a portrait of the man that it would be impertinence in me to attempt another. He begins:

> No comedy of situation, not farce itself, can provide a stranger encounter than that between Bottom and Titania; but it belongs to the purest comedy of character, and Bottom is as much the life of this scene as he is of the Interlude to follow.

And then, noting that there is a

> robust independence in all Bottom's thoughts and actions that is not to be extinguished even by the ass's head,

Alexander continues:

> What lucidity and sanity are his, how just and straightforward his fashion of thought, whether in Athens or fairyland!
> QUINCE.—Is all our company here?
> BOTTOM. —You were best to call them generally, man by man, according to the scrip.

And then, as Quince still fumbles with the business,

> First, good Peter Quince, say what the play treats on; then read the names of the actors, and so grow to a point.

True, he is sometimes himself discursive, even vagrant, for, as in many brilliant commentators, the energetic current of his thought eddies at times into a backwater. If there is no difficulty he must invent one,

> There are things in this comedy of Pyramus and Thisby that will never please.

But only that he may restore the situation by some happy stroke,

> I have a device to make all well.

And what an eye for the right authority he discovers when Quince poses the problem of bringing in moonshine,

> SNUG. —Doth the moon shine that night we play our play?
> BOTTOM. —A calendar, a calendar! Look in the almanack; find out moonshine, find out moonshine. . . .

Bottom's commonsense corresponds to his manly cast of mind. Though deserted by his terrified companions he will sing,

> I will walk up and down here, and I will sing, that they may hear I am not afraid.

And he will argue resolutely even with his fancies,

> The finch, the sparrow, and the lark,
>     The plain-song cuckoo gray,
> Whose note full many a man doth mark,
>     And dares not answer nay;

for indeed, who would set his wit to so foolish a bird? Who would give a bird the lie, though he cry 'cuckoo' never so? But there is nothing overbearing or boorish in the man; and he treats Pease-blossom, Mustard-seed, and their companions with the same patient courtesy he extends to the Duke himself:—

THESUS. —The wall, methinks, being sensible, should curse again.

BOTTOM. —No, in truth, sir, he should not. 'Deceiving me' is Thisby's cue; she is to enter now, and I am to spy her through the wall. You shall see, it will fall pat as I told you. Yonder she comes.

Naturally, he is not appreciated except by those who know him. To them he is 'Sweet bully Bottom', with simply the best wit and best person, too, in Athens, 'a very paramour for a sweet voice'. To Puck, untouched by human toil and infirmity, he is merely

The shallowest thick-skin of that barren sort.

And even the enchanted Titania seems a shade unappreciative, unless it is pure solicitude that makes her say,

Tie up my love's tongue, bring him silently.

It is easy to laugh at Bottom, and Johnson was able to put his old friend Garrick and the actors in their place, when he noted on Bottom's choice of beard:

Here Bottom again discovers a true genius for the stage by his solicitude for propriety of dress, and his deliberation which beard to choose among many beards, all unnatural.[1]

Bottom was invented for Titania to fall in love with— Shakespeare's inspired version of the old tale of Beauty and the Beast, with help from Apuleius.[2] And Titania and the Fairies were invented for the world to fall in love with the play. If one could imagine it without them, what would it be?—a caddis-case, with all its iridescent loveliness gone. Most of its music and its movement belong to them also.

But their songs and voices are as small and wildly sweet as that of the wind in seeding grasses or of water chiming[3] in a well.... And the very breath of the south wind over Titania's woodland thyme and violets —Shakespeare's most-favoured flower—is sweet with her presence[4].

[1] Alexander, *Shakespeare's Life and Art*, pp. 106–8.          [2] See p. 216.
[3] I.e., tinkling. Cf. Cowper, *The Task*, I, 193, 'rills chiming as they fall upon loose pebbles'.
[4] See p. xxx of the Introduction by Walter de la Mare to an edition of *A Midsummer Night's Dream* by C. Aldred (1935). The essay was reprinted in *Pleasures and Speculations*, 1940.

So writes the modern poet laureate of Fairyland, his own imagination kindled by that of Shakespeare. But—a ticklish point, and one that must give us pause—were the Fairies entirely a production of Shakespeare's own? This, at least, is the question posed in a learned book entitled *The Elizabethan Fairies: the Fairies of Folklore and the Fairies of Shakespeare*, by Minor White Latham, 1930. It is clear that before Shakespeare, fairies were traditionally regarded as beautiful but often malevolent beings and of stature not dissimilar to that of adult men and women; and Dr. Latham holds therefore that though all the other references to fairies in the plays,[1] with the exception of Mercutio's Queen Mab, agree, or can be reconciled, with this traditional conception, the tiny butterfly-like fairies of *A Midsummer Night's Dream* are 'spirits of another sort'.[2] To quote his summing-up:

> Whatever is homely or substantial or dangerous has been removed from the picture of them which Shakespeare paints, and only their rulers are still invested with formidable powers and uncertain tempers. Diminutive, pleasing, and picturesque sprites, with small garden names and small garden affairs, associated with moon-beams and butterflies, they present themselves as a new race of fairies.[3]

And he claims that the influence of the *Dream* was so great that, at any rate in literary productions, Shakespeare's fairies almost completely took possession of human imagination with the result that the previous existence of their life-size malevolent predecessors is now forgotten. In substance Dr. Latham is undoubtedly correct. But he has, I think, stated the case too absolutely. He is obliged of course to admit that benevolent fairies could exist before *A Midsummer Night's Dream* because, to prove it, there was Spenser's *Fairie Queene* in which, though the poem was never finished enough to give us a picture of the fairy court, all England knew that its queen symbolized Elizabeth herself. Moreover Oberon, king

---

[1] See *Merry Wives*, V, 5, 47; *Hamlet*, I, i, 163; *I Henry IV*, I, i, 86–8; *Winter's Tale*, III, iii, 112; *Cymbeline*, II, ii, 9; *Macbeth*, IV, i, 42.

[2] *Midsummer Night's Dream*, III, ii, 388.

[3] P. 180.

of the fairies, 'the little dwarf Oberon with his unapproachable beauty and gentle carriage' who came from his kingdom of Faerie somewhere east of Jerusalem,[1] is an important figure in the romance of *Huon of Bordeaux* which Shakespeare is known to have used for his play; and he appears again, attended by 'armies of little elves', in Christopher Middleton's romance of *Chinon of England*,[2] published in 1597 but probably based upon popular tradition. For as Chambers well says,

> Oberon and his eastern realm are to be found in *Huon of Bordeaux*; and every English country-side knew of the little green dwarfs who dwelt in the earth-knolls and danced by night in the fairy rings, and of Robin Goodfellow, the tricksy house spirit, who performed domestic labours for cleanly maidens, and played malicious pranks upon slatterns or upon such as neglected the simple observances which he regarded as his due.[3]

All things considered, it looks safe enough to believe, as has always been believed, that Shakespeare learnt all about tiny fairies or elves in Warwickshire, one may guess as a little boy sitting on his mother's knee; and then, being of 'imagination all compact', went out into the forest of Arden at his door, and *saw* them[4]. In any case either then or later he must have learnt to think of the elves as almost infinitesimal, for Mercutio describes Queen Mab, the midwife of dreams, as

> In shape no bigger than an agate-stone
> On the forefinger of an alderman,
> Drawn with a team of little atomies
> Over men's noses as they lie asleep;

and *Romeo and Juliet* was written a year or two before the *Dream* play itself, that is, if the interlude of Pyramus and Thisbe and Wall was, as seems likely, a comic palinode to

[1] See Introduction by Sidney Lee to *Huon of Bordeaux*, translated by Lord Berners, Early English Text Society, Extra Series, 1882–  .
[2] Ed. by W. E. Mead for the Early English Text Society, orig. series, 1925. See p. 30 for the 'elves'.
[3] *Shakespeare: a Survey*, p. 77.     [4] See p. 214.

the garden scene in *Romeo and Juliet*,[1] as Shaw's *How He Lied to her Husband* was to *Candida*. It stands to reason of course that such tiny beings could not be represented on the stage. Titania is attended by four 'elves', Pease-blossom, Cobweb, Moth, and Mustardseed, to whom are given monosyllabic speeches that could be readily learnt and repeated by quite small children, perhaps little bridesmaids of the married couple for whom the play was originally written, and there would be nothing ridiculous in supposing that such elves might for fear

> Creep into acorn-cups and hide them there.

But Puck, Oberon, the Fairy who is introduced at the opening of Act II to inform the audience who Puck is and what the quarrel between Oberon and Titania is about, Titania herself, and the trains that follow Oberon and Titania and sing the blessing at the end of the play, were all clearly played by professionals, mostly by boys, and probably singing boys maintained by the lord of the house.

## II. OBERON'S VISION AND THE OCCASIONS OF THE PLAY

No scholar seems to doubt that *A Midsummer Night's Dream* is a marriage play and written to be performed at a grand wedding in some nobleman's house. There seems no reason why for Shakespeare and his company, it should not have been *the* marriage play which could be brought out, after a little touching up, whenever they were called upon to provide the evening's entertainment that normally terminated the festivities on such occasions. The Elizabethans missed no opportunity for feasting and merry-making, and for revelry no time was more auspicious than a wedding-day. Nor would a single day suffice. For as Theseus goes off to bed with Hippolyta at the end of the play he proclaims:

> A fortnight hold we this solemnity
> In nightly revels and new jollity.

[1] See Chambers, *William Shakespeare*, I, 345.

And a fortnight seems to have been a not unusual period for the revels to continue;[1] while on the day itself such revels might last far into the night, if we once again accept Theseus as a credible witness. 'Come now' he says to Philostrate at the beginning of the same last scene,

> . . . what masques, what dances shall we have,
> To wear away this long age of three hours
> Between our after-supper and bed-time?

The 'tedious brief scene' of young Pyramus and his love Thisby would barely occupy a third of this time, but 'three hours' would amply suffice for the *Dream* as a whole and is clearly meant to denote the normal duration.

That the play, though the title page of the Quarto shows that it found its way on to the public stage in or before 1600, was originally written or re-written for a wedding at a house with a hall large enough for its proper performance and not for some other occasion at court or elsewhere, needs no arguing. Its whole atmosphere proclaims the fact; and in particular the fairy masque that forms its conclusion would otherwise hardly make sense, since it clearly points to a performance in the house of the bridegroom himself who has just been celebrating his marriage to a great lady.

So far most scholars are, I think, agreed. But when it comes to the question of what was the grand wedding for which Shakespeare first produced the play, all agreement vanishes. Chambers, we shall see, gives a list of six possibilities, advanced by different authorities at different times. But before discussing these it will be well to examine a passage upon the interpretation of which the choice of the wedding must depend. I refer to the famous allusion to the Queen, and the vision that precedes it. Thus it runs:

OBERON. My gentle Puck, come hither. Thou rememb'rest
Since once I sat upon a promontory,
And heard a mermaid, on a dolphin's back,
Uttering such dulcet and harmonious breath

[1] See *Shakespeare's England*, ii, 147–8.

That the rude sea grew civil at her song,
And certain stars shot madly from their spheres
To hear the sea-maid's music.
PUCK.                                I remember.
OBERON. That very time I saw—but thou couldst not—
Flying between the cold moon and the earth,
Cupid all armed: a certain aim he took
At a fair Vestal, thronéd by the west,
And loosed his love-shaft smartly from his bow,
As it should pierce a hundred thousand hearts:
But I might see young Cupid's fiery shaft
Quenched in the chaste beams of the wat'ry moon:
And the imperial Vot'ress passéd on,
In maiden meditation, fancy-free.
Yet marked I where the bolt of Cupid fell.
It fell upon a little western flower;
Before milk-white; now purple with love's wound—
And maidens call it Love-in-idleness.[1]

No one questions that the 'fair Vestal thronéd by the west' is Queen Elizabeth. Nor do I think it can be denied that the lines about Cupid are as a whole intended to symbolize a well-planned and ardent, not to say vigorous, assault upon the royal heart. For note that Cupid is 'all armed', that is to say, in full panoply; that he takes a 'certain' (i.e. a steady and deliberate) aim; and that—here comes the climax—he looses his love-shaft so 'smartly'

As it should pierce a hundred thousand hearts.

A courtship of the Queen thus described must, one would suppose, have been public property and recognizable not only to Shakespeare's immediate audience but to any audience of Elizabeth's subjects. To which, then, among her many suitors, is Oberon alluding? The answer is given in the earlier part of the passage which, as again no one questions, describes in poetical language one of those pageants or entertainments offered to the Queen almost any year as she went in progress to some nobleman's house or other; and in this case, as the second half of the passage shows,

[1] II, i, 148–68.

offered by the suitor who was at that very time laying siege to her heart. The pageantry in fact was part of his campaign, as is plain from Oberon's words, which signify that he saw Cupid shooting while he and Puck were watching the pageant. Now there is one occasion and only one that fits the conjunction of events to which Shakespeare is here alluding, namely the Queen's visit to the Earl of Leicester at Kenilworth for three weeks, July 9th–27th, in 1575. And in particular Oberon's lovely vision of the mermaid on the dolphin's back is clearly a poetical reflexion of the water pageant, which was the most striking of the shows Leicester then provided. Two detailed descriptions of this pageant by eye-witnesses are extant, one by George Gascoigne, the poet who helped to prepare some of the shows, and the other by Robert Laneham, door-keeper to the Privy Council, whose report makes as racy a piece of Elizabethan journalism as we possess. The two naturally differ slightly on minor points, as Shakespeare's version does from them, but how close Oberon's vision comes to the reality will be seen when corresponding passages are set down together.[1]

SHAKESPEARE. . . . a mermaid on a dolphin's back.

LANEHAM. Her Highness now returning [from the chase and reaching a bridge across an artificial lake] there came, upon a swimming mermaid, Triton, Neptune's blaster, who with his trumpet, etc.

GASCOIGNE. Triton in the likeness of a mermaid came towards the Queen's Majesty.

SHAKESPEARE. Uttering such dulcet and harmonious breath.

LANEHAM. [the approach of the Queen to the lake releases the Lady of the Lake from prison, and she in gratitude sends as a gift] Arion, that excellent and famous musician, in tire and appointment strange, riding aloft upon his old friend the dolphin, . . . [who] began a delectable ditty of a song well apted to a melodious noise, compounded of six several instruments, all covert, casting sound from the dolphin's belly within, Arion the seventh sitting, thus singing without.

GASCOIGNE has much the same account, but speaks of 'Triton in likeness of a mermaid'.

[1] I give the contemporary accounts in modern spelling. A similar table was set forth by N. J. Halpin in his *Oberon's Vision*, the Shakespeare Society, 1843.

# A Midsummer Night's Dream

SHAKESPEARE. That the rude sea grew civil at her song.

LANEHAM. [After the release of the Lady of the Lake] Arion moving herewith from the bridge and fleeting more into the pool, charged in Neptune's name Aeolus with all his winds, the waters with his springs, his fish and fowl, and all his clients in the same, that they be not so hardy in any force to stir, but keep them calm and quiet while this queen be present.

GASCOIGNE gives the same command to his 'Triton, in the likeness of a mermaid'.

SHAKESPEARE. And certain stars shot madly from their spheres
        To hear the sea maid's music.

LANEHAM [recording the second day of the visit, a week or more before the foregoing]. At night late, as though Jupiter the last night had forgot . . . part of his welcome unto her Highness appointed . . . at last the Altitonant [i.e. Jove the High Thunderer] displays his main power, with blaze of burning darts flying to and fro, leams [flashes] of stars coruscant, streams and hail of fiery sparks, lightnings of wild-fire on water and land, flight and shoot of thunderbolts, all with such continuance, horror, and vehemency, that the heavens thundered, the waters scourged [? lashed], the earth shook.

GASCOIGNE gives a somewhat different version of the fireworks.

Shakespeare runs the events of two days together, but he had no call to be precise and was writing some twenty years later than the visit. Both Laneham's and Gascoigne's accounts were in print for him to read. But is it not possible that he was drawing upon his own memory? Dr. Percy of the *Reliques of English Poetry* thought so, pointing out that the dramatist was eleven years old at the time of the Queen's visit and Kenilworth only fifteen miles from Stratford.[1] A boy of 'imagination all compact', as we have insisted already, could not have stayed at home while these great affairs were afoot close by. It is even possible that he himself took part in song or dance or other display, since those responsible must have raked the countryside for miles around for likely boy talent.

In any case Oberon's vision is undoubtedly a poetic version of the Kenilworth pageantry. It is true that similar

---

[1] *Reliques* (Bohn's Library), i, 98.

shows are described in the accounts of other Elizabethan progresses by Nichols,[1] and the entertainment offered by the Earl of Hertford at Elvetham in 1591 bears a rather close resemblance, and is even favoured by Chambers as the origin of Oberon's lines.[2] But none of these was combined with an attempt to secure Elizabeth's hand; certainly not that at Elvetham, since Hertford was a married man and his countess made the queen a present at the time of the visit.

To return then to Cupid all-armed. The fiery love-shaft, despite the force and skill of the archer, failed to reach the heart of the fair Vestal, and so,

> Quenched in the chaste beams of the wat'ry moon . . .
> It fell upon a little western flower;
> Before milk-white; now purple with love's wound.

This little flower, as we have seen above, is essential to the plot of the play, its function being to bewitch Titania and Lysander; and its name 'love-in-idleness' was most apt, since although it sounds innocent and pretty to our ears, it meant to the Elizabethans love-madness, a sudden passion or overwhelming desire.[3] Shakespeare only uses the term once elsewhere and clearly with this meaning. Says Tranio to Lucentio in *The Shrew*:

> I pray, sir, tell me, is it possible
> That love should of a sudden take such hold?

To which his master replies:

> O Tranio, till I found it to be true,
> I never thought it possible or likely;
> But see, while idly I stood looking on,
> I found the effect of love in idleness;
> And now in plainness do confess to thee . . .
> Tranio, I burn, I pine, I perish, Tranio,
> If I achieve not this young modest girl.[4]

[1] Nichols, *Progresses of Queen Elizabeth* (1788–1821).
[2] Chambers, *William Shakespeare*, i, 358; *Shakespearean Gleanings*, pp. 63–4.
[3] Cf. the proverb 'idleness begets lust' (Tilley, I9) and 'idle' = mad (*Hamlet*), III, ii, 88.
[4] *Taming of the Shrew*, I, i, 145–51, 154–5.

The flower Oberon sends for and later calls 'Cupid's flower' stands therefore for that irrational, irresistible type of love that may take possession of a man or woman often quite suddenly—and for the purposes of the play need mean nothing more, while its empurpling by love's wound is just a commonplace of classical mythology. Indeed it looks as if Shakespeare had in mind the story, as told by his favourite Ovid, of Hyacinthust the boy beloved of Apollo from whose life-blood sprang a flower 'which took the form of the lily save that it was purple, the lily silvery white'.[1] Moreover, it had its antidote in the other flower, 'Dian's bud' Oberon calls it, needed for the plot as well, since, as we have also seen, it was the instrument for resolving the double imbroglio effected by Cupid's flower; restoring to both Titania and Lysander normal sight, sanity of vision and fidelity of love. What more was needed? The fable was complete and every modern audience goes home satisfied and asking no further questions. Perhaps the spectators at the Globe in 1600 accepted it in similar fashion, for by then the Kenilworth affair was twenty-five years old and Leicester a dozen years in his grave, so that for most people the whole business must have completely dropped out of mind. As for the lines about the fair Vestal, they would be taken as nothing more than a pretty piece of homage to the great queen, as they are by most critics still today.

But for the Queen herself and for members of her court, the Herberts, the Earls of Essex and Southampton, and their families, all of whom remembered Leicester well and some of whom even twenty years later no doubt could recall the doings at Kenilworth in 1575, Oberon's vision must have implied something very different and far more pointed. For the pageant being recognizable as one of the 'princely shows' at Kenilworth, and Cupid's aim at the fair Vestal betokening Leicester's ardent courtship of Elizabeth, the little western flower upon which the 'fiery shaft' fell could only be the woman with whom Leicester consoled himself

[1] Ovid, *Metamorphoses*, X, 212 ff.

whẹn Elizabeth repulsed his advances; in a word, Lettice Knollys, Lady Essex, mother of the Earl of Essex, whom Leicester married in 1576, a few months after the Queen left Kenilworth, and who for some years had been his mistress; who had, as the London gossips had been reporting in 1575, borne him two children while her husband, the old Earl of Essex, was still alive and over in Ireland. At about the same time Lady Sheffield, another mistress, was also presenting him with a son. For if ever a man was subject to, or guilty of, 'love-in-idleness', it was Leicester. He had the decency to marry his Lettice when her husband died in 1576, but the wedding was kept secret since he was still ostensibly paying court to the Queen. The courtship of the Duke of Alençon had now, however, become Elizabeth's chief preoccupation, and the French ambassador struck a shrewd blow for his master by whispering Leicester's secret[1] into her ears. That Elizabeth's anger was 'open and devastating' is history's version of Oberon's

> But I might see young Cupid's fiery shaft
> Quenched in the chaste beams of the wat'ry moon.

Yet though 'the imperial Vot'ress passéd on', she was not quite 'fancy free', for as long as he lived she cherished a tenderness for the lover who had so outrageously slighted her, and a 'loathing' for the woman whom he had married.[2]

Finally, if Lettice Knollys, Countess of Essex, be the little flower, the point of the epithets 'western' and 'milk-white' becomes clear, for 'western' stands for 'English' as in the case of the 'fair Vestal'—Oberon is of course speaking in Greece, and what 'milk-white' does not owe to Ovid's wounded Hyacinth the noble audience would readily supply from the lady's name, since 'Lettice', though derived from Laetitia, might be taken as a quibble on 'lettuce', the English form of the Latin *lactuca*, 'the milky plant', so called from the colour of its juice.

[1] For these facts and the political situation see Neale, *Queen Elizabeth* (1934). p. 245. Neale does not relate this to the Kenilworth visit.
[2] See Neale, op. cit., p. 288.

# A Midsummer Night's Dream

The suggestion that Oberon's vision reflects the pageantry at Kenilworth was first made by James Boaden[1] in 1838, and was considerably developed five years later by N. J. Halpin,[2] who was also the first to advance the theory that in the 'western flower' Shakespeare was pointing at the Countess of Essex. Halpin's interpretation was, I think, generally accepted until E. K. Chambers set his great authority against it. Yet his only ground for so doing that I can discover is the beauty of the tribute to the Queen which he assumes must have been intended for her ears, and that therefore: (i) the wedding for which the play was written must have been one at which Elizabeth was present, and (ii) Oberon's vision could not possibly have any reference to the courtship of Leicester. 'The attempt', he asserts,

> to turn the mermaid and the falling stars and the little Western flower into an allegory . . . of the intrigue of Leicester with the Countess of Essex may be summarily disregarded. Whatever else complimentary poetry is, it must be in the first place gratifying to the person complimented. . . . The marriage [of Leicester] had caused her bitter mortification in its day, and if Edmund Tilney [the censor of plays] had allowed Shakespeare to allude to it before her, he would have signed his own warrant for the Tower and Shakespeare's for the Marshalsea.[3]

Now, however, that it has become clear that Oberon's vision *is directly* connected with the marriage that Elizabeth detested, these arguments of Chambers cut just the other way. The Queen can never have heard the offensive passage, and had there been the slightest chance of her turning up for the performance, the whole thing (viz. l. 149 to the middle of l. 169) must have been cut out of the prompt-book,[4]

[1] *Essay on the Sonnets of Shakespeare*, etc. by James Boaden, 1837.

[2] *Oberon's Vision in the 'Midsummer Night's Dream'* by N. J. Halpin, The Shakespeare Society, 1843.

[3] Chambers, *Shakespearean Gleanings* (1944), p. 63, reprinting an essay, *On the Occasion of 'A Midsummer Night's Dream'* first published in Gollancz's *Homage to Shakespeare*, 1916.

[4] As will be seen in section III below, the Quarto of 1600 was printed from Shakespeare's draft, the so-called 'foul papers'. This would contain all that Shakespeare had written of the play. Alterations and excisions for any particular performance would naturally be made in the prompt-book.

and could have been with the greatest possible ease. The text
would then read

> My gentle Puck, come hither. Thou remembrest
> The herb I showed thee once . . .

And no one would notice anything amiss.

In a later treatment of the topic, Chambers seems less
absolute; for he concedes that 'the flattery', as he calls it,
'does not of course prove that Elizabeth was at the wedding'.[1]
Nevertheless he continues to assume it, for he goes on to
give the list (spoken of above) of the six noble weddings for
which previous critics had suggested the play might have
been composed, and writes off three of them, either because
the wedding was secret, like the third, or like the other two
brought the bridegroom into disfavour. Yet these three
weddings—those of Robert, Earl of Essex, of the Countess
of Southampton, and of the Earl of Southampton himself,
were all connected with the Leicester–Essex circle at court;
that is to say, they were just those at which Oberon's vision,
as just interpreted, would not only have seemed apt but
might have been warmly applauded. It is true that the reference to the little western flower goes rather near the bone,
yet there is nothing in it that need have brought a blush to
the good lady's cheek, seeing that 'before milk-white' might
be taken quite literally as a tribute to her chastity before
the marriage with Leicester.

But the initial error on the part of Chambers, an error he
shares with other critics, is the description of the tribute to
Elizabeth as 'obvious flattery'. How was William Shakespeare, the player, to speak of the Queen to an audience of
courtiers (one of whom, as we shall presently see, was probably the Queen's vice-chamberlain), except in terms of the
greatest reverence? Or how could William Shakespeare, the
supreme poet, have failed to pay to his sovereign lady the
finest tribute a monarch has ever received? Yet the lines are
*not* flattery; there is not a hint of insincerity or falsehood

---

[1] *William Shakespeare,* i, 358–9.

about them, and the proof of this is that modern Englishmen still feel that they speak the truth. But they were not written for Elizabeth to hear, and they were never spoken from the stage when she was present. It is noticeable incidentally that the publisher of the 1600 Quarto did not claim that it had been graced by a royal auditor as those that published the Quartos of *Love's Labour's Lost*, *The Merry Wives* and *King Lear* were able to do.

The vision of Oberon being thus explained, we can now turn to the problem of the wedding or weddings for which the play was designed. For as I have said, it may have served for more than one occasion of the sort; though, if so, we must be prepared for the possibility of slight adjustments and additions to suit different circumstances, a possibility Chambers himself seems to admit.[1] But as in a discussion of this kind the question of date is of first importance, let us begin by having Chambers's list of six noble weddings and their dates before us. They are:

(1) Robert, Earl of Essex to Frances, widow of Sir Philip Sidney, secretly, April or May, 1590.

(2) Sir Thomas Heneage to the Countess of Southampton, May 2, 1594.

(3) William Stanley, Earl of Derby to Elizabeth Vere at Greenwich or at Lord Burghley's house in the Strand, 26 January 1595.

(4) Sir Thomas Berkeley to Elizabeth Carey at Blackfriars, 9 February, 1596.

(5) Earl of Southampton to Elizabeth Vernon, secretly, 'about February or August' (Chambers) but probably near 30 August (see Stopes, *Southampton*, pp. 122–3), 1598.

(6) Henry, Lord Herbert, brother of William Herbert, Earl of Pembroke, to Anne Russell at Blackfriars, 16 June, 1600.

And there may be added for completeness a suggestion of Sidney Lee's (*Shakespeare*, p. 232):

---

[1] *William Shakespeare*, I, 361 (top). And for No. 3 see *Shakespearean Gleanings*, pp. 61–2.

(7) Earl of Bedford to Lucy Harington 'the universal patroness of poets', 12 December, 1594.

Assuming that this exhausts the possibilities, let us now see whether there are any date-clues in the play itself which might point to one or more of them; and we may begin with a very obvious clue, which strangely appears to have been almost unnoticed by English commentators,[1] although Elze drew attention to it in his *Life of William Shakespeare*, 1876. The marriage of Theseus and Hippolyta takes place on May Day; for they go hunting one morning, and finding the lovers sleeping in the forest, Theseus remarks to his bride

> No doubt they rose up early to observe
> The rite of May; and hearing our intent,
> Came here in grace of our solemnity.
> (IV, 1, 131–3.)

And if this points to the season of the real wedding, as it well may, the opening words of the play would suggest the very year, for Theseus tells us that he and Hippolyta are to be wedded in four days' time, when there is a new moon in the heavens. And she replies (I, i, 7–11):

> Four days will quickly steep themselves in night:
> Four nights will quickly dream away the time;
> And then the moon, like to a silver bow
> New-bent in heaven, shall behold the night
> Of our solemnities.

Turn now to our list of weddings and one, the most natural one in the world to be associated with this play, as the industrious Mrs. Carmichael Stopes pointed out in 1922,[2] stares us in the face: that of the Countess of Southampton, mother of Shakespeare's patron, who was being married to Sir Thomas Heneage on 2nd May 1594, there being in that

---

[1] An exception is the half-serious, half-scoffing reference to Elze's suggestion in a footnote on p. xi of Aldis Wright's Clarendon Press edition of *A Midsummer Night's Dream* (1887).

[2] C. C. Stopes, *Life of Henry, Third Earl of Southampton*, pp. 75–8.

year a new moon a week later.[1] And when we recollect that 1594 is the year in which Shakespeare published *The Rape of Lucrece*, entered in the Stationers' Register on May 9th and dedicated to Southampton in far more intimate terms than the humble dedication of *Venus and Adonis* the previous year, the evidence seems to be accumulating. Lastly, Sir Thomas Heneage having been Elizabeth's Vice-Chamberlain since 1589,[2] what more appropriate company of actors to play at his wedding than the newly-formed Lord Chamberlain's men who first appear in London exactly a month later?[3] We do not know where the wedding took place, but the great lady who ruled England had not approved, so it is certain that she was not present. On the other hand Heneage, an old gentleman, had been present at Kenilworth in 1575 and would have taken every point in Oberon's vision; while as a devoted servant of the Queen he would have appreciated the lovely reference to her. The insistence upon four days in Theseus's opening speech I'take to be a piece of dramatic clockwork, since if we stop and reckon, there is only an interval of some twenty-four hours between the beginning and end of the play.[4] But four days will seem none too long for all the events and ups-and-downs that the audience will be expected to follow in the play.

There are, however, several better-known date-clues which point in a different direction altogether, namely to a wedding that took place several months later, in 1594–5. One of these clues is a pleasant little jest at the expense of the Scottish court. The pageant to accompany a grand dinner

[1] On 10th May 1594, as Professor Brück, the Astronomer Royal of Scotland, is good enough to inform me. Aldis Wright (op. cit.) notes that May 1st coincided with a new moon in 1592, and if a suitable wedding offered that year, it might have a strong claim to be the first occasion on which Shakespeare's play was performed.

[2] *Elizabethan Stage*, I, p. 42.

[3] *Elizabethan Stage*, II, p. 193.

[4] See my Introduction to *Othello*, section v, for dramatic clockwork, of which that play offers an extreme example.

following upon the baptism of Prince Henry (later Prince of Wales) on the 30th August 1594 included a triumphal car, originally intended to be drawn in by a lion, until it occurred to (or was suggested to) those responsible that some of the party at the table, the ladies no doubt, might take fright; and so a blackamoor had to be substituted as cart-horse. The nervousness about Lion (*alias* Snout) on the part of Bottom and his fellow Mechanicals is an obvious reflection of this. Equally well known, though not, I think, fully appreciated, is the long description, almost overlong, of the bad weather in the summer of 1594 which Titania accounts for (at II, i, 88–114) as due to the quarrel between Oberon and herself. Two points, neither I think, hitherto observed, may be made about this. In the first place, the Oberon in *Huon of Bordeaux*, from which Shakespeare took some hints for his *Dream*[1], was said to be able when in anger to cause

> reyne and wynde and snowe and . . . meruelous tempestes with thonder and lyghtenynges so that it shall seme to you that all the world sholde pereshe.[2]

It is possible therefore that Titania's long speech may be a development of something shorter in the text at an earlier stage. And, in the second place, the passage fixes the period of the unseasonable weather almost to the very month. It began, she tells us, at the 'middle summer's spring' which I suppose may be April or May; and she is herself speaking not long after the beginning of 1595, since she is clearly referring in the final section to recent disturbances of the Christmas festivities when she says,

> The human mortals want their winter here:
> No night is *now* with hymn or carol blest.[3]

—a reference of capital importance since it implies that the play was being performed about that season.

[1] See above pp. 189–90.
[2] Latham, op. cit., p. 187. *Huon of Bordeaux*. An alternative source is suggested on pp. 216–17.
[3] II, i, 101–2. I now believe 'here' to be a misprint for 'cheer' (Hanmer conj.)

The third, less certain, clue to the same period is suggested by Alexander, who points out that the names of Theseus's four mistresses, Perigouna, Aegles, Ariadne and Antiopa, whom Oberon mentions in his short speech immediately before Titania's about the weather, all occur in the opening pages of North's *Plutarch*, a new edition of which was being printed by Shakespeare's fellow-Stratfordian, Richard Field, at the very time that the same man was printing *The Rape of Lucrece*.[1] What more natural than that Shakespeare, being in the shop to discuss business, should turn over the first two or three pages of the new *Plutarch* to refresh his memory about Theseus who of course was already the Duke of Athens when the play was first drafted.

Once more our list shows a wedding exactly suited to these internal dates: namely, that of William Stanley, Earl of Derby, to Elizabeth Vere on the 26th January 1595. Chambers records that Queen Elizabeth was present on this occasion and that the Chamberlain's men then gave a play which was almost certainly *A Midsummer Night's Dream*.[2] There is, however, some doubt whether the wedding took place at Greenwich or at Lord Burghley's house in the Strand, so that her presence does not seem absolutely certain. Yet its possibility, if not likelihood, must have been contemplated, and the prompt-book adjusted to prevent her being offended by having to hear the dangerous vision of Oberon. By the excision of lines 149–68, the play, a short one in any case, would have lost twenty-four lines. It seems possible, therefore, that something like the same number of lines were worked into what Titania had to say about the weather and this would account for the inordinate length of that speech.

[1] Alexander, op. cit., p. 105. Can this have been the first occasion upon which Shakespeare had looked at North? Everything else in the play about Theseus he might have found in Chaucer's *Knight's Tale*.

[2] See *Eliz. Stage*, iv, p. 109. Stowe, *Annales*, p. 768 under 1595, runs: 'The 26 of Januarie William earle of Darby married the Earle of Oxfords daughter at the court then at Greenwich which marryage feast was there most royally kept.'

Acting on the assumption that Elizabeth was present to receive the oblation of 'flattery' in Oberon's vision, Chambers decides that the effective choice lies between marriages (3) and (4) in his list of marriages. After so much disagreement it is pleasant to agree with him on the selection of (3), though he would never have allowed my reasons for so doing. And I now propose to go one better by choosing, not '*between* (3) and (4)', but both of them. In other words I now suggest that Shakespeare's *Dream* was performed at yet a third wedding, that of Thomas Berkeley to Elizabeth Carey at Blackfriars on 19th February 1596. In this instance there are no supporting internal date-clues, but the elaborate dance and song of the Fairies at the end of the play are clearly a late addition designed for performance at a private establishment, since the song of the Fairies begins

> Now, until the break of day,
> Through the house each fairy stray,

and ends

> And each several chamber bless,
> Through this palace, with sweet peace,
> And the owner of it blest,
> Ever shall in safety rest.

All this points not merely to a noble house, but to one possessed of a choir of singing boys to supplement the usual professional company's resources. And though unfortunately no details are known of the Berkeley wedding, the fact that it was given at Blackfriars, which meant the house of the bride's father, Sir George Carey, next door to Burbadge's Blackfriars playhouse; that Carey's father was the Lord Chamberlain; and that Carey himself had a musical establishment which would probably be able to supply all the singing boys needed, as it seems to have supplied the dancing and singing fairies in the forest scene of *The Merry Wives*', a play pretty obviously connected with the Garter feast that celebrated the Garter installation of the same George Carey who then became Lord Chamberlain—all this is enough to justify a strong presumption that a play belonging to the Lord Chamberlain's company was given, and that the play chosen was *A Midsummer Night's Dream*.[1]

Nor is that the end of this conjectural textual history of the play. For, it will be recollected, the title page of the 1600 Quarto informs us that it had been 'sundry times publickely acted by the Right honourable the Lord Chamberlaine his servants', and for such performances the fairy dance and song would be at once inappropriate for a public theatre and out of the question for a professional company of players. That would accordingly be omitted and Puck's last speech, 'If we shadows have offended', etc. composed as an epilogue in its place.[2]

At this point the reader will probably be feeling that he has had enough of 'disintegration'. Yet there remains one more passage in its history to be considered, a pre-Shakespearian one. But this must be relegated to another section, which reprints the article written in 1948, as stated above.


## III. THE ORIGINAL PLAY

(First published in *Tribute to Walter de la Mare
on his Seventy-fifth Birthday*, 25th April 1948)

In 1924 Quiller-Couch and I published our edition of *A Midsummer Night's Dream*, in a bibliographical note of which I claimed that eight passages of verse at the beginning of Act V had been written as additions in the margin of the manuscript used by the printers of the first Quarto, who, being without the regular verse-divisions to guide them, had to fit these marginal lines into the text as best they might; and further, that since the rest of the dialogue reads straight on when the passages are omitted, they were evidently additions made to the first draft and made by Shakespeare himself. A reprint of the opening speeches will show the reader how the business works. The text is repro-

---

[1] Cf. pp. 105, 126 of Alexander, *Shakespeare's Life and Art*.
[2] Chambers, *William Shakespeare*, I, 360–1, agrees in the main with this.

duced exactly as it appears in the Quarto, except that the disarranged verse has been italicized and slanting strokes have been inserted to show where the lines should rightly end.

> HIPPOLYTA. Tis strange, my Theseus, that these louers speake of.
> THESEUS. More straunge then true. I neuer may beleeue
> These antique fables, nor these Fairy toyes.
> Louers, and mad men haue such seething braines,
> *Such shaping phantasies, that apprehend/ more,*
> *Then coole reason euer comprehends./ The lunatick,*
> *The louer, and the Poet/ are of imagination all compact./*
> One sees more diuels, then vast hell can holde:
> That is the mad man. The louer, all as frantick,
> Sees Helens beauty in a brow of Ægypt.
> *The Poets eye, in a fine frenzy, rolling,/ doth glance*
> *From heauen to earth, from earth to heauen./ And as*
> *Imagination bodies forth/ the formes of things*
> *Vnknowne: the Poets penne/ turnes them to shapes,*
> *And giues to ayery nothing,/ a locall habitation,*
> *And a name./* Such trickes hath strong imagination,
> That if it would but apprehend some ioy,
> It comprehends some bringer of that ioy.
> Or in the night, imagining some feare,
> How easy is a bush suppos'd a Beare?

It will be noticed that in the mis-lined portions of his speech Theseus introduces 'the poet'; in the correctly arranged blank verse he laughs, somewhat woodenly, at the 'seething brains' of lovers and madmen, but says nothing about poets at all. Clearly 'the poet' was an afterthought on Shakespeare part's.

So far the case is unassailable, and has not been seriously challenged by later critics. But I did not stop there. Textual irregularities in other parts of the Quarto seemed at least open to the interpretation of having been caused by a general revision of the whole MS, while when the style of the indubitable additions in Act V was compared with that of their context, I found the difference so striking that I could not believe them written at the same time or even in the same year. In a word I came to the conclusion that *A Mid-*

*summer Night's Dream* is a play revised by Shakespeare, especially as regards the scenes in which the Fairies and the Mechanicals disport themselves, several years after it had been originally plotted. And I may now confess that, had I been then able to summon up sufficient pluck, I should have gone further still and declared it my belief that the original play was not written by Shakespeare at all. I went so far as to point out that 'though the eight patches of dis-arranged verse[1] are unnecessary to the bare sense, they contain all the beauty, all the life, all the memorable things of the passage'; that 'their masterly diction and vigorous sweep, which pays no attention to line-termination but runs on until the idea which impels it is exhausted, introduce a note of intellectual energy that makes the whole glow with poetic genius'; and that 'the remaining fifty-five lines, on the other hand, are simple, end-stopped, just a little monot-onous', while 'the last two lines of Theseus' first speech are so poor that they have even been regarded as an interpola-tion by some critics'. But I was a coward, a prey to 'the initiate fear that wants hard use', being in 1924 'yet but young in deed'; and so I described the fifty-five lines as 'early Shakespearian verse', feeling certain that most of them were nothing of the kind.

Perhaps it was as well, for I was shortly told on the highest authority that I had gone much too far already. Writing on the *Dream* in his *William Shakespeare* (1930) Sir Edmund Chambers, prince of Shakespearian scholars, would have no truck whatever with any theory of a general revision, while on the matter of the additions in Act V he remarked:

> In 5.1.1–84 correctly lined passages alternate with others which are mislined, and I agree with Wilson that the latter probably represent additional matter written without lineation in the margin of the manuscript. They are a little more freely written than the original lines which they supplement. This hardly excludes the possibility that they were afterthoughts at the time of original composition.[2]

[1] The rearranged passages extend over the first 84 lines of the Act.
[2] *William Shakespeare*, i, 360.

'A little more freely written'; I rubbed my eyes at that, and might have beat at my ears too; for see and hear those additional lines as Chambers did I could not. Yet if two educational officials (he was Second Secretary and I a humble H.M.I. of the Board of Education) had begun wrangling in public on aesthetic distinctions, nobody would have marked them; and the rest of the canon stretched out before me, to be edited, as it seemed to the crack o'doom. So I kept silence and pressed on, leaving my critic to win his case by default, as for lack of eternity a general editor of Shakespeare must often do.

And then suddenly and quite unexpectedly, Walter de la Mare delivered his verdict; the poet above all others of this age who, sharing the very spirit of Shakespeare's fairy-land, had the best right, I felt, to be heard on the matter at issue. And now it has been made available in reprint, Walter de la Mare's essay is there for all to read.[1] I need, therefore, do no more here than quote a few sentences from it by way of illustrating the main argument. He notes that the four lovers of the *Dream*, as most critics have agreed, are 'only intermittently real', that 'whole scenes in the play', citing one of the critics,[2] 'are hardly worthy of Shakespeare's 'prentice hand, yet seem to bear the unmistakable mark of his unmistakable pen'; and, having asked 'But do they consistently bear this mark?' he proceeds as follows:

> When Quince, having looked up moonshine in the almanac, which he keeps in his bag, declares that 'on the night' she will be at full, Bottom chimes in with, 'Why, then you may leave a casement of the great chamber window, where we play, open: and the moon may shine in at the casement.' 'Ay,' says Quince, 'or else one must come in with a bush of thorns, and a lanthorn, and say he comes to disfigure, or to present, the person of Moonshine.' Now this, pure prose though it is, is faintly suffused with poetry. One has only to listen to the rhythm and matching assonances of the sentences to discover that. . . . It is too Shakespeare's moon that is shining, and

[1] See his *Pleasures and Speculations*, 1940, and above p. 187, n. 2, for the edition referred to.
[2] S. R. Grant White.

it is his lanthorn. Compare this prose with such verses as,

> 'Do not say so, Lysander, say not so.
> What though he love your Hermia? Lord! what though?
> Yet Hermia still loves you: then be content.'
> 'Content with Hermia? No: I do repent . . .'

or with

> 'Lysander, keep thy Hermia: I will none.
> If e'er I loved her, all that love is gone.
> My heart to her but as guest-wise sojourned,
> And now to Helen it is home returned'—

or with

> 'Nor is he dead, for aught that I can tell.'
> 'I pray thee, tell me then that he is well.'
> 'An if I could, what should I get therefore?'
> 'A privilege, never to see me more,
> And from thy hated presence part I so:
> See me no more, whether he be dead or no.'

Far from there being any hint of poetry in lines such as these, they have uncommonly little sense. What order of bright wits and tender feelings indeed ever expressed itself in strains so jejune?

He then turns to the verse of the fairy scenes for comparison.

Titania's speeches are poetry in essence, 'potable moonlight', the lovers', though not invariably, are 'poetical' merely in tincture. The former are compact with beauty and meaning; the latter are shallow, stumbling, bald, and vacant. The stubborn words quoted above are being compelled to fit the metre, to occupy the lines—that 'Lord! what though?', that 'guest-wise sojourned', that 'part I so'—as the feet of the Ugly Sisters were made to fit Cinderella's glass slipper. So we have the truly-Shakespearian in

> Fair Helena! who more engilds the night
> Than all yon fiery oes and eyes of light,

and it is followed immediately by lines so faintly Shakespearean as

> Why seek'st thou me? could not this make thee know
> The hate I bear thee made me leave thee so?

Can we recall any other play written at one time and by one author that reveals discords in style and inequalities of mere intelligence so extreme? Did ever a fine poet indeed—let alone that pre-eminent prince of poets, Shakespeare—when once his imagination and his gift of expression had come of age, thus indulge, now in excellent, and now in dull and characterless verse?

## Variations on the theme of

He also cites the long speech in the first scene of 'the old,
permanently indignant, and minor character, Egeus'.

> It is a speech, like many of those bestowed on the young lovers,
> that resembles a duet between two distinguishable voices. 'Thou
> hast', he charges Lysander,
>> Thou hast by moonlight at her window sung,
>> With feigning voice, verses of feigning love;
>> And stol'n the impression of her fantasy
>> With bracelets of thy hair, rings, gauds, conceits,
>> Knacks, trifles, nosegays, sweetmeats—messengers
>> Of strong prevailment in unhardened youth . . .
>> With cunning hast thou filched my daughter's heart . . .
> So far, so good. We recognize whose mind it is that can thus
> squander its wealth in verbal music. But suddenly, and almost in the
> same breath, this tiresome old man is babbling lines as rudimentary
> as those which a mere schoolboy might thump out upon his desk,
> lines 'pretty much like a child's finger playing on two notes altern-
> ately on the piano':—
>> I beg the ancient privilege of Athens;
>> As she is mine, I may dispose of her;
>> Which shall be either to this gentleman,
>> Or to her death, according to our law,
>> Immediately provided in that case.
> 'In that case'! It is little better than mere sampler work, and its plain-
> ness is oddly out of keeping with the skilful embroidery of the
> conceits above. What can be the reason for this abrupt change both
> in form and content?

At this point Walter de la Mare discussed the theory of
revision outlined above. To my delight, however, he took
without hesitation the step I had funked; he would not for
a moment entertain a solution which explained the jejune
and insipid verse as early Shakespeare.

> Surely, to accept as Shakespeare's, at any age, what is provably not
> merely scamped or heedless but poverty-stricken verse—verse that
> advertises a dull and stubborn pen—is more extravagant than to
> discredit its being his at all. The former forces us to believe that a
> hand capable in 1592 of—
>> No? then I well perceive you are not nigh:
>> Either death or you I'll find immediately . . .
> and an abysmal *descent* to—

> Or in the night imagining some fear,
> How easy is a bush supposed a bear!

could in 1594, by some astonishing legerdemain, be faintly but per-
ceptibly pre-echoing, so to speak, the grand-mannered Milton's
characteristic accent and cadence:

> How canst thou thus for shame, Titania,
> Glance at my credit with Hippolyta,
> Knowing I know thy love to Theseus?
> *Didst thou not lead him through the glimmering night*
> *From Perigouna, whom he ravishéd?*
> *And make him with fair Aegles break his faith,*
> *With Ariadne, and Antiopa?*

There is more, much more, I should like to quote from
this essay, profound in critical discernment and rich in the
understanding of Shakespeare; an essay generously written
to help one friend with the production of his school edition,
and of even greater help to another friend responsible for an
edition of a duller kind. But enough has been quoted, I
believe, to convince all who have eyes and ears to distinguish between poetry and chopped prose, between the
flight of Pegasus in the empyrean and 'the forced gait of a
shuffling nag' in the village pound, that Shakespeare's work
on *A Midsummer Night's Dream* was one, not of plotting and
scaffold-building, but of partial transformation; and that the
irregularly divided passages of verses in the first eighty-four
lines of Act V allow us a glimpse of a portion of the manuscript after that transformation had taken place.

I am proud to think it was the dissecting out of these
passages which first led Walter de la Mare to inquire into
the processes of his predecessor's creation, and so to trump
—how gloriously!—my small card. In the hope of inducing
him to partner me in a second rubber at the same table, I
now tried another suit, thinking that even if he lacked time
or inclination to take a hand, he would approve the lead,[1]
since it links *A Midsummer Night's Dream* with one of its
chief rivals for mythological loveliness in the literature of

---

[1] But, O the heavy change now thou art gone,
Now thou art gone, and never must return!

the world, the story of *Cupid and Psyche*, as told in *The Golden Ass* of Lucius Apuleius, and translated from the Latin into fine Elizabethan prose by William Adlington in 1566.

The learned commentators have never got very far with the sources of *A Midsummer Night's Dream*, and the total of their labours has been adequately summed as follows by Q, friend and fellow-editor, in his Introduction to the play:

> The story ... is woven of three threads, which we can disentangle with ease into (i) the main, sentimental, plot of the court of Theseus and the four lovers, (2) the grotesque, buffooning plot of Bottom and his fellows, with the interlude of *Pyramus and Thisbe*, and (3) the fairy plot. For the first, Shakespeare may have used floating hints from Chaucer's *Knightes Tale* of Palamon and Arcite, afterwards the set theme of *The Two Noble Kinsmen*; and from North's Plutarch's *Life of Theseus*. For the second, Ovid includes the legend of *Pyramus and Thisbe* in the 4th Book of his *Metamorphoses*, and we know that Shakespeare knew his Ovid—if not, as many contend, in the original, at any rate in Arthur Golding's translation (1575).[1]

As for the third, what is more likely, he asks, than that Shakespeare

> brought all this fairy-stuff up to London in his own head, packed with nursery legends of his native Warwickshire? When will criticism learn to allow for the enormous drafts made by creative artists such as Shakespeare and Dickens upon their childhood? They do not, as Wordsworth did, write it all out in a story and call it *The Prelude*; but surely they use it none the less.[2]

To which I fancy I can hear our poet reply 'They do!' Yet for all this the foregoing, as I said, carries us a very little way. It tells us nothing, for instance, of the Transformation of Bottom which is the link between plots 2 and 3, or of the magic flower employed to infatuate Titania with her Ass, which is also the cause of the imbroglio in plot 1, and therefore, flower as it is, the very linch-pin of the whole dramatic structure. Now all these things and a good deal more may be traced to Apuleius; and Q came within an ace of discovering it when, a little later in the same Introduc-

[1] Cf. above, p. 185.  [2] See Introduction pp. xiii–xiv and below p. 187.

tion, he imagined Shakespeare puzzling over the problem of knitting his three plots together until he suddenly asks himself, 'What is the story in Ovid about Midas and the ass's ears? Or am I confusing it with a story I read the other day, in a book about witches, of a man transformed into an ass?'

But before going further let me make one thing clear. Walter de la Mare's demonstration of how the play came into being renders it no longer necessary to suppose Shakespeare drawing upon any source except the old play-book he transformed. He may of course have read Plutarch's *Life of Theseus* before making his revision;[1] but the haphazard use of the names taken from Plutarch—Aegeus, Theseus's aged father according to Plutarch, becomes for example Egeus, Hermia's old father, in the play—suggests that the *Parallel Lives* were followed more fully and more closely in the original draft, and that Shakespeare had freely abridged and pulled the material about in the rehandling.[2] Similarly, while he *may* have read Adlington's translation of Apuleius, we can feel pretty confident that magic and a man-ass were needed from the beginning to tie the three plots together; and it helps us considerably to understand the relations between *The Golden Ass* and *A Midsummer Night's Dream* as we now have it, if we believe those relations to be indirect; if we suppose, that is, Shakespeare's knowledge of Apuleius to have been limited to what he found of him in the old *Dream* play.

As everyone knows, *Cupid and Psyche* is a tale related by one of the characters in Apuleius's main story, which deals with the various adventures of one Lucius, a young Greek, who is at the beginning of things transformed by a witch into an ass and regains his human shape at the end by eating

---

[1] The same holds good of *The Knight's Tale* from which, it is now clear to me, 'Egeus' must be derived. He is there also the 'olde fader' of Theseus, but is treated very differently (see lines 2838, 2905).

[2] For another suggestion about Plutarch made by Peter Alexander, see p. 204 above.

a rose. Here then is the germ of the magic flower and the transformation of Bottom, and I do not see how anyone reading in Apuleius the account of the lascivious matron making love to the ass[1] can fail to perceive a coarse adumbration of Titania's delicate courtship of Bottom, while when, earlier in the romance, the charming captive princess promises her 'little ass' a life of ease and glory if he will restore her to liberty, we have yet another pre-echo of Titania's endearments. Take this for example:

> First, I will finely comb thy mane and adorn it with my maiden necklaces, and then I will bravely dress the hair of thy forehead, and tie up thy rugged tail trimly, whose bristles are now ragged and matted by want of care: I will deck thee round about with golden trappings and tassels, in such sort that thou shalt glitter like the stars of the sky, and shalt go in triumph amid the applause of the people. I will bring thee every day in my silken apron the kernels of nuts, and will pamper thee up with dainty delights.[2]

We shall presently discover suggestions elsewhere for Titania's attendant fairies and their ministrations, but does not the sentence last quoted give us a foretaste of

> Feed him with apricocks and dewberries,
> With purple grapes, green figs, and mulberries.—
> > (III, i, 157-8.)

and

> I have a venturous fairy that shall seek
> The squirrel's hoard, and fetch thee thence new nuts
> > (IV, i, 34-5.)

Or do not the first two suggest

> Come, sit thee down upon this flowery bed,
> While I thy amiable cheeks do coy,
> And stick musk-roses in thy sleek smooth head,
> And kiss thy fair large ears, my gentle joy?
> > (IV, i, 1-4.)

Did these parallels stand alone, they might perhaps be written off as accidental. But they are supplemented and

[1] See pp. 506 ff. of Lucius Apuleius, *Golden Ass*, in the Loeb Classics, ed. by Stephen Gaselee, who uses Adlington's translation, from which I quote below.
[2] Loeb Classics, p. 291.

confirmed by a number of parallels with the *Cupid and
Psyche* story. If Q is right in asserting that it was Shakespeare
himself who brought Puck and the Fairies to Court from
Warwickshire—and who can doubt it?—then the old *Dream*
was in all probability a classical mythological play throughout, like Peele's *Arraignment of Paris* and Lyly's plays. And
that being so, it follows that the criss-cross confusion with
the four Lovers, which is certainly part of the original plot,
must have been brought about there by Cupid, true and
rightful mischief-maker in that kind, as Puck himself acknowledges, when he exclaims:

> Cupid is a knavish lad,
> Thus to make poor females mad.
> (III, ii, 440–1.)

I believe too that the fairy plot as a whole at one time re-
sembled, perhaps closely, the story of *Cupid and Psyche*, in
which, allowing for Shakespeare's subsequent changes,
Venus played the part of Oberon and Psyche of Titania. And
this belief seems corroborated by the following parallels:

(1) Puck is introduced at the opening of Act II with an
account of his Warwickshire mischief-making; Cupid is
likewise introduced by Apuleius as the mischief-maker of
Greek city life,

> who by his evil manners, contemning all public justice and law,
> armed with fire and arrows, running up and down in the nights
> from house to house, and corrupting the lawful marriages of every
> person, doth nothing (and yet he is not punished) but that which is
> evil.[1]

(2) As the jealous Oberon summons Puck to help in his
punishment of Titania, so the jealous Venus summons Cupid
to help her to punish Psyche.

(3) The jealous anger of Oberon is the cause of disastrous
seasons in the countryside which *we* see as a reflection of the
rain and storms of 1594 and for which we found a possible
source in *Huon of Bordeaux*.[2] But the jealousy of Venus

---

[1] Loeb Classics, p. 191.          [2] See above p. 204.

brings disaster to the sea-faring Greeks, for, as a 'wordy and curious gull' relates, she

> doth use to riot on the sea, whereby they say there is now nothing any more gracious, nothing pleasant, nothing gentle but all is become uncivil, monstrous, and horrible; moreover, there are no more loving marriages, nor friendships of amity, for all is disorderly, and there is a very bitter hatred of weddings as base things.[1]

(4) Psyche is wafted by Zephyrus 'into a deep valley', where she is sweetly couched amongst the soft and tender herbs, as in a bed of dewy grass and fragrant flowers,[2] which looks like a direct suggestion for Titania's bower and the 'bank where the wild thyme grows' (II, i, 249).

(5) As Titania is sung to by tiny attendant sprites, who feed her love with delicate fruits, so Psyche is waited upon by invisible spirits who serve her with 'all sorts of wines like nectar' and 'plentiful dishes of divers meats', furnishing her too with 'the harmony of a large concourse' which

> did so greatly thrill her ears that though there were no manner of person, yet seemed she in the midst of a great quire.

(6) Oberon and Venus prescribe the same punishment for the victim. 'And this beyond all, I pray thee without delay', enjoins Venus upon Cupid,

> that she may fall in desperate love with the most miserable creature living, the most poor, the most crooked, and the most vile that there may be found in all the world of like wretchedness.[3]

Bully Bottom would not have recognized that portrait, but Shakespeare's judicious and noble audience undoubtedly would. And though the Psyche of Apuleius does not in fact fall in love with a monster, she was intended so to do, while it was as a monster her evil sisters represented the husband, whose face she had never seen. It seems likely, then, that the equivalent of Psyche in the old play did love something vile and detestable, the more so that Bottom's ass-head is clearly

---

[1] Loeb Classics, p. 241.
[2] Ibid., pp. 191–201; ibid., p. 206.
[3] Loeb Classics, p. 191.

derived, as we have seen, from that of the transformed Lucius.

(7) Lastly, and perhaps most interesting parallel of all, Oberon's well-known lines at II, i, 148 ff., which begin

> Thou remembrest
> Since once I sat upon a promontory,
> And heard a mermaid, on a dolphin's back,
> Uttering such dulcet and harmonious breath,
> That the rude sea grew civil at her song,

and continue a little later with the great tribute to the Maiden Queen, though undoubtedly, as we have seen above, a reference as it stands to the royal 'entertainment' presented to Elizabeth by Leicester in 1575, are discovered to be almost a distillation of Apuleius's scarcely less lovely description of Venus taking to her native element.

> When she had spoken these words, she embraced long and kissed often her son, and took her voyage towards the shore hard by, where the tides flow to and fro: and when she was come there and had trodden with her rosy feet upon the top of the trembling waters, then the deep sea became exceeding calm upon its whole surface, and at her will, as though she had before given her bidding, straightway appeared her servitors from the deep; for incontinent came the daughters of Nereus singing with tunes melodiously; Portunus with his bristled and rough beard of azure; Salacia with her bosom full of fish; Palaemon the little driver of the dolphins; and the bands of Triton's trumpeters leaping hither and thither, the one blowing on his shell with a heavenly noise, another turning aside with a silken veil the burning heat of the fierce sun, another holding a mirror before his lady's eyes, others, yoked two together, swimming beneath her car. Such was the company which followed Venus marching towards the middest Ocean.[1]

Assuredly, the original *Dream* contained something akin to Oberon's vision. Who wrote it? One can guess. For whose wedding was it written? One might guess that also. But our meddling intellect has asked, and tried to answer, questions

---

[1] Loeb's Classics, pp. 191–3. Gaselee's translation differs here a little from that of Adlington, who omits the words referring to the sea becoming 'exceeding calm'. My reprint of the Walter de la Mare article ends here.

enough. Let us rather follow Venus to the island of the blest in middest ocean by re-reading, or better still by re-hearing, the Happy Comedies themselves once again. For as an unknown admirer of our ever-young Shakespeare wrote in 1609:

'So much and such savoured wit is in his comedies that they seem (for their height of pleasure) to be born in that sea that brought forth Venus.'[1]

---

[1] Prologue to the first quarto of *Troilus and Cressida*.

# Index

# Index

McNair, A. D., Lord, 83 n.
Macready, 107
Malory, 40, 46 n.
Malone, Edmond, 88 n., 91 n.
Mare, R. de la, 11 ff.
Mare, Walter de la, 184, 188 n., 207, 210 ff.
Marsh, Edward, 74
Mead, W. E., 190 n.
Menander, 20, 22
Meredith, George, 14, 19 ff., 26, 32, 51, 108, 134, 153, 162
Molière, 21 f., 24, 27, 29, 32, 91, 153, 174
Montemayor, Jorge de, 41 f., 50, 53, 146 ff., 150, 152, 166
More, Sir Thomas, 24, 110 ff., 132
Morris, William, 148
Moulton, Richard D., 97 n.

Neale, Professor J. E., 198 n.
Nichols, John, 196
Nicholson, Brinsley, 173 n.
Noble, Richmond, 100 n.
Normand, Lord, of Aberdour, 106 n.
North, Sir Thomas, 149, 205

Ovid, 144, 197

Pater, Walter, 56
Peele, George, 217
Percy, Thomas, 195
Plato, 17, 117
Plautus, 22 f., 27, 29, 32, 91, 152, 174
Plutarch, 215
Pollard, A. W., 64
Pope, Alexander, 69, 169 n.
Pruvost, Professor, 41

Quiller-Couch ('Q'), Sir Arthur, 11, 38 n., 55, 96 n., 101 ff., 186 n., 207, 214, 217

Rabelais, 21
Ralegh, Sir Walter, 148, 151
Rapin, 30 n.
Reyher, Professor Paul, 41 n., 43 n.
Rutland, The Earl of, 145

Saintsbury, Professor George, 30 n.
Sampson, George, 124 n.
Sampson, Dr. John, 152
Sannazzaro, 149
Shaw, G. B., 21 f., 24, 134, 191
Sidney, Sir Philip, 30, 94, 145 f., 148, 167 n., 169 n.
Sisson, Professor Charles, 165 n., 204 n.
Smart, Dr. J. S., 50 n., 93
Southampton, The Earl of, 113, 145, 197 ff., 201 ff.
Spenser, Edmund, 45, 149, 189
Steevens, George, 169 n.
Sterne, Laurence, 153
Stoll, Professor E. E., 23 n., 107 n
Stopes, Mrs. Carmichael, 202
Stowe, John, 205 n.
Strachey, Lytton, 173
Straparola, 81
Strype, John, 49

Terence, 22 f., 27, 37, 82, 166
Theobald, Lewis, 204 n.
Theocritus, 148
Thomas, Sir Henry, 177 n.

Virgil, 148

# Index

Walker, Dr. Alice, 84 n.
Warner, William, 39 f.
Welsford, Dr. Enid, 29 n.
White, Richard Grant, 210 n.
Whitehead, Professor A. N., 16
Willcock, Professor G. D., 49 n.,
   59 n., 87

Wilson, J. Dover., 33 n., 100 n.,
   192 n.
Wordsworth, William, 24

Yates, Dr. Frances A., 67 n.
Young, Bartholomew, 41, 42 n.,
   146 n., 147 f.